# *On Taqlīd*

# On Taqlīd

## *Ibn al Qayyim's Critique of Authority in Islamic Law*

ABDUL-RAHMAN MUSTAFA

OXFORD
UNIVERSITY PRESS

OXFORD
UNIVERSITY PRESS

Oxford University Press is a department of the University of Oxford.
It furthers the University's objective of excellence in research, scholarship,
and education by publishing worldwide.

Oxford New York
Auckland Cape Town Dar es Salaam Hong Kong Karachi
Kuala Lumpur Madrid Melbourne Mexico City Nairobi
New Delhi Shanghai Taipei Toronto

With offices in
Argentina Austria Brazil Chile Czech Republic France Greece
Guatemala Hungary Italy Japan Poland Portugal Singapore
South Korea Switzerland Thailand Turkey Ukraine Vietnam



Published in the United States of America by
Oxford University Press
198 Madison Avenue, New York, NY 10016



Library of Congress Cataloging-in-Publication Data
Mustafa, Abdul-Rahman.
On taqlīd : Ibn al Qayyim's critique of authority in Islamic law / Abdul-Rahman Mustafa.
p. cm.
Includes bibliographical references and index.
ISBN 978-0-19-993751-6 (hardcover : alk. paper) 1. Taqlīd. 2. Ibn Qayyim al-Jawziyah,
Muhammad ibn Abi Bakr, 1292–1350. I'lam al-muwaqqi'in 'an rabb al-'alamin. 3. Islamic
law—Interpretation and construction. I. Ibn Qayyim al-Jawziyah, Muhammad ibn Abi Bakr,
1292–1350. I'lam al-muwaqqi'in 'an rabb al-'alamin. English. Selections. II. Title.
KBP454.M87 2013
340.5'9—dc23
2012020492

1 3 5 7 9 8 6 4 2

# *Contents*

# *Acknowledgments*

THIS WORK WOULD have been impossible without the support of Shaykh Mashhūr Ḥasan. His scholarship has set a very high standard for those who follow in his footsteps. His help and encouragement is greatly appreciated.

Hafiz Hasan Madni was an extremely generous teacher and colleague, who helped at various stages to make this work a reality.

Hafiz Naeem was very helpful with the referencing and translation. H. Khan reviewed the manuscript several times and was always a source of great help and much inspiration.

Mr. Anwar Kamal deserves special thanks for his generous assistance.

I would also like to thank everyone at Oxford University Press, particularly Cynthia Read, Charlotte Steinhardt, Rick Stinson, and the copyeditors for their valuable assistance.

Yassin Rashid knows how thankful I am to have him as a fellow traveler.

Finally, this work is dedicated to my parents, Farida and Tariq, and to my brother, Saad.

# *On Taqlīd*

# *Introduction*

AN OLD ARAB proverb says that things are known by their opposites. The best place, then, for us to begin our introduction to Ibn al-Qayyim's (d. 751/1350) essay on *taqlīd* is with one of its most substantial refutations:

> In the worst of times, a misguided group arose—insulting the Imāms, condemning *taqlīd,* and calling on others to do the same, even though most of their criticisms and all their proofs are based on *taqlīd* of their predecessors. . . . In reality these people are greater *muqallids* than the *muqallids* themselves. For the *muqallids* only oblige a non-*mujtahid* to imitate a *mujtahid,* while these people obligate the *mujtahid* to imitate them. . . . They call people to abandon *taqlīd* of the *mujtahid* scholars and imitate themselves instead. . . . No rational person was left in any doubt about the ignorance and deviance of these people, for it did not lead anywhere except self-contradiction in their opinions and actions. For they condemned the practice of others while choosing something far worse for themselves. They forbade others from doing something but then obliged them to do that which was far more repulsive. However, since their doubts and deceptions have misled those who lack knowledge and because they have spread among them, we have deemed it appropriate to expose their deception.
>
> Now, since the debate over *ijtihād* and *taqlīd* is the fundamental and greatest battle between us and them, we took up this matter here, in this introduction, presenting it in the most complete and perfect way. That is because we observed that Ibn al-Qayyim, who is the father of this group, spoke at great length on this issue in the *I'lām al-muwaqqi'īn,* to the extent that he has left nothing to say for those who come after him.[1]

The main topic addressed by Ibn al-Qayyim in the essay presented in this volume is *taqlīd* and its validity in Islamic law. It is remarkable that, despite the seminal importance of this text of Ibn al-Qayyim, which ranks as one of the most significant works on Islamic legal theory ever written, it has not been the subject of much commentary or discussion in any European language. In fact Ibn al-Qayyim's works in general, despite their immense popularity in the Muslim world, have not, until now, been considered worthy of serious study by Western scholars.[2] One reason for this is that Ibn al-Qayyim has been obscured by his master Ibn Taymiyyah (d. 728/1328), whose forceful personality, lively intellect and contested legacy have aroused greater interest amongst later scholars.[3] Ibn al-Qayyim, in turn, has often been seen as a mere mouthpiece for the thoughts of Ibn Taymiyyah, and it has been assumed that Ibn al-Qayyim himself was not a particularly interesting or original author. Yet another reason for Ibn al-Qayyim's lack of popularity in the West has to do with the fact that there has been, in general, so little Orientalist scholarship on the Ḥanbalī school, to which Ibn al-Qayyim belonged.[4]

In the Islamic world, by contrast, Ibn al-Qayyim continues to be acknowledged not just as one of its most prolific authors but also as one of its most influential and original theologians and jurists.[5] He composed several works on exegesis, Prophetic traditions, theology, and Islamic critiques of Judaism and Christianity. His works in the fields of legal and political theory (*I'lām al-muwaqqi'īn* and *Ṭuruq al-ḥukmiyyah*), Sufism (*Madārij al-sālikīn*) and Prophetic biography (*Zād al-ma'ād*) are ground-breaking, as each marks a new way of thinking and writing in its respective genre. His views on procedural law and the role and function of the judiciary in an Islamic state have proved enormously influential in the Muslim world and have provided the underpinning for the legal systems of countries such as Saudi Arabia, Egypt, and Pakistan. In the extract cited above, which comes from a refutation of Ibn al-Qayyim written almost seven centuries after his death by Ḥabīb Aḥmad Kīrānwī, a Deobandī Ḥanafī scholar living in colonial India in the 1930s, we can see that Ibn al-Qayyim continues to play a very significant role in ongoing debates between contemporary Islamic movements in South Asia and the broader Muslim world. Entitled *al-Dīn al-qayyim* (The Upright Faith), Kīrānwī's refutation proclaims by its very title that it is meant as a full-fledged attack on Ibn al-Qayyim's essay on *taqlīd*, playing, as it does, with Ibn al-Qayyim's patronymic (*naṣab*). *Al-dīn al-qayyim* appears as an independent essay in the grand Deobandī Ḥanafī summa composed primarily by Zafar 'Uthmānī (d. 1974), the multi-volume

*I'lā' al-sunan.*[6] Together with Ashraf 'Alī Thānwī (d. 1943), the leading Deobandī scholar of the day, who encouraged and supervised the project, 'Uthmānī, Kīrānwī and other Deobandī luminaries involved in the composition of the *I'lā'* sought therein to present a rigorous defense of the Ḥanafī school's substantive law and its jurisprudential principles, which were under heavy attack by the South Asian Ahl-e Ḥadīth. Both the Ahl-e Ḥadīth and the Deobandīs were revivalist movements that started in colonial India in the nineteenth century, with the aim of revitalizing Islamic thought and practice, but the two groups had very different ideas about how to bring about this much desired Islamic renaissance. The Deobandīs (named after the area where the first seminary disseminating the views of this school of thought was established) advocated strong and uncompromising *taqlīd* of the Ḥanafī school as the way for Muslims in the nineteenth century to recreate a link with an authentic Islamic religious tradition, a link that they believed had been severed in their own time. By contrast, the Ahl-e Ḥadīth (who as their name suggests, identified themselves as followers of *ḥadīth*) identified *taqlīd* itself as one of the reasons for the crisis of nineteenth-century Islam. Their prescription for the ills of Muslim society thus included an abandonment of *taqlīd* of the established schools of Islamic law, some of whose rulings they criticized for not being based on the *ḥadīth*. The stage was thus set for a sustained and bitter debate between these two South Asian sects which, to this day, shapes Islamic cultural and intellectual life on the Indian subcontinent and beyond. As we shall see, Ibn al-Qayyim's writing on *taqlīd* made him one of the most influential personalities to feature in this debate.

The fact that privileged medieval scholars of the Mamluk period, as well as their marginalized twentieth-century counterparts in British India, should see it as their scholarly duty to expound on the concept of *taqlīd* says something about the centrality of the topic to Muslim identity. More than any other jurisprudential topic, a scholar's or even a layman's position on *taqlīd* continues to act as a sign of their individual and collective identity in the Muslim community. It is thus not only South Asian scholarly circles that have seen, since the late nineteenth century, particularly bitter debates on the topic of *taqlīd*: almost every traditional revivalist Islamic movement and thinker since the eighteenth century has, to some extent, criticized the *taqlīd* practiced by their contemporaries. This is true of the founder of the so-called Wahhābī sect, Muḥammad b. 'Abd al-Wahhāb (d. 1792), the Yemeni "Salafī" revivalists al-Ṣan'ānī (d. 1182/1768) and al-Shawkānī (d. 1250/1834), the Mughal-era revivalist Shāh Walī

Allāh of Delhi (d. 1762), and the Egyptian thinker Rashīd Riḍā (d. 1935), to name a few.[7]

This should not be taken to mean that criticism of *taqlīd* is a phenomenon of late modernity, for, as we shall see, medieval Muslim jurists had almost as much to say against *taqlīd* as did later Muslim revivalists. What does distinguish modern debates on *taqlīd* from earlier ones is the presence, in later periods, of a group of reformists (as opposed to revivalists) who simply reject the method of argumentation employed by classical scholars in arguing for or against *taqlīd*. Instead, the reformists seek to introduce "modern" thought and practice to the Islamic legal tradition, and it is for this reason that they reject the notion of *taqlīd*. This is something that distinguishes these reformists from those classical and modern scholars whose arguments for and against *taqlīd* are based primarily on their understanding of scripture and traditional Islam. Among the latter are critics of *taqlīd*, such as the South Asian Ahl-e Ḥadīth, the Wahhābīs, traditional Salafīs such as the late *ḥadīth* expert Nāṣir al-Dīn al-Albānī (d. 1999), internationally renowned scholars such as Yūsuf al-Qaraḍāwī, as well as leading Islamists such as Sayyid Quṭb (d. 1966) and Abū l-Aʿlā Mawdūdī (d. 1979).[8] On the other hand, scholars such as Taqī ʿUthmānī, al-Būṭī, and al-Yāfiʿī (see bibliography) continue, with varying degrees of emphasis, to keep alive a tradition of pro-*taqlīd* scholarship.[9] Almost all the authors mentioned above, both for and against *taqlīd*, do refer at some point to Ibn al-Qayyim's discussion on *taqlīd*, and most assert that it is one that cannot be surpassed, an opinion expressed also by Kīrānwī in the extract quoted above.

Outside of South Asia, the participants in the debates over *taqlīd* may be different, but the basic ideas being discussed are similar. In South Africa and the United Kingdom, a growing number of Deobandī seminaries continue to advocate the Deobandī position in favor of *taqlīd*. In turn, they are opposed by various Salafī groups and by Islamists influenced by the Egyptian Ikhwān or the Pakistani Jamāt-e Islāmī (although these groups also differ among themselves on the topic of *taqlīd*). In recent years it has also become de rigueur for famous Western converts to Islam to expound on the topic of *taqlīd*, which they all, despite their differing judgments on it, see as one of the central issues facing the Muslim community. While some, such as Muhammad Asad (d. 1992), have taken a broadly anti-*taqlīd* stance, others, such as Nuh Ha Mim Keller and Tim Winter (who also writes under the pseudonym Abdal Hakim Murad), have taken a strongly pro-*taqlīd* stance.[10]

In the political realm too, their varying positions on *taqlīd* explain, at least in part, the divisions among various Islamist groups vying for political influence in Muslim countries. In Egypt, the Salafist al-Nūr party and the Muslim Brotherhood accuse each other of adopting incorrect positions on the issue of *ijtihād* and *taqlīd*. In Pakistan, too, the Jamāt-e Islāmī and other Deobandī and Ahl-e Ḥadīth political parties—such as the Jamīʿat ʿUlamā-e Islām and the Markazī Jamīʿat Ahl-e Ḥadīth—continue to differ over the extent to which *taqlīd* ought to be the governing principle of the legal system of an Islamic state. Such differences have prevented Pakistan's religious political parties from agreeing on a program for the Islamization of the country's laws and given the country's rulers a convenient excuse for their inability to bring about greater Islamization. Differences over *taqlīd* also account for a significant part of the internal debate that takes place among various militant organizations, such as al-Qāʿidah and the Taliban, who adopt radically different positions on the issue of *taqlīd*. Abdullah Azzam, the leading scholarly advocate of *jihād* in the 1980s and the mentor of Osama bin Laden, wrote an influential book, *Join the Caravan*, encouraging non-Afghans to participate in the Afghan *jihād* against the Soviet Union. He felt compelled to warn his readers, however, of the Afghan proclivity for *taqlīd* of the Ḥanafī school which made the Afghans intolerant of other schools of law which they believed "were not part of Islam."[11] It is not surprising, then, that in recent years even the US government, or at least what might mordantly be called its "thinking arm," has become involved in determining how best the debates among the various schools of Islamic law and their positions on *taqlīd* can be used to its advantage. For example, in a report published by the RAND Corporation, Cheryl Bernard, the wife of a former US ambassador to Iraq and Afghanistan, advises the United States to "encourage" Ḥanafī law, in order to "weaken the authority of backward Wahhabi religious rulings."[12] The RAND corporation's understanding of Islam does not mark the nadir but only the continuation of a tradition of Western commentary on Islam and *taqlīd*, for many Western intellectuals have seen their own culture primarily in terms of its opposition to the kind of *ijtihād* or *taqlīd* that they believed to be prevalent in Islamic law. This is true of jurists such as the distinguished American legal scholar Roscoe Pound and sociologists such as Max Weber, who showed little awareness of the importance of *taqlīd* in Islamic thought and were dismissive of what they saw as unregulated *ijtihād* of Islam. On the other hand, those English judges of the Privy Council who adjudicated cases dealing with Indian Anglo-Muhammadan law did so with the conviction that, unlike the common law, which was based on judicial discretion and equity, Islamic law did not allow for *ijtihād* and was an entirely formalistic *taqlīd*-bound system.[13] *Taqlīd* and *ijtihād*, then, are not only concepts by which Muslims mark their own identities but by which their identities are marked by "others." Those "others" in turn have often defined themselves in terms of their own opposition to *ijtihād* or *taqlīd*.

## Why *Taqlīd*?

As with all intense and lengthy arguments, the longevity of the debate on *taqlīd* has much to do with the conflicting ways in which the underlying ideas have been understood and discussed. Etymology alone offers little help. *Taqlīd* is derived from the Arabic root *q-l-d*, meaning "to bind an animal." In technical use it means "to copy, imitate." *Ijtihād* is from the root *j-h-d*, meaning "to struggle, persevere." For classical Muslim jurisprudents and theologians, *ijtihād* thus represented a variety of activities that, at their core, involved exerting oneself to arrive at the correct answer to a given question, often with reference to scripture. *Taqlīd* was, by contrast, seen as accepting and following the views of someone whose opinion was not itself considered a proof. Knowing that Muslim scholars were, by and large, working with these definitions in mind does not explain the longevity and intensity of the debate on *taqlīd*. To understand that, we have to understand why *taqlīd* assumed such a great importance in Islamic intellectual life.

This is, however, a subject on which there is little agreement, as scholars, both Muslim and non-Muslim, disagree not only on the definition of *taqlīd* but also on the reason it gained such prominence in Islamic legal culture. Part of the explanation clearly lies in the level of passion the topic raises amongst individual Muslims. To adopt a particular position on *taqlīd* is to adopt a particular view on questions of right and wrong and to make a statement about one's right and ability to adopt such a view. With the rise of literacy and the spread of scholarly literature and discourse in the public realm, it is hardly surprising that vast numbers of Muslims should take an interest in such questions.

Scholars have also tried to account for the rise of *taqlīd* with reference to other social factors. Some suggest that the institution of *taqlīd* was used in an attempt to solidify religious law and prevent it from being interfered with by political authorities.[14] Others believe that the rise of *taqlīd* was a result of the desire of the scholarly class to limit the discretionary powers of legal officials at the bottom of the legal hierarchy, by obliging them to adhere to a particular school of law.[15] Yet others argue that the emergence of a regime of *taqlīd* was an inevitable result of the pressures that push all legal systems toward greater institutionalization. Evidence for this institutional pressure in favor of *taqlīd* can be seen in most legal systems, even those in which there is a widespread distaste for rigid *taqlīd*. In Saudi Arabia, for instance, despite the anti-*taqlīd* stance of the majority of the Ḥanbalī religious elite, there have been calls from some members of that elite for a set of codified laws that all judges would be obliged to follow.[16] In this light, Professor Sherman Jackson's observation hits the mark—*ijtihād* and *taqlīd* are not mutually exclusive moments in Muslim history but competing hegemonies that stood and continue to stand in perpetual competition with each other.[17]

The institutionalization of *taqlīd* has also been defended, as we shall see, on the grounds that it prevented ordinary Muslims (and scholars), from seeking legal loopholes by following isolated opinions and legal dispensations from the various schools of law. Instead, the doctrine of *taqlīd* supposedly compelled ordinary Muslims to obtain legal rulings from a particular school of law, while compelling scholars to follow a particular set of jurisprudential principles, on which they could base their legal rulings consistently, rather than relying on contradictory principles from the various schools.

We shall return to Ibn al-Qayyim's specific responses to some of these arguments below. Here, we need only point out that these arguments do lose some of their force in view of the fact that scholars from nearly every school did actually accept the practice of combining the rulings of two schools to validate an act whose individual parts would not be recognized as valid by either one of them, a practice known as *talfīq*.[18] That this doctrine was associated particularly with the strongly pro-*taqlīd* Ḥanafīs and that some of its strongest opponents were the *taqlīd*-wary Ḥanbalīs, suggests that the more insistent a school was on *taqlīd*—as the Ḥanafīs were, by and large—the greater its recourse to *talfīq* in order to provide some flexibility for ordinary Muslims who could not be expected always to know, let alone adhere to, the opinions of their school on all matters. *Talfīq* thus allowed a ritual act of worship—such as prayer, marriage, or even a contract of sale, all of which would be regarded as acts of worship if performed in accordance with the *sharīʿah*—to be validated by having the individual parts of such acts approved by different schools. By contrast, a school that emphasized obedience to scripture over the necessity of *taqlīd*, as the Ḥanbalīs generally did, would be more likely to regard *talfīq* as unnecessary or illegitimate. Unnecessary, that is, if *talfīq* validated an act that was legitimate in light of scripture anyway—and illegitimate if it validated an act not in harmony with scripture in the first place.[19]

## *Taqlīd*: The Layman's Boon?

The rise of *taqlīd* has also been seen as an inevitable development in Islamic law, because it provided the layman with a definitive answer to all his legal queries, thus keeping him from becoming lost in the bewildering complexity of disagreement (*ikhtilāf*) that existed on almost every legal question discussed by Muslim scholars. But this explanation of the rise of *taqlīd* too is unsatisfactory, for it assumes that the regime of *taqlīd* ends the confusion and bewilderment of the layman and legal officials, whereas complexity continues, in fact, to be a feature of the regime of *taqlīd*. In terms of complexity, then, the only difference between the regime of *ijtihād* and the regime of *taqlīd* is that in the latter, instead of (supposedly nonexistent) *mujtahids*, it is *muftīs* within the school who now have to deal with increased complexity, leading to a great deal of scholarly disagreement or *ikhtilāf*. Jackson has rightly pointed out that the regime of *taqlīd* fits the definition of the kind of legal system that, for all its sophistication and "advancement," is marked by an increased rigidity, an inability to respond to the practical needs of society, horrendous complexity, and remoteness and confusion for lawyer and layman alike.[20]

Muslim scholars such as Ibn Daqīq al-ʿĪd (d. 702/1303) point out that a layman's burden could actually be said to increase under the regime of *taqlīd*. In the regime of *ijtihād*, a layman could assume that the legal verdicts (*fatāwā*, sing. *fatwā*) he obtains are based on scripture, not just on the prevailing opinion of a school. In a regime of *taqlīd*, he would have to make certain that the *fatāwā* he obtains are based on scripture, because many *fatāwā* in this regime would be based simply on the prevailing opinion of a school.[21] Ibn al-Qayyim, too, argues that, when faced with disagreement between scholars, a non-scholar would bear the burden of determining whether one of the scholars was more knowledgeable than the other and would then be required to follow him.[22] Even pro-*taqlīd* Ḥanafī scholars often celebrate Prophetic traditions (*aḥādīth*, sing. *ḥadīth*) that speak of a person obtaining a *fatwā* from his heart, thereby accepting that there is, in the end, little else a layman can do when faced with the bewildering complexity of the *madhhab* system and the reality of *ikhtilāf* within his own school.[23] Ibn ʿĀbidīn (d. 1252/1836), the towering figure of authority in the Ḥanafī school, refers to a protracted debate in his school over the question of whether or not a layman is obliged to identify the most knowledgeable scholar and imitate him. The mere existence of this debate shows the great confusion experienced by both laymen and scholars under the regime of *taqlīd*.[24] Even scholars who absolve the layman of this responsibility, such as the great Shāfiʿī *ḥadīth* commentator Ibn Ḥajar (d. 852/1448), often require the layman to use specific criteria for selecting one scholarly opinion over another. Ibn ʿĀbidīn—while arguing that laymen need not even have a *madhhab* and could, moreover, change their *madhhab* every day—insists that they may not do so on invalid grounds, which suggests that valid grounds would have to be presented (even if only to oneself) to justify such a decision. This, too, suggests that, for both the ordinary Muslim and the scholar, the regime of *taqlīd* was at least as complex as the regime of *ijtihād*.[25] Indeed, Ibn al-Qayyim reports that there are as many as seven divergent scholarly positions on how a layman should act when faced with *ikhtilāf* between two *muftī*s—hardly what one expects of a system designed to make things less complex for the layman.[26]

It is true that scholars in the regime of *taqlīd* often spoke about the judgment of the *qāḍī* (judge) or the verdict of the *muftī* acting as a scriptural text (*naṣṣ*) for an ordinary Muslim, suggesting that he could rely completely on these and not concern himself with the objective truth.[27] Statements such as these must, however, be balanced against the opinions of many scholars (with the notable exception of the Ḥanafīs) who also held that a judge's ruling, even if issued validly by him, in accordance with his school, would not render lawful that which was actually impermissible in the *sharīʿah*. This would mean that an ordinary litigant who obtained an objectively incorrect judgment in his favor could not lawfully rely on it if he knew it to be incorrect, even if it was based on the valid opinion of a school of law.[28]

Perhaps the strongest argument against the idea that the rise of *taqlīd* can be explained by the fact that it made life easier for the lay person by obliging him to follow a single school is that the vast majority of Muslim scholars never required the layman to adhere to a single *madhhab*—in fact, they regarded it as improper for him to do so.[29] Even the Ḥanafī school, traditionally the most dedicated to the concept of *taqlīd*, produced several scholars who argued that a layman could not claim to belong to a specific *madhhab*, as this was a privilege of the scholar or the student of law.[30] The Ḥanafī scholar Muḥammad Saʿīd Albānī (not to be confused with the famous Salafī *ḥadīth* scholar Nāṣir al-Dīn al-Albānī), bases his arguments in favor of *talfīq* on the fact that ordinary Muslims in his age and earlier never performed their prayers strictly according to a particular school and should not be burdened with having to know the technical rules regarding the validity of their prayer according to a single school.[31] Albānī was, of course, aware that, by making that argument, he was associating himself with Ḥanbalīs such as Ibn al-Qayyim, who had long argued that a layman does not adhere to a specific *madhhab*.[32]

## *Taqlīd*: The Scholar's Bane?

The aforementioned explanation of the rise of *taqlīd* has proved so enduring because *muqallid* scholars themselves regularly invoked the figure of the layman to justify the institution of *taqlīd*. In fact, they would even include themselves in this category, pleading that as mere *muqallid*s they could celebrate the ideal of *ijtihād* but could not employ it to change the rulings of their *madhhab*s. Their status as *muqallid*s meant that they could only narrate and transmit the rulings of their predecessors, an argument made repeatedly in Ibn ʿĀbidīn's *Radd al-muḥtār* and ʿUthmānī's *Iʿlāʾ al-sunan*.[33] This argument had already been considered, and rejected, by Ibn Rushd (d. 520/1126, the grandfather of the Ibn Rushd famous in the West as Averroës), who insisted that transmission could not count as *fatwā* and that someone who could only narrate a *fatwā* therefore had no authority to issue one. Ibn al-Qayyim too, argues that a person who is asked to relate *madhhab* rulings may transmit them but cannot call himself a *muftī* of Islam, because the religion is not confined to a single school of law.[34]

*Muqallid* scholars tended to insist, however, that they could not go outside the jurisprudential principles on which the legal rulings of their predecessors were based without succumbing to inconsistency. In reality there has always been, as critics of *taqlīd* have pointed out, considerable disagreement over whether the legal rulings of the schools are deduced on the basis of preexisting jurisprudential principles, or whether these principles themselves were invented by *muqallid* jurists to harmonize and justify previous legal rulings. The renowned Indian traditionist Shāh Walī

Allāh, for instance, argued that *madhhab* principles were invented later, in order to justify the existing rulings of the *madhhab*:

> Amongst them (the new developments) are that I have found some of them claiming that the basis of disagreement between Abū Hanīfa and al-Shaāfi'ī, may God be pleased with both of them, is founded on those principles which are mentioned in the book of al-Pazdawī and other similar ones. Rather the truth is that most of them are principles derived on the basis of their opinions.

Shāh Walī Allāh then goes on to list various principles that were upheld in the Ḥanafī school, such as preferring a *ḥadīth* because of the greater number of its narrators, distinguishing between those who are legal experts and those who are not when accepting their *ḥadīth*, and specifying general legal statements in light of specific ones. Having discussed these principles, Shāh Walī Allāh argues that these and similar issues:

> . . . are principles derived from the statements of the founders (of the legal schools). These are not soundly transmitted from Abū Hanifa and his associates, and holding to them and taking troubles to refute what contravenes them among the practices of the earlier ones in their references as al-Pazdawī and others did, is not more correct than holding what opposes these and responding with what refutes them.[35]

The debate over whether or not jurisprudential principles preceded substantive legal opinions shows the extent to which jurists operating in the regime of *taqlīd* themselves had trouble deciphering the exact implication of terms such as *ijtihād*, *tarjīḥ* (preferring one opinion over another), *muqallid*, and *mujtahid*. While some *muqallid* scholars did see *taqlīd* as a form of *ijtihād* because *muqallid* scholars engaged in the exercise of preferring certain legal opinions over others (*tarjīḥ*), others held that *taqlīd* meant that all the legal opinions handed down from the early scholars of their schools had to be followed. The latter trend reflects, as Jackson suggests, a kind of despair and disillusionment generated by the loss of a legal system in which *ijtihād*, not *taqlīd*, was the archetypal juristic activity. The loss of this *ijtihād*-based legal system pushes some jurists to insist that everything the *mujtahid imāms* say must be accepted and made the subject of imitation, including their legal rulings, their verdicts on *ḥadīth*, and their interpretations of the Qur'an. According to Jackson, such claims reflect the fact that a legal structure consisting of several tiers has become too complex and is therefore reduced to just a few, such as *taqlīd*, which are then taken to constitute the entire system.[36] This is, in fact, one of Ibn al-Qayyim's main criticisms of the regime of *taqlīd*—it begins to treat *taqlīd* not just as a type of legal activity side by side with *ijtihād*, or as "legal scaffolding," as Jackson would describe it, but to use Kelsen's terminology, as the *Grundnorm* on which the whole legal edifice rests:

> The basic principle is that the opinion of another may not be accepted without proof, except in cases of necessity. You have made this case of necessity your basic capital." (Argument 65)

It has also been suggested by some scholars that the discourse on *taqlīd* was part of an attempt by Muslim jurists to employ the methodology of *uṣūl al-fiqh* (jurisprudence) to conceal the inherent subjectivity of legal interpretation, while securing those legal outcomes that the jurists themselves deemed preferable. For even while advocating imitation of the doctrines of his Imām, a *muqallid* jurist could make a finding of fact that would allow his Imām's doctrines not to be applied to the facts before him without actually challenging those doctrines as such.[37] One example of this approach can be found in a series of *fatāwā* issued by Ashraf ʿAlī Thānwī and other Deobandī *ʿulamā'* in the early twentieth century. The problem they faced was that Ḥanafī law required wives whose husbands had deserted them to wait for almost 100 years before they could have their marriages dissolved by judicial decree. Some Ḥanafī *muftī*s had therefore begun to advise such women to circumvent the strict Ḥanafī doctrine by committing apostasy, which, under Ḥanafī, law automatically nullified their marriages. Having freed themselves of their husbands, these women could then immediately return to Islam by proclaiming the declaration of faith (the Ḥanafī punishment of apostasy could not be applied to the wives in this case, because it had been outlawed by colonial law). In response to this situation, Thānwī and other Deobandīs issued *fatāwā* requiring Ḥanafīs to adopt the opinion of the Mālikī school on the judicial dissolution of marriage, which allowed women in such circumstances to obtain a judicial dissolution within four years. But even as they transformed the prevailing opinion of their school, the Deobandī scholars presented the adoption of the Mālikī opinion as something that did not make them *mujtahids*. The official *fatwā* of the Ḥanafī school on the matter was likewise never renounced as incorrect law. Rather, a particular factual situation was presented in terms that made the application of the Ḥanafī opinion to it unfeasible.[38]

In cases such as this, *taqlīd* is clearly working as a legal fiction that allows jurists to work substantial change in the law while keeping alive the myth that the law is unchanging and consistent.[39] But to what extent were the scholars who engaged in this legal fiction aware of the fact? Perhaps the greatest proponent of the view that *muqallid* scholars deliberately manipulated the concept of *taqlīd* to suit their agendas was the late Orientalist Norman Calder, who was considered one of the foremost authorities on the subject of *taqlīd* and wrote an article on the subject in the *Encyclopaedia of Islam*.[40] Calder repeatedly referred to the deliberate "manipulation" of hermeneutical techniques and Prophetic traditions by later scholars to support their juristic opinions.[41] Using the rhetoric of *taqlīd* was, for Calder, part of this manipulation. While Hallaq had suggested that many *muqallid* jurists were confused by the various ways in which terms like *ijtihād* and *taqlīd* were being used, Calder countered that, "the majority of scholars were not confused; they knew how to manipulate and serve the tradition of discourse which had constituted their training and their intellectual and literary tools."[42] According to Calder, then, learning the rhetoric of *taqlīd* was an integral part of the discipline of *uṣūl* by which scholars engaged in mass deception, attempting to portray the law as an unchanging and objective discipline, when it was not so.[43] On this issue, Orientalist scholars, following their Muslim counterparts, basically divide into two camps: Some, such as Jackson, argue that even when *muqallid* scholars employ the techniques of *ūṣul al-fiqh* to derive law from scripture directly, their activities should be termed *taqlīd* unless the *muqallid* scholars in question actually claim that they are basing their opinions on the application of *ūṣul al-fiqh* to scripture.[44] On the other hand, scholars such as Hallaq argue that one ought to refer to the juristic activities of *muqallid* jurists as *ijtihād*, which they were in everything but name.[45]

Clearly, this debate has huge implications for our understanding of the role of *uṣūl al-fiqh* in Islamic legal reasoning. Accepting the claim that *muqallid* scholars used, and continue to use, *uṣūl* as a discipline through which they justified their own legal and political preferences means that the purpose of *uṣūl* is not to facilitate linguistic interpretation and principles-based legal reasoning but to justify the legal and political preferences of jurists. Therefore, *uṣūl* plays little role in actually developing substantive law, and it has little to teach students, beyond the art of concealing their subjective political preferences.[46] According to this view *uṣūl* should be thought of as a science of justification or a form of intellectual play—or just something that must be studied as a religious obligation.[47] There is some evidence to support this view. *Uṣūl* begins to look very much like a science of justification, when we consider the work of *muqallid* scholars such as the famous Ḥanafī-Muʿtazilī Abū l-Ḥasan al-Karkhī (d. 340/952), who claimed that any verse of the Qur'an or any *ḥadīth* that went against his school would be held to be abrogated or would be set aside as the less preferred view.[48] In this view, it is clear that the purpose of *uṣūl* is not just to discover or derive rulings from scripture but to justify the rulings of one's own school. The same point is made much more explicitly by Kīrānwī, in his polemical refutation of Ibn al-Qayyim's essay on *taqlīd*, in which he states that a *muqallid* can never admit that his *madhhab* is weak, because analyzing the strength and weakness of different opinions is the task of the *mujtahid*. The task of the *muqallid*, therefore, would be to use *uṣūl* to establish the superiority of his school, a task Kīrānwī and his fellow Deobandī collaborators perform with great skill.[49]

On the other hand, for critics of *taqlīd* such as Ibn al-Qayyim, *uṣūl* played a vital role in giving Muslims the tools needed to deduce law from scripture, thus keeping scripture alive as a source of law for successive generations of Muslims. They were thus critical of *muqallid* scholars who used *uṣūl* merely to defend the opinions of their schools, as we shall see later.[50] Al-Dhahabī, another critic of rigid *taqlīd*, asks sarcastically why *muqallids* continue to engage in the study of *uṣūl al-fiqh*, which was beneficial only to someone engaged in *ijtihād*, which *muqallid* jurists held they were not.[51]

## *Taqlīd* and the Rule of Law

It has also been argued that *taqlīd* represents the triumph of the ideal of the rule of law over the ideal of judicial discretion, by replacing the subjective conscience of the *mujtahid* with the group sensibility of the school.[52] Another account of *taqlīd* argues that the regime of *taqlīd* ensured that all the schools were guaranteed respect for their opinions by the state and that no one *madhhab* would dominate all others. The *madhhab* thus forms the basic "constitutional unit" through which the individual rights and liberties of those belonging to politically marginalized schools are protected.[53]

It is true that the regime of *taqlīd* provided mechanisms for reducing the potential for tyranny that it fostered in the first place. For the problem of how to protect politically marginalized schools only arises when a particular *madhhab* has gained political or legal prominence and then seeks to institutionalize its own *taqlīd*, while marginalizing other schools. Only in a regime of *taqlīd*, in which judges and legal officials feel bound to uphold the opinions of their own schools, does the danger of domination by one such school become a possibility.

This is not to deny that the regime of *ijtihād*—in which a *qāḍī* had the responsibility of carrying out *ijtihād* for himself—had the potential to foster its own kind of tyranny. It is precisely because of their recognition of the possibility of such an outcome that scholars writing under the regime of *ijtihād* not only explicitly instructed *qāḍīs* to leave their own school when they found another Imām's rule to be more correct but also spoke against a rigid system of judicial precedent that would bind judges to the opinions of their predecessors or contemporaries. Instead, judges were encouraged to take into account the specifics of the case before them, in order to achieve a substantially just outcome in each case.

Thus, while Professor Jackson is undoubtedly right to draw attention to the ways in which the outstanding scholar al-Qarāfī (d. 684/1285) attempted to present a vision of *taqlīd* that would make it a bulwark against tyranny, defined by Jackson as "the tendency to appropriate law or the authority that backs it to the end of making false or mistaken claims of authority," it is by no means certain that al-Qarāfī's sophisticated definition of *taqlīd* was the one eventually accepted by most *muqallid* scholars.[54] Indeed, those scholars who criticize rigid *taqlīd*, such as Ibn al-Qayyim, do so precisely because in their view, it allows "false or mistaken claims of authority" to be made for views that ought not to have any such authority. For traditionalist critics of *taqlīd* in all four schools of law and beyond, it is scripture alone, as understood by the Prophet and his Companions, that is the standard by which the authoritativeness of any claim of authority can be judged. By contrast, as Jackson shows, jurists under the regime of *taqlīd* surreptitiously carried out *ijtihād* "disguised" as *taqlīd* in order to project their own view back in time, in order to render good faith challenges to them more difficult.[55] Furthermore, as Jackson points out, under *muqallid* jurists, jurisprudential doctrines such as *ijmā*ʿ (consensus) would be reduced to a fiction perpetuated by *muqallid* scholars to bolster their own opinions. This explains why scholars such as Ibn al-Qayyim railed against such false claims of authority, which to them amounted to a form of tyranny by *muqallid* scholars to further their own views. They simply refused to celebrate a rule of law built on such noble lies.

Moreover, the idea of protecting liberty by establishing the freedom of legal schools from review by an external authority is one that could itself be abused by the executive branch of government for its own ends. For in a situation where the legal opinions of the schools are protected and cannot be displaced by outsiders and where judges of a *madhhab* are bound to uphold its opinions in public, a shrewd ruler would be tempted to seek justification for his tyrannical measures in the legal doctrines of a particular *madhhab* and thereby bestow on such measures the level of protection and freedom from external legal review enjoyed by the legal schools themselves. Paradoxically, governments would, under this system, have a greater incentive to involve themselves in the previously off-limits world of the legal schools than they would in the regime of *ijtihād,* where a *madhhab* is not worth co-opting, because its legal opinions are not protected from judicial review and therefore cannot bestow much protection on the executive. The process of state co-option of the *madhhab* arguably reached its apogee in the Ottoman period, by the end of which the Ḥanafī *madhhab* was, at least at an official level, no longer independent of the government in any meaningful sense. Astute defenders of the regime of *taqlīd,* such as al-Qarāfī, seem to have feared this and did their best to counter such an outcome by insisting on the distinction between the executive and religious functions of government, limiting the role of the *madhhab* to the latter. But even the efforts of an outstanding scholar such as al-Qarāfī were unable to create a workable division of authority and responsibility between the ruler's law and *madhhab* law, leaving open the possibility of co-option of one by the other.

In the *Nukat al-ẓarīfah* of Akmal al-Dīn Muḥammad b. Maḥmūd al-Ḥanafī (d. 786/1384), we can see clearly how the regime of *taqlīd* exerted pressure on each *madhhab* to portray itself as the most accommodating of executive discretion and as the one that would grant the greatest discretion to the executive. The *Nukat* was a Ḥanafī apologetic work, which was thoroughly refuted by the renowned Ḥanafī traditionalist, Ibn Abī al-ʿIzz al-Ḥanafī (d. 792/1390?), in his *al-ʾIttibāʿ*. The *Nukat,* large sections of which are reproduced in Ibn Abī l-ʿIzz's text, attempts to convince the political authorities of the day to support the Ḥanafī *madhhab.* One of the arguments presented to persuade them to do so is that the Ḥanafīs, unlike the Shāfiʿīs, allow a sinful ruler to continue in his post.[56] For Sunnīs such as Ibn al-Qayyim, the worst possible form of adulteration of *madhhab* and state would be one in which non-orthodox schools such as the Shīʿīs allied themselves with the state and thereby gained protection for themselves and their tyrannical protectors. The Fāṭimid Empire was the prime example of this for Ibn al-Qayyim, but it was by no means the only one. In Ibn al-Qayyim's own time, the appeal of Shīʿism among the Mongols was attributed in part to the efforts of the Shīʿī scholar al-Ḥillī (d. 726/1326), whose work was criticized at great length by Ibn Taymiyyah in his *Minhāj*. By giving a *fatwā* to the Mongol ruler Qayshan Gülük, circa 709/1309, which allowed him to go back to his thrice-divorced wife—a *fatwā* that none of the Sunnī *muqallids* at the time would issue—al-Ḥillī was supposed to have created a soft spot for Shīʿism in the ruler's heart. It is significant that both Ibn Taymiyyah and Ibn al-Qayyim actually opposed the majority Sunnī opinion on the issue of the triple divorce. For them, the refusal of the Sunnī scholars to abandon *taqlīd* was therefore creating an unwholesome alliance between a corrupted religion and a corrupted political authority.

The potential for tyranny present in a state-*madhhab* alliance is fully and startlingly expressed in the writings of fundamentalists such as the Pakistani founder of the Jamāt-e Islāmī, Abū l-Aʿlā Mawdūdī, who justifies his stance that the state can impose one *madhhab* on the population by drawing on the example of the Ottoman Empire, which imposed Ḥanafism as the state *madhhab*. Mawdūdī's argument is that, because the views held by the established schools are by definition orthodox, there can be no grounds for objecting to them, if a state were to impose them at an official level.[57] For both Mawdūdī and the defenders of the regime of *taqlīd*, the *madhhab*'s views need not be subjected to a further test of legitimacy. While opposed to rigid *taqlīd* in his other writings, here Mawdūdī's views seem similar to those held by defenders of the regime of *taqlīd*, who argued that a *muqallid* had only to discover what his Imām's rule was and could ignore the question of what actually constituted God's rule for the legal problem facing him.[58] This is precisely the stance objected to by those scholars of the classical period who criticized rigid *taqlīd*. For them, all authority had to be subject to the test of compatibility with scripture. Any authority or law, religious or secular, that was not justified by scripture was not law but tyranny. For these critics, the problem with the regime of *taqlīd* was that it sought to immunize itself from being challenged for its conformity to scripture, which for these scholars was the sole and thus ultimate source of authority and legitimacy in Islam. To refuse to refer all authority to the test of compatibility with scripture would mean allowing non-scriptural—and therefore (in the Muslim view) tyrannical—views to be treated in exactly the same way as those for which such scriptural proof was available.

## *Taqlīd* as Authority

Some recent discussions of *taqlīd*, such as those of Haim Gerber, have argued against calling it "imitation" of the doctrines of past authorities on the grounds that *taqlīd* involves accepting the intellectual authority of another jurist and is therefore distinct from imitation.[59] If this view is correct, it is difficult to reconcile with the account of *taqlīd* as presented by one of the most astute writers ever to address the subject, al-Qarāfī. In Jackson's summary of al-Qarāfī's thought, it is clear that for the latter, *taqlīd* is certainly not just the acceptance of someone else's intellectual authority. Rather, the *muqallid* scholar accepts that his knowledge and understanding of *uṣūl* matches that of the eponym, and that it might even be greater than his.[60] *Taqlīd*, then, is simply the process of acquiring some necessary authority—not necessarily intellectual—that could act as the force behind the law.

While jurists in the regime of *ijtihād* would be able to locate the authority of the law in its content, those in the regime of *taqlīd* would find it necessary to locate such authority elsewhere: in the person of an individual jurist of the past, or in a school, either of which could be used to validate the legal opinions of a *muqallid* scholar. The *muqallid* scholar could not, however, acknowledge this fact, because doing so would expose the extent to which the law was subject to constant change and innovation, thus destroying the legitimacy it claimed by virtue of being unchanging and consistent.[61]

The suggestion that legal opinions in the regime of *taqlīd* derive their authority not from the content of the law but from the legal and scholarly tradition to which the *muqallid* scholar belongs is therefore problematic for several reasons. First, such a neat division between authority and content in Islamic law is untenable, for the authority of any legal opinion continues to be determined in part by the extent to which its content is based on scripture. It is for this reason that *muqallid* scholars continued to challenge both the authority and the content of scholarly opinions by offering different interpretations of scriptural proofs relied on by their opponents or dismissing the *aḥādīth* relied on by the latter as inauthentic.[62] The content of the law thus continued to function as a mark of its authority, even in the regime of *taqlīd*, as *muqallid* scholars continued to present the rulings of their Imāms as more authoritative because the substance of their rulings matched the *aḥādīth*. This is the case, for example, in the attack of Ibn al-Labbād (ʿAbd al-Laṭīf al-Baghdādī, d. 629/1231) against al-Shāfiʿī and in the defense of Abū Ḥanīfah in the *Iʿlāʾ al-sunan*.[63] Both works aim to show that it is the *content* of Mālik and Abū Ḥanīfah's doctrines—in particular their being in harmony with scripture—that makes them more worthy of being followed and bestows more authority on them.

Presenting the regime of *taqlīd* as a system in which the authority of a legal opinion derives not from its content but from its place in a particular legal tradition also creates a misleading dichotomy between a regime of *taqlīd* based on tradition and authority and a regime of *ijtihād* that appears to lack these qualities. In fact, authority and tradition are always among the core features of any legal culture, as seen in the works of both traditionalist Salafī critics of *taqlīd* and their opponents.[64] The real question, then, is, why should the search for authority, which is an animating feature of almost every legal culture, so often take the form of *taqlīd* in Islam? Why is it that the authority of scripture, which seems to suffice for some scholars, proves insufficient for *muqallid* scholars in the regime of *taqlīd*, even as *muqallid* scholars such as al-Qarāfī assert that *muqallids* and *mujtahids* are absolutely equal in their mastery of the interpretive sciences.[65] It is, after all, precisely their opponents' concept of authority that the critics of rigid *taqlīd* are denouncing, when they criticize dicta that the *madhhab* of the Imām is like the Qurʾan for his followers—a statement attributed to Ibn al-Ṣalāḥ al-Shahrazūrī (d. 643/1245) which is roundly condemned by Ibn Qayyim.[66] Instead, Ibn al-Qayyim argues that a *muftī* should mention the scriptural evidence for his *fatwā*—even to the extent of trying to incorporate words used in scripture in his *fatwā*—precisely to emphasize the latter's *authority*.[67]

The trend of conflating *taqlīd* with tradition and with Islam itself is perhaps most visible in the work of the late Norman Calder. In his work on Ibn ʿĀbidīn's *Chaplets on the Mufti's Task*, Calder explicitly contrasts the Islamic legal tradition with the Protestant legal vision of the English Restoration poet John Dryden and confidently asserts that Islam "was otherwise."[68] He sees similarities between Dryden's concepts of "reasonable faith" and his "everyman's direct approach to scripture," and the reformist thought of Muḥammad ʿAbduh (d. 1905) and Jamāl al-Dīn al-Afghānī (d. 1897). The legal vision of all three, he maintains, is opposed to the justified acknowledgment of authority, the commitment to tradition and the doctrine of *taqlīd* that is the hallmark of Islamic legal practice. In Islam, he says, neither scripture nor common sense, but only the interpretations of established figures, carried authority. Scripture, he asserts, did not speak itself.[69] The fact that, despite Calder's confident assertions, the following essay of Ibn al-Qayyim, as well as works by renowned scholars such as al-Ṭabarī (d. 310/923), Ibn Baṭṭah (d. 387/997), Ibn Ḥazm (d. 456/1064), and al-Khaṭīb al-Baghdādī (d. 463/1071), all refer to "speaking scripture" (*kitāb nāṭiq*) alerts us to the common mistake of transposing our knowledge of one school (in Calder's case, the Ḥanafī), to the whole Islamic tradition.[70]

Scholars such as those mentioned above criticized rigid *taqlīd* precisely because they saw it as undermining the primary source of authority in Islam—scripture. The debate on *taqlīd*, then, is not about authority versus the lack of authority but about how certain sources of authority come to be valued as others are devalued.[71] For instance, Ibn al-Qayyim repeatedly refers to the Companions and their students living in various centers of learning throughout the early Islamic state as individuals whose status as legal authorities is accepted across sectarian lines.[72] Recent studies of early *ḥadīth* collections, such as that by Lucas on the *Muṣannaf* of Ibn Abī Shaybah, also suggest that the early *ahl al-ḥadīth* and *ahl al-rā'y* were in agreement over the identity of the individuals who were considered to be legal authorities.[73] Critics of Ibn al-Qayyim's arguments on *taqlīd* seldom miss an opportunity to accuse him and his fellow Salafīs of imitating earlier authorities.[74] How then, does there come to be disagreement about the extent to which the opinions of these authorities are authoritative? Why is it that early jurists, such as the eponyms of the *madhhabs*' followers, can be celebrated for their legal ingenuity and novelty, while later ones are seen as suspect, unless they derive their opinions by reference to past authorities? These questions can only be answered if we explore the way the authority of the *madhhab* is constructed.

## Seeking Authority for the *Madhhab*

To explain adequately the rise and functioning of the regime of *taqlīd*, we have to explain how different modes of authority emerge and develop as the regime of *ijtihād* transforms into the regime of *taqlīd*. The shift from a system in which interaction with revelation was seen as an essential feature of a jurist's work to one in which it was not was a radical one, and this transformation occurred at the same time as other major transitions in Islamic culture, particularly the rise of popular Sufism. As Makdisi has argued, one of the ways in which the new regime of *taqlīd* compensated for the diminished role of scripture in legal reasoning was by developing a cult of piety around the figure of the eponym and the *madhhab* itself. For giving up the blessing of interacting with scripture, a *muqallid* was compensated with the blessings of being associated with the *madhhab* of his eponym.[75] In many cases, the *madhhab* began to take on some of the features of the developed Sufi orders (*ṭuruq*, sing. *ṭarīqah*), becoming a self-contained traditional and pietistic tradition. This happened while the concept of piety itself was being contested between those who argued for strict adherence to the Sunnah and the practices of the *salaf* (pious forefathers) and those who celebrated the extraordinary and rigorous feats of worship and reported miracles of later figures of authority, which, for them, provided the firmest link with the spirituality of the Prophet. Extraordinary spiritual feats were thus also associated with the founding Imāms of the schools of law just as they were with major saints and the founders of Sufi orders.

With the entrenchment of the regime of *taqlīd*, scriptural, theological, and eschatological arguments and proofs in favor of *taqlīd* came to wield as much influence as jurisprudential arguments. These arguments continue to be seen in contemporary debates on the topic in the Muslim world. The change in the nature of the argument not only suggests a transformation in the way scripture is understood, it also explains why those Muslim scholars who dared to challenge the *taqlīd* practiced by their peers were persecuted so severely by the latter. For the critics of *taqlīd* were challenging not just an abstract jurisprudential doctrine but a Weltanschauung, one that regarded ongoing *ijtihād* as impious and sinful. Ibn al-Qayyim is clear about what he believes to be the implications of the belief of the *muqallid* scholars that there had been no *mujtahid*s since the days of the Imāms:

> According to them, it is acceptable for there to be a time when the earth is devoid of those who stand on the path of God with evidence, and for it to be empty of those who speak on the basis of knowledge. They regard it as impermissible for anyone after that time to look to the Book of God or the Sunnah for the purpose of acquiring rulings from them. Nor do they deem it permissible for one to judge and render verdicts based directly on what is in the Qur'an and Sunnah, unless this corresponds to the opinion of the principal and the one he imitates.

We must understand this in order to understand the ferocity of the debate on *taqlīd* and appreciate the significance of Islamic revivalist thought that condemned *taqlīd*.[76]

To get some sense of the intensity of the debate and the way *madhhab* authority is constructed, let us consider the introductory section of the *Radd al-muḥtār* of Ibn ʿĀbidīn, which outlines the basic principles on which the rest of this most authoritative of Ḥanafī works rests. *Taqlīd* figures prominently as one of those basic principles, and, in addition to explaining the superstructure of the Ḥanafī school, the author draws on several earlier Ḥanafī authorities to build his case for the authority of the Ḥanafī *madhhab*. Ibn ʿĀbidīn's account demonstrates vividly how the authority of the *madhhab* was developed and sustained against its critics in later Islamic legal history. The ferocity of the debates on this issue can be gauged by Ibn ʿĀbidīn's discussion of poetic verses attributed to the celebrated scholar ʿAbdallāh b. al-Mubārak (d. 181/797) by early Ḥanafī authorities. At the end of the poem comes a curse on anyone who rejects the sayings of Abū Ḥanīfah: "May Our Lord curse, by an amount equaling the number of grains of sand in the world / The one who rejects the opinion of Abū Ḥanīfah" (*Fa laʿnat rabbina aʿdād raml/ʿAlā man radd qawl Abī Ḥanīfah*).[77] The famous dictum of al-Karkhī, the Muʿtazilī-Ḥanafī jurist, that every verse of the Qurʾan and every *ḥadīth* disagreeing with the interpretation of the Ḥanafīs would have to reinterpreted or would be considered abrogated, is also cited at the outset.[78]

As stated earlier, the authority of the eponym of a *madhhab* was constructed in ways that also legitimized his school. Hurvitz has described the cult of piety that developed around the figure of Aḥmad b. Ḥanbal and contributed to the construction of his school.[79] Al-Shāfiʿī's descent from the Quraysh, the clan of the Prophet, played a great role in developing his authority. His closeness to the Prophet is reported by *madhhab* authorities to be so great that, like the Prophet, he suffered more than ordinary believers during his illness.[80] Outstanding scholars such as al-Nawawī (d. 676/1277–1278) and Ibn Qudāmah (d. 620/1223) do not see themselves simply as heirs of the intellectual tradition of their Imāms, they also believe themselves to be part of a spiritual chain going back to the founders of the schools. Al-Nawawī asks God to bless him on account of his affiliation with al-Shāfiʿī.[81] Ibn Qudāmah alludes to the blessing (*tabarruk*) he hopes to gain from being associated with Ibn Ḥanbal and also from commenting on a Ḥanbalī text as renowned as the *Mukhtaṣar* of al-Khiraqī (d. 334/945).[82] Abū Isḥāq al-Shirāzī (d. 476/1083) and other scholars frequently report seeing the Prophet in dreams in which he approves of their Imāms and condemns others (in al-Shirāzī's case, Abū Ḥanīfah's use of *rā'y* is condemned by the Prophet). Various dream reports also have Abū Ḥanīfah assuring people that they would enter paradise.

*Madhhab* authority was also bolstered by the creation of a religious figure of knowledge and authority, the eponym, with his own disciples (*aṣḥāb*), much like the Prophet and his Companions.[83] At the same time, another aspect of the construction of scholarly and *madhhab* authority, particularly visible in the case of the Ḥanafī school, which has historically been the most inclined to insist on *taqlīd*, involved constructing an image of the eponym and his followers that was influenced by contemporary developments in Sufism. After a certain date, arguments in support of *taqlīd* involved the skillful appropriation of aspects of the developing Sufi tradition, as can be seen in the works of authors such as al-Sha'rānī (d. 973/1565), Ibn 'Abidīn, and 'Uthmānī, whose arguments in favor of Abū Ḥanīfah exemplify this trend. Likewise, scholars who criticized rigid *taqlīd* were often thereby also criticizing what they regarded as the cults of personality that had become a hallmark of popular Sufism in their days, which had been appropriated by the legal schools.

In literature that uses a Sufi phenomenology to reinforce the authority of the *madhhab*, both the *mujtahid* and the Sufi *shaykh* come to be seen as "rarer than red sulphur." This metaphor, common among Sufis, bemoans not only lost knowledge but also the lost qualities of spiritual insight and virtue embodied in the eponyms. In the absence of the eponym and individuals like him who possess these qualities, it becomes essential to hold on to their transferred authority as represented by those who belonged to their "schools," whether in law or Sufism—those who, by following their Imām, would rekindle and enliven the dormant spirituality and religiosity of their followers. Recreating that missing spirituality in later generations demanded strict conformity to the practices of deceased figures around whom a cult of spirituality and piety had developed, for they were regarded as having ascended heights of piety that were impossible to reach for those coming later. Ibn 'Aqīl (d. 513/1119), the renowned Ḥanbalī jurist, records the argument of his opponents, who insist that, even if people meeting the prerequisite of *ijtihād* can be found in their time, they are corrupted by their sins, implying that the early *mujtahids* themselves were above that.[84] Attitudes like this would prompt al-Ṣan'ānī to exclaim that the *muqallids* exalted earlier scholars to such an extent that they began to think of them as creatures who were "not made of the essence of clay" (*annahum ghayr makhlūqīn min ṣulālah min ṭīn*).[85] Al-Ṣanʿānī's choice of words, drawing on the Qurʾanic account of the creation of all men from clay (*ṣulālah min ṭīn*, Q., al-Muʾminūn, 23:12), indicates the strong disapproval this glorification of mere mortals would evoke in some scholars, for whom such exaltation of men "made of the essence of clay" would come dangerously close to an elevation of man above the station in which God had placed him.

Law schools also appropriated from Sufism the idea of the inner or intuitive knowledge of the eponyms and past *mujtahids*. Thus, in later apologetic works on *taqlīd*, what distinguishes the earlier generations of scholars is their *dhawq* (intuition) or *kashf* (unveiling of the truth), both heavily charged Sufi terms used repeatedly by ʿUthmānī, in his *Iʿlāʾ al-sunan*, to describe the process of *ijtihād* carried out by a *mujtahid*. The art or science of *ijtihād* was not, in this view, something to be learned but rather to be experienced in the way divine gnosis is experienced in Sufi thought. By the same logic, anyone who disagreed with the *ijtihād* of a *mujtahid* on rational grounds could be dismissed easily, because, whatever his level of knowledge, he could not argue against the *dhawq* of the eponym. Using *dhawq* and *kashf* as arguments for the veracity of a *mujtahid*'s opinion was, however, a double-edged sword. Some Ḥanafī critics of rigid *taqlīd* would use the same techniques to "prove" that *taqlīd* of one *madhhab* was not obligatory, claiming that this was a truth that had been "unveiled" to them.[86]

The process of constructing an eponym's mystic and spiritual authority can be seen, once again, in the opening section of the *Radd al-muḥtār*, which is significant precisely because it brings together several layers of Ḥanafī scholarship devoted to a discussion of the authority of the Ḥanafī school and its eponym. In this section, Abū Ḥanīfah's spiritual authority is valued as much as, if not more than, his legal acumen, and it is clearly the meta-principle that shapes the main work, which is concerned with the presentation, elucidation, and justification of Ḥanafī opinions. Several reports are cited, in which Abū Ḥanīfah's disciples mention seeing him in the highest ranks of paradise in their dreams. Combining the authority of a religious scholar and a gnostic, Abū Ḥanīfah is reported to have seen God 100 times in his dreams, a feat seldom accomplished by even the most adept mystics. He is also reported to have been taught the words to a religious formula that, if recited, will save people from divine punishment. Even Abū Ḥanīfah's worship is presented in unmistakably mystical terms. During his last pilgrimage to Mecca, he is reported to have entered the Kaʿbah and prayed a two-unit prayer, in which he recited one half of the Qur'an while standing on his right foot alone, and the other half while standing on his left foot, after which he claimed to have achieved gnosis (*ma'rifah*). The connection between his mystic power and his legal status is solidified when we learn that, as a result of his extraordinary feats of worship, he received divine assurance that he and those who followed his school would be forgiven.[87] Abū Ḥanīfah's status as a mystic saint is cemented by the report that al-Shāfi'ī himself would pray at Abū Ḥanīfah's grave when he wanted his prayers to be answered.[88] Not only does this report show the way in which *muqallid* scholars used Sufi practices, such as offering prayer at the burial places of saints, to consolidate the authority of their own schools, it also neatly establishes a hierarchy between the two eponyms whose schools developed such an intense rivalry over time. Other Ḥanafīs had gone so far as to report *aḥādīth* in which the Prophet himself predicted that there would be in his community a man known as Muḥammad b. Idrīs (i.e., al-Shafi'ī), who would be more harmful to it than the Devil and that there would be a man in his community called Abū Ḥanīfah, who would be its light.[89]

The importance of such reports should not be underestimated. In the course of his lengthy refutation of Ibn al-Qayyim's essay, the Deobandī scholar Kīrānwī argues that Ibn al-Qayyim is wrong in asserting that the very act of a *muqallid* choosing the Imām and school to which he subscribes involves a kind of *ijtihād*. Kīrānwī argues that, unlike issues of substantive law (*furū'*), in which specific evidence and *ijtihād* are required before one can act on a scholarly opinion, one could choose one's Imām not on the basis of any evidence but merely on the basis of an "inclination of one's heart." Similarly, a *muqallid* could defend his Imām not on the basis of evidence but on the basis of being charitable towards the latter, again without carrying out any *ijtihād* himself.[90] The effect of reports such as those mentioned by Ibn 'Ābidīn and his Ḥanafī predecessors in procuring an "inclination of the heart" and "charitableness" towards one's Imām would be considerable, especially in the case of the layman who could not be expected to appreciate the subtle legal differences between the schools but who could certainly grasp the significance of reports such as those related above. In fact, reports such as these would reinforce the ties of loyalty that bound large numbers of ordinary people to a school, such ties being perhaps the greatest resource any school could have.[91] The selection of one's Imām on such grounds is exactly what leads critics of *taqlīd* such as al-Ṣan'ānī to dismiss such choices as a form of caprice (*shahwah*).[92] Ibn al-Qayyim also points out that such accounts in support of particular eponyms lose their potency once nearly all the schools develop them to bolster the authority of their own Imāms:

> If every sect from the imitators argues for the primacy of its principal for any possible reason such as his belonging to an earlier time, his asceticism and piety, his meeting with venerable and ordinary scholars whom those after him could not meet, or the large number of his followers who are not rivaled by anyone else, another group is able to argue for the primacy of their principal with these same arguments—or similar ones—or those even better. (Argument 81)

Acknowledging the way Sufi discourse was used to promote *taqlīd* does not mean that all, or even most, scholars in the regime of *taqlīd* actively subscribed to a Sufi worldview in which saints guaranteed one's entry to heaven or praying at the graves of dead saints was encouraged. The fact that *muqallid* scholars employed Sufi metaphors to construct the authority of their eponyms and schools probably represents their recognition of the popular appeal of Sufism and their attempts to present their own tradition in terms that would transcend their own jurisprudential world and find resonances in Sufi circles.[93] This would explain the *muqallid* scholars' continued celebration of the unique contribution of their eponyms as jurisprudents who also happened to be masters of Sufism, and not as Sufis who also happened to be masters of jurisprudence.

At the same time, we can see that traditionalists amongst the Ḥanbalīs and others generally avoided constructing the authority of their scholars by using the discourse of mystical Sufism. On the contrary, they saw the authority of their scholars as lying in the fact that they submitted to the intellectual authority of the Prophet, in comparison to whose intellect the intellect of the whole of humanity (including those scholars whose legal acumen was so celebrated by *muqallid* jurists) was merely "a speck of dust." This argument was widespread in early traditionalist circles, and Wahb b. Munabbih (d. 110/728?) reports as many as seventy of his teachers using it.[94] In addition to relying heavily on the intellectual authority of the Prophet, traditionalists cultivated the idea that piety consisted of close adherence to his word.[95] This principle meant measuring the authority of a scholar not on the basis of the novelty of his legal approach nor on the basis of how often he could be shown to be correct in matters of *ikhtilāf* but on whether he had the correct approach to legal problems, that is, by searching for answers in the *aḥādīth*, a test which the traditionalist *ahl al-ḥadīth* were bound to pass and their rivals were bound to fail.[96] In fact, Aḥmad b. Ḥanbal was himself reported to have advised people to obtain verdicts from the *ahl al-ḥadīth* rather than the *ahl al-rā'y* even if the former were not very knowledgeable, due to the soundness of their approach.[97] In his essay on *taqlīd*, Ibn al-Qayyim also points out the strength of the methodology of the *ahl al-ḥadīth*, which he credits for the relative lack of dissension in their ranks:

> This is why you will find that the people who have the least disagreement among themselves are the people of the Sunnah and *ḥadīth*. There is not, in the whole world, a faction more in harmony and with lesser disagreement in their midst than them because they base themselves on this principle. The more a sect is removed from the *ḥadīth*, the greater and more severe is the disagreement in their midst. (Argument 51)

The above reveals once again that, in the debate on *taqlīd*, it is not just two legal theories that are competing for acceptance but two competing views on how to recapture the piety, knowledge, and authority of the Prophet—two competing *religiosities*. This also explains the Salafī opposition to rigid *taqlīd*. Classical Salafīs such as al-Bukhārī (d. 256/870), Ibn Taymiyyah, and al-Ṣanʿānī believed that their contemporaries' understanding of rigid *taqlīd* went beyond the practice and beliefs of the Prophet and the early generations (including especially the Companions). This made it both dangerous and misguided, a point we shall return to later.[98] Their criticism of rigid *taqlīd* was thus based on the same arguments that they used to condemn speculative theology (*kalām*) and extremist Sufis. It is for this reason that traditionalists such as Ibn Taymiyyah, unlike the anti-*taqlīd* Ḥanafī scholars, never base their arguments on *kashf*, preferring to rely instead on scriptural or rational arguments.

As we have seen, a crucial ingredient of the construction of the extraordinary spiritual authority of the eponym was the notion that such spiritual authority disappeared from the world as time progressed and was replaced by immorality and sinfulness. Many defenders of *taqlīd* based their arguments on *aḥādīth* that spoke of the spread of corruption and the disappearance of knowledge, as the end of the world drew near.[99] This made it preferable to rely on authorities of the past. In light of these traditions, they argued, it was unseemly and impious for later authorities to challenge the views of earlier ones.

The critics of rigid *taqlīd,* such as Ibn al-Qayyim and al-Ṣanʿānī, did not altogether reject the idea of worsening times, which had substantial support in the *ḥadīth* literature. Instead, they argued that disagreeing with earlier scholars did not mean that one believed oneself to be superior to them in rank nor that one would be rewarded as much for his *ijtihād* as they were for theirs.[100] Rather, both early and late scholars could disagree with each other and with their predecessors on the basis of scriptural proof, without holding themselves to be superior to their opponents.[101] Alongside this, critics of rigid *taqlīd* placed great importance on the existence of *aḥādīth* that spoke of the victorious group in the *ummah* (Muslim community) that would continue to remain firm on the truth, and the *mujaddid* who would revive Islam at the turn of each century.[102] The victorious community and the *mujaddid* would fight innovations and non-scriptural influences that had crept into the religion and would act as the "proof of God on earth."[103] From the popular traditionalist identification of ʿUmar b. ʿAbd al-ʿAzīz, al-Shāfiʿī, and Aḥmad b. Ḥanbal as possible *mujaddids*, we can see that the *mujaddid* tradition was understood, at least by traditionalists, as referring to individuals whose calls for renewal (*tajdīd*) emphasized the authority of the Qurʾan and the Sunnah over *taqlīd* of previous authorities. It was thus argued that the *mujaddid* must also be an absolute *mujtahid.* The frequently cited lists of *mujaddids* thus often include scholars such as ʿIzz b. ʿAbd al-Salām (d. 660/1262), who were renowned for their criticism of the rigid *taqlīd* practiced by their contemporaries and for their call to eschew scholarly and popular beliefs and practices not supported by scripture. Ḥanbalī traditionalists, however, did not rely as much as their Shāfiʿī counterparts on the *mujaddid* tradition, partly because, as a school, they were generally the least inclined toward *taqlīd* in the first place and so did not feel the need for a *mujaddid* figure to liberate them from rigid *taqlīd.* Hodgson has correctly described the Ḥanbalī tradition as a radical movement that challenged established authority on principle:

> Hanbalism . . . remained a comprehensive and essentially radical movement, which had elaborated its own fiqh in accordance with its own principles, but whose leaders were often unwilling to acknowledge the kind of *taqlīd* as provided the institutional security of the other schools, and replaced the ijmāʿ tradition of the living community on principle. *Ijtihād* inquiry remained alive among the Hanbalīs; each major teacher felt free to start afresh, according to the needs of his own time to reform in a puritan direction.[104]

The Ḥanafīs, for their part, were just as comfortable employing eschatological arguments in defense of their own positions on *taqlīd*. While other schools saw in the return of the Messiah an opportunity to return to a pristine form of Islam free of *madhhab* boundaries, the renowned Ḥanafī scholar al-Haṣkafī's (d. 1088/1677) assertion that the Messiah would be a Ḥanafī *muqallid* (an assertion based on a mystical unveiling, or *kashf*), demonstrates the way in which almost all schools could use the same eschatological material to reinforce their own positions on *taqlīd*.[105]

## Theological Rationale for *Taqlīd*

Within the range of what might be termed non-jurisprudential arguments for *taqlīd*, we need to pay special attention to the theological paradigm. Theological concerns were always crucially important in any Islamic jurisprudential debate, and the debate on *taqlīd* was no exception.[106] In fact, one of the most enduring battles in *uṣūl al-fiqh* was that between traditionalists and *kalām* scholars who sought to develop Islamic theology in light of Hellenistic philosophy and science. The penetration of *kalām* scholars into the ranks of the scholars of *uṣūl* early in the history of the discipline was something that traditionalists fought against. In his insightful work on the theological significance of al-Shāfiʿī's *uṣūl al-fiqh*, Makdisi suggests that, after Shāfiʿī, one of the reasons for the popularity of *uṣūl* as a field of study was the opportunity it gave *kalām* theologians to practice their craft in the garb of traditionalism.[107] The traditionalists, however, viewed *uṣūl al-fiqh* as an antidote to *kalām*, and later traditionalists, particularly those of the Shāfiʿī school, would go to great lengths to distinguish their *uṣūl al-fiqh* from those of the *kalām* theologians, particularly the Ashʿarīs, who represented the greatest threat to traditionalism.[108]

We can see theological concerns at the forefront of the debate on *taqlīd*, as scholars argued over whether it was possible for an age to be altogether devoid of *mujtahids*. Because it was agreed in principle that carrying out *ijtihād* was a divine command, which could be fulfilled only by *mujtahids*, jurisprudents found themselves involved in a theological debate on whether God could issue an impossible command, to carry out *ijtihād*, while depriving humanity of the *mujtahids* who would be required to do so.[109]

More generally, the theological affiliations of certain scholars often prompted them to promote or condemn certain conceptions of *taqlīd* and *ijtihād*. This can be seen in the legal works of Muʿtazilī scholars such as Abū Ḥuṣayn al-Baṣrī (d. 436/1044–1045) and ʿAbd al-Jabbār (d. 415/1024), which take an anti-*taqlīd* stance.[110] Early Ḥanafīs such as al-Jaṣṣāṣ (d. 370/980–981) also refuted *taqlīd* on theological grounds, arguing, in broadly Muʿtazilī terms, for the obligation to use one's own reason to understand scripture.[111] In fact, positions on *taqlīd* came to be so aligned with positions in theology that that the renowned Ḥanafī scholar Ibn ʿĀbidīn candidly refers to the "position of the *ahl al-sunnah wa-l-jamāʿah*" (referring primarily to the Māturīdīs and Ashʿarīs) on *taqlīd*.[112]

In many cases, scholars were forced to adopt conflicting positions on *taqlīd* because of their theological affiliations. Al-Māwardī's (d. 450/1058) theological leanings forced him to conclude that, because a Prophetic tradition that is not reported through numerous chains of narration (*tawātur*) cannot generate positive knowledge, all such reports are to be followed by way of *taqlīd*—this despite his general condemnation of *taqlīd*.[113] Theological considerations are responsible also for some of the more glaring tensions in the Ashʿarī al-Subkī's (d. 771/1370) biography of Juwaynī (d. 478/1085), whose deathbed repentance of *kalām* al-Subkī is forced to recast as a retraction of his legal *ijtihād*, in which he differed with the Shāfiʿī school.[114] In reality, al-Juwaynī's condemnation of those who did not follow "the path of the *salaf*" could not have been a retraction of his legal independence from the Shāfiʿī school, because following a school did not really prevent al-Juwaynī or al-Subkī himself from disagreeing with the earlier scholars from the same school.[115] Al-Juwaynī's retraction of *kalām* was, on the other hand, something the Ashʿarī al-Subkī could not support. He thus presents al-Juwaynī as a pure *muqallid*, who repented of his *ijtihād*. If we are to understand the topic of *taqlīd* properly, it is crucial that we consider the theological dimension of the debates surrounding it.[116]

The unity of the *ummah* and its protection from error were also theological factors that figured prominently in jurisprudential debates on *taqlīd*. For *muqallids*, the unity of the *ummah* would be destroyed by people being given the freedom to adopt novel positions on seemingly settled questions of law. For critics of rigid *taqlīd*, there was ample proof of the evil consequences of rigid *taqlīd* in reprehensible innovations such as the establishment of a separate congregation for each of the four schools in the Sacred Mosque in Mecca, not to mention *fatāwā* in which, for example, the marriage of Ḥanafī women to Shāfiʿī men was analogized to a marriage between Muslim women and non-Muslim men and therefore declared prohibited.[117] Even some broad-minded jurisprudents, such as the great al-Ghazālī (d. 505/1111), had argued that a *muqallid* could not pray behind an *imām* belonging to another school, if the latter's prayer would be invalid according to one's own school.[118] This was also one of the arguments presented by Ibn al-Qayyim in his essay on *taqlīd*:

> Certainly disagreement has arisen and worsened because of imitation and its proponents. They are the ones who divided the religion into factions, each one glorifying and turning to its principal and condemning those who oppose him. They do not believe in the correctness of acting by the others' views, as if the others belonged to an entirely different community. They exert and outdo themselves in refuting each other. They say, "Their books and our books differ, as do their scholars and ours and their schools and ours." All this they have done despite the fact that there is one Prophet, one Qur'an, one religion and one God. (Argument 51)

Ibn ʿAqīl also argued that the idea that there were no more *mujtahids* further damaged the notion of a divinely protected and unified *ummah*, which reached authoritative consensus or *ijmāʿ* (because consensus can only issue from the *mujtahids* of a particular age).[119] For other scholars critical of *taqlīd*, such as Ibn Taymiyyah and al-ʿIzz, who both issued verdicts allowing prayers behind an *imām* from another school, the rulings issued by *muqallid* scholars prohibiting such prayers went against the theological imperative of keeping the *ummah* united. Such explicit theological reasoning was an essential part of the jurisprudential arguments on *taqlīd*, and many scholars were motivated to write against *taqlīd* simply because of their abhorrence for the dissension it caused in congregational prayer.[120] At the same time, those theological doctrines that united the Sunnī community, such as their opposition to the Shīʿīs, were also used to convince the community of the invalidity of particular stances on the issue of *taqlīd*. The Ḥanafī traditionalist Ibn Abī al-ʿIzz would argue that, by selecting individual scholars as their sources of authority, Sunnī *muqallids* had started to act like the Shīʿīs, who had also arbitrarily chosen particular Companions as the sources of all authority.[121] Discussing *taqlīd*, Ibn al-Qayyim also argues that the Sunnī position on the deference due to scholars is distinct from that of the Shīʿīs and their extreme opponents, the Nāṣibīs, whose opposition to the former made them belittle ʿAlī and refuse to give him his due.[122] We can thus say that the influence of theological principles on the institution of *taqlīd* was significant, as will be seen from Ibn al-Qayyim's discussion of the subject.[123]

## Ashʿarī Skepticism and *Taqlīd*

The issue of theology is even more intricately linked with *taqlīd* than the above account suggests. In his masterful study of the legal and political thought of al-Qarāfī, one of the most outstanding scholars ever to write on the topic of *taqlīd*, Professor Jackson demonstrates that al-Qarāfī was motivated to defend the system of *taqlīd* because of his belief that the divine origin of scripture imposed no limitation whatever on the range of its possible interpretations.[124] Without any hope of arriving at an objectively correct interpretation of scripture, *muqallid* scholars could legitimately continue to defend the opinions of their predecessors, which were as likely to be correct as those of their rivals.

This skepticism about the possibility of an objectively correct interpretation of scripture was one of the hallmarks of late Ashʿarī theology. While early Ashʿarīs such as al-Juwaynī (d. 478) had argued that only one out of many conflicting juristic views could be correct, at least in matters of *uṣūl*, many later Ashʿarīs such as al-Ghazālī tended to hold that, in matters of speculative *ijtihād*, *mujtahids* who held mutually contradictory views were all correct.[125] The act of carrying out *ijtihād* thus bestowed a sort of immunity, both legal and spiritual, on the *mujtahid* and all those who imitated him. Other Ashʿarīs, such as al-Qarāfī and Fakhr al-Dīn al-Rāzī (d. 606/1209), did not accept the doctrine of all *mujtahids* being correct, but nevertheless held that disagreement among the *mujtahids* meant that, generally, no objectively correct theological or legal view could be identified without reference to established schools or scholars.[126] Rāzī, for instance, argued not only that it was impossible to find the solution to all possible legal problems (which were potentially infinite) within scripture (which was finite), but also that it was impossible to assert that scripture had an objectively correct meaning. To do so would be to concede that God intended to achieve certain objectives and purposes with His acts and speech. However, the idea of God having aims and objectives had already been ruled out by Ashʿarī theology, as seen in the writings of al-Rāzī, who in his renowned commentary on the Qurʾan, rejected the idea that God's actions (including His speech and His legislative commands contained in the Qurʾan) could have an objective or purpose.[127] Among later Ash'arīs, this belief fuelled a great deal of skepticism about the possibility of arriving at an objectively correct and straightforward interpretation of scripture. The Ash'arī al-Subkī would claim that the denial of identifiable purposes in the divine law was the most popular view among the scholars of *kalām*, as opposed to the jurists who, according to al-Subkī, held the view that speaking of divine purposes in the law was valid.[128] Even some Ḥanbalīs, despite their opposition to Ash'arism, would come close to holding al-Rāzī's position.[129]

Rejecting the idea that there are authoritative, objectively verifiable interpretations of scripture has profound effects on legal theory and jurisprudence, not to mention theology.[130] These effects are quite visible in the works of some Ash'arī scholars.[131] For when Ash'arī scholars such as al-Qarāfī wrote on the subject of *taqlīd*, they did so partly under the influence of al-Rāzī's view that one could not speak of an objective purpose in scripture, and that one must therefore be skeptical about the possibility of preferring one of several competing scholarly inferences by referring to the underlying rationale of scripture itself.[132] Instead, *muqallid* scholars were automatically driven to locate authority for their legal opinions outside of scripture, for instance, in a *madhhab* or a super-*mujtahid* figure whose spiritual authority silences his opponents and makes his opinions worthy of imitation by later scholars. This explains, in part, why *muqallid* scholars found it so convenient to embellish the spiritual authority of their eponyms.[133] Scholars such as Sha'rānī, for instance, would employ Sufi terminology to argue that each *mujtahid* has an intuition (*dhawq*) and a novice (*sālik*, a term used for Sufi novice) who aspires to knowledge of the *sharī'ah*, once he attains gnosis or *ma'rifah*, will see that all the *mujtahids* are correct and that he may follow any of the schools that he desires.[134] Similarly, scholars who rejected the idea of an objective meaning of scripture would try to justify their views with sources of authority such as consensus, because the latter would remove the debate over the correct interpretation of scripture by demonstrating that a particular interpretation had been accepted as normative by all scholars. In this way, as Jackson shows, *muqallid* scholars would often reduce *ijmā'* to the considered opinion of their own school.[135]

Traditionalists such as Ibn al-Qayyim, however, insisted that revelation was to be accepted according to its straightforward and objectively correct meaning, and it was important for a scholar to strive to grasp that meaning.[136] They also affirmed the existence of purposes in God's law and remained firmly opposed to the idea that scripture could be used to justify mutually contradictory opinions. As Ibn al-Qayyim says, in the course of his refutation of the position of the *muqallid* scholars:

> We oppose the practice of saying, "Both of them [scholars who disagreed with each other] were right in their interpretation of the Book and Sunnah," even while their opinions are contradictory. Thus, the one who says this holds the evidences of the Book and the Sunnah to be contradictory and conflicting, holding that God and His Messenger command a thing and its opposite at the same time. The one who says this also maintains that His religion is subject to the opinions of men and that, in the meantime, there is no specific ruling for him to act on. So he either follows this approach or he declares incorrect the one who disagrees with his principal. He has no choice but to follow one of these two courses—this is among the blessings of imitation on him.

Like other traditionalists, Ibn al-Qayyim also rejects the new standard of orthodoxy created by the Ashʿarī view. For as Professor Jackson shows, in the absence of any notion of objective meaning, the acceptance of a legal opinion would not depend on its intrinsic content but on its endorsement by a recognized school. In fact, endorsement by a school would automatically make an opinion orthodox.[137] Ibn al-Qayyim expresses his opposition to the *muqallid* scholars' use of the concept of *ijmāʿ* thus:

> When this trend started, the practice of abandonment of texts by relying on supposed consensus came into being. Then, claims in support of this began to surface. Now, when someone among the imitators who does not know of the disagreement [in a particular area of law] is argued against on the basis of the Qurʾan and the Sunnah, he says: "This is against consensus." This is precisely what was rejected by the Imāms of Islam. They denounced the one who did this, and said, "Anyone making such a claim [of the existence of consensus] is a liar." (Argument 52)[138]

For traditionalists, the mere fact that an opinion was followed by way of *taqlīd* could not make that opinion orthodox. Orthodoxy did not depend upon the figure of a *mujtahid* or the institution of a *madhhab*, but upon scripture and the articulations of faith and law made by the *salaf*. Ibn al-Qayyim, for instance, argues in his critique of *taqlīd* that "an opinion is not correct by virtue of its bearer but because of the soundness of the proofs that establish its validity."

Furthermore, the Ashʿarīs also attracted a lot of criticism for being critical of the claims to objective knowledge made by the Muʿtazilīs and the traditionalists, while not always applying their rigorous moral relativism to themselves. For even as Ashʿarī jurists denounced the idea of objectively correct interpretations of scripture, they often argued that their own scriptural interpretations were in fact objectively correct. For instance, Al-Qarāfī—while basing his argument for *taqlīd* on the fact that the legal stance of one school cannot be established as preferable to that of another on the basis of scripture—is severely critical of some Ḥanafī scriptural interpretations that he holds to be simply wrong, despite the fact that they fulfill his criterion of validity: acceptance by an established school of law.[139] Here, al-Qarāfī's stance on such issues is not substantively different from that of his master, al-ʿIzz, who refused to recognize the validity of those views of the other schools that he held to be incorrect, even if they could be supported by a far-fetched interpretation of scripture.

Similarly, the Ashʿārī theological stance on the impossibility of holding that God's law was based on purposes and objectives was clearly at odds with the legal doctrines of leading Ashʿarī scholars who upheld the idea that the purpose of God's law was the welfare of humanity. Al-Rāzī, who denied in his *tafsīr* the possibility of imputing a rationale to God's law, nevertheless accepts in his writings on *uṣūl* that the rule that God has established his law for the benefit of human beings should guide the scholar who undertakes *qiyās,* because serving human interests is the purpose of God's law. Ashʿarīs, such as al-Ghāzalī and al-Juwaynī, went so far in affirming the existence of wise purposes in God's law that they were actually condemned by their Mālikī opponents for extending the scope of *maṣlaḥah,* or the welfare underlying divine law, further than even the Mālikīs would.[140] Al-Qarāfī too, while resting his argument for the regime of *taqlīd* on the fact that in the absence of any authoritative interpretation of scripture the interpretations of each school should be protected, nevertheless has no trouble claiming that "whenever we find a thing to be beneficial, we assume it to be a benefit which the law seeks to promote."[141] Elsewhere, al-Qarāfī criticizes his fellow Malikī *muqallids* who disagreed with his views and argues that anyone who contemplates his own views with "a sound mind and a critical eye free of the partisan bias of the madhhabs, which is unfitting for anyone who truly fears God

Almighty" will come around to his view.[142] To the extent that al-Qarāfī's argument here is accepted, it damages his argument in favor of *taqlīd*, which challenged the very possibility of arriving at an objective and non-partisan view. Similarly, in his *uṣūl* work, *al-Maḥṣūl*, al-Rāzī first lampoons those who deny the existence of purposes in God's law, pointing out that the Qur'anic text leaves no way of denying the existence of such purposes. However, a few paragraphs later, al-Rāzī goes on to insist that the existence of purposes in the law of God is something to be denied absolutely.[143]

Ibn al-Qayyim was very familiar with the works of Ashʿarī theologians and jurists. He had studied the works of al-Rāzī with leading Ashʿarī scholars such as Ṣafī al-Dīn al-Armawī as well as with Ibn Taymiyyah.[144] He thus formulates a comprehensive traditionalist response to Ashʿarī theology and jurisprudence in his most famous jurisprudential work, the *Iʿlām* and devotes a large part of the *Iʿlām* to pointing out the errors of the doctrine of *taqlīd* as developed and understood by his opponents.

## Ibn al-Qayyim's *Iʿlām*

Ibn al-Qayyim's critique of *taqlīd* forms a crucial part of his larger discussion of Islamic legal theory in the *Iʿlām*. He begins his work by providing a traditionalist account of Islamic legal history and legal theory, before moving on to dismiss what he regards as the misguided legal philosophy of the *ahl al-rāʾy* and the textualists/literalists (Ẓāhirīs) on the question of the relationship between divine law and rationality. Traditionalists such as Ibn al-Qayyim had long accused these two groups of allowing either unrestricted rationality in law or none at all. This discussion is followed by a lengthy refutation of those scholars who obligate all *muftīs* to perform *taqlīd* of a particular school of law. Instead, Ibn al-Qayyim argues both for the sufficiency of the Qur'an and Sunnah as sources of authority and also for the proposition that every rule found in the Qur'an and Sunnah is rational and serves a wise purpose. Therefore, Ibn al-Qayyim argues, it is not only logically impossible for the Qur'ān and the Sunnah to contradict themselves or each other but also impossible for them ever to be irrational, as mistakenly asserted by some scholars. This leads into a lengthy section that is devoted to a refutation of scholarly attempts to circumvent clear rules of the Qur'an and Sunnah through the use of *ḥiyal* (legal loopholes or stratagems). In the last section of the work, Ibn al-Qayyim discusses general principles underlying *iftā'* (the discipline of issuing verdicts) and then ends his work with a collection of Prophetic sayings, which he presents as Prophetic *fatāwā*, organizing them by subject. The *I'lām* thus differs from Ibn al-Qayyim's *Ṭuruq al-ḥukmiyyah*, which is addressed to the *qāḍī* (judge) as opposed to the *muftī*—although Ibn al-Qayyim points out that a *qāḍī* could also be involved in issuing verdicts—and both works share a concern with enabling those engaged in these fields to act according to the letter and spirit of scripture.[145]

The fact that Ibn al-Qayyim is writing a book for *muftī*s who will be asked to speak on behalf of God shows that he does not regard it as possible for every believer to derive from scripture all the legal rulings he will be required to live by. It is precisely because he accepts that the ordinary person will refer to a *muftī* that Ibn al-Qayyim also regards it as necessary for the *muftī* to guide the questioner to what scripture says and not to the position of a school, for Ibn al-Qayyim shares the view of most Muslim scholars, who insist that the layman is not obliged to adhere to a specific *madhhab*.[146] *Muftīs* must also rule according to what they perceive to be the correct position on any legal matter, because it is that and not the intricate inter-*madhhab* debates that an ordinary person comes to learn from them.[147] Only when the *muftī* is asked specifically regarding the ruling of his *madhhab* on a particular issue is it permissible for him to narrate just that, instead of what he believes to be the correct answer.

## Ibn al-Qayyim's Traditionalist Critique of *Taqlīd*

Ibn al-Qayyim's critique of the institutionalization of *taqlīd* forms part of his overall defense of traditionalism and his attack on the legal culture prevalent in his time. The main traditionalist principles Ibn al-Qayyim was attempting to defend and which he felt were under attack by his *muqallid* critics were the supremacy and self-sufficiency of scripture, the harmony of reason and revelation, and the authority of the practice and opinions of the earliest generation of Muslims, the *salaf*. For Ibn al-Qayyim, the institutionalization of rigid *madhhab*-based *taqlīd* challenged each of these principles and was associated with a host of other theological and jurisprudential errors. This is one reason that legal and theological arguments are interwoven in almost every section of the *I'lām*, not least the section on *taqlīd*.[148] Let us examine the significance of *taqlīd* to each of these principles.

## First Traditionalist Principle: The Supremacy and Self-Sufficiency of Scripture

Traditionalists such as Ibn al-Qayyim had long argued that scripture contained an answer to all legal questions which could ever arise, but they were opposed by two main theological and legal camps: the *ahl al-rā'y* and the Zāhirīs

### *Scriptural Text and Scriptural Intent: The Zāhirīs and the Ahl al-Rā'y*

The *ahl al-rā'y* held that basing the law on the Qur'an and Sunnah alone was too restrictive an approach to legal reasoning and did not allow sufficient room for human discretion in arriving at just legal outcomes. The *ahl al-ẓāhir* argued, in terms opposite from those of the *ahl al-rā'y*, that employing any kind of human reasoning in deriving law undermined God's *sharī'ah* and replaced it with subjective human desires and biases. The *I'lām* is basically an attempt to chart a middle path between these two approaches. Ibn al-Qayyim's main argument is that, while opposing the *ahl al-rā'y* and the *ahl al-ẓāhir*, the traditionalists combine, in their own legal and theological theory, all that is best in the approach of the *ahl al-rā'y* and the ẓāhirīs. For the *ahl al-ḥadīth*, Ibn al-Qayyim's party, are masters not only of traditional disciplines such as *ḥadīth* but also of a scripturally inspired *rā'y* (personal reasoning or opinion), a fact that makes them better jurisprudents than the *ahl al-rā'y*, even though the latter celebrated their own legal acumen and dismissed the traditionalists as simple-minded literalists.[149]

Ibn al-Qayyim's main concern, then, is to find a way of reading revelation that upholds its status as the uncreated word of God—or, in the case of the Sunnah, the inspired word of God—while allowing it to provide guidance for ever-changing and contingent human needs. In fact, the whole *I'lām* can be read as a commentary on al-Shāfi'ī's meta-principle, outlined in his *Risālah*, that the Qur'an and the Sunnah contain the solution to every problem a Muslim could ever face: "On all matters touching [the life] of a Muslim there is either a binding decision or an indication as to the right answer."[150] Although Ibn al-Qayyim champions the dictum of al-Shāfi'ī, he does make it clear that the latter's reference to scripture refers not only to its finite text, as argued by the Zāhirīs, but also to those general rational principles on which the religious and legal edifice rests, which are derived inductively from close observation and an overview of scripture.[151]

Against the Zāhirīs, Ibn al-Qayyim argues first, that the use of rational principles such as *qiyās* (analogy), *istiḥsān* (juristic preference), *sadd al-dharāʾiʿ* (blocking the means to a proscribed end), and *maṣlaḥah* (welfare) in legal reasoning is justified, because it is based on the practice of the earliest generation of Muslims (*salaf*), which should be accepted as normative by all Muslims. It is the Companions of the Prophet, Ibn al-Qayyim reasons, who, with their perfect understanding of the purposes of the Lawgiver, displayed the soundest form of rationality in their legal reasoning, while remaining true to scripture.[152] Those closest to them in methodology are the great traditionists and *ḥadīth* scholars who, although they used their rationality to understand better the purposes and objectives behind God's law, never set their rationality against scripture.[153] For Ibn al-Qayyim, the fact that the *sharīʿah* seeks to promote certain values, such as the removal of oppression and excessive hardship, simply cannot be denied.[154] Therefore, the term "scripture" does not refer just to the text of the Qurʾan and Sunnah but also to the spirit (*rūḥ*), underlying wisdom (*ḥikmah*), and higher objectives (*maqṣad*/*maqāṣid*) behind the text.[155] Because the text and its underlying rationale are part of scripture, a *muftī* must not neglect either when issuing religious verdicts.[156] Inductively derived legal principles are not, as claimed by the Zāhirīs, an impious form of speculation about the will of God. Rather, they are necessary and religiously obligatory procedures needed to deduce scriptural solutions to new problems. A *muftī* who does not accept this undermines scripture itself.

Having argued against the Zāhirīs that the institution of *iftāʾ* would not function properly unless *muftīs* issue opinions that uphold the spirit and rationale as well as the text of the law, Ibn al-Qayyim turns the same argument against the *ahl al-rāʾy* and the *kalām* groups influenced by them. He criticizes many of these groups for believing that scripture, at least in its expression in the form of the Qurʾan and the Sunnah, is limited and that human intellect therefore has a role to play in determining (as opposed to inferring) the law.[157] An even more dangerous doctrine that Ibn al-Qayyim attributes to the *ahl al-rāʾy* is their belief that many religious rulings are actually irrational or, at least, a-rational. As a result, they are left with three choices when faced with a scriptural text that commands what they perceive to be an irrational obligation. The first is to obey the command as a matter of pure ritual. The second is to reinterpret it. The third is to refuse to act in accordance with it.[158] Each of these approaches is erroneous, according to Ibn al-Qayyim, because, to begin with, there can never be a contradiction between reason and revelation.

It is precisely because they do not believe in any underlying rationale in the law, Ibn al-Qayyim suggests, that the *ahl al-rāʾy* are such strong advocates of *ḥiyal*, or legal stratagems, whereby a *muftī* allows an act that preserves the formal appearance of conformity to the law but discards the law's underlying wisdom and purpose, an example being the infamous *ḥalālah* marriage, whereby a triply divorced wife enters into a marriage contract only to allow her to return to her previous husband.[159] For if the law is seen to be non-rational to begin with, the question of preserving its internal logic does not even arise—one need worry only about preserving its external form as an act of ritual worship. Lest we think that Ibn al-Qayyim's discussion was based on abstract legal theory, we should bear in mind that the validity of the *ḥalālah* marriage was one of the most contentious issues debated between *muqallid*s and critics of *taqlīd* in Ibn al-Qayyim's time and remains so to this day, as seen by the voluminous literature on the subject by Deobandīs, who regard *ḥalālah* marriages as licit, and the Ahl-e Ḥadīth, who insist that they are forbidden.

### *Jurisprudential Principles*

Having dealt with the objections of the Ẓāhirīs and the *ahl al-rāʾy*, Ibn al-Qayyim moves on to address the status of jurisprudential principles attributed to the founders of the schools of law that were often used by *muqallid* scholars to justify their refusal to follow scriptural proofs that went against them. Ibn al-Qayyim maintains that a scholar who sets aside a scriptural obligation on the basis of its supposed contradiction with reason or with a jurisprudential principle attributed to his Imām or his school has committed a grave theological and jurisprudential error.[160] *Muftī*s must not issue *fatāwā* that are contradicted by clear and authentic *aḥādīth*.[161] They must also avoid the practice of relying on vague scriptural texts whose legal import is unclear, in order to prove the validity of their *madhhab*, while rejecting clear and explicit texts because they stand in conflict with the same.[162] It is also not permissible for them to distort the straightforward meaning of scriptural texts to make them conform to the opinions of their schools, something *muqallid* scholars are guilty of.[163]

> If the opinion of their own principal should go against a clear text of God and His Messenger, they [the *muqallid* scholars] regard it as obligatory to sport with the divine texts and use every artifice to take them out of their proper meaning, circumventing them in every possible way, until the opinion of their principal is proved correct.

> By God, what would have become of His religion, His Book, and His Messenger's Sunnah when faced with an innovation that, if successful, would almost ruin the throne of faith and destroy its pillar? (Argument 16)

It is to emphasize the importance of issuing *fatāwā* that accord with scriptural texts that Ibn al-Qayyim concludes his tract with a collection of the *fatāwā* of the Prophet.[164] He comments that in his own time, the authority and importance of these verdicts has diminished in favor of verdicts based on opinions that were not always supported by strong scriptural proofs.[165] He reminds *muftīs* that their primary loyalty is to scripture, not to their own clique or *madhhab*, even when they can see that the latter is incorrect.[166]

Ibn al-Qayyim argues that all the founding Imāms regarded it as forbidden to issue verdicts except on the basis of positive knowledge, by which they meant scripture.[167] The practice of his contemporaries, Ibn al-Qayyim argues, is different.[168] For *muqallid muftīs* issue *fatāwā* based on the mere absence of known disagreement on an issue among the scholars of the past, without looking into the Qur'an, the Sunnah or the opinions of the *salaf*, thereby devaluing the role of scripture:

> When it came to the later generations, their practice was contrary to this and they said, "If a new problem is presented before a *muftī* or a ruler, he must first see whether there is any disagreement in this area or not. If there is no disagreement, he does not need to look into the Book or the Sunnah. Rather, he is to issue a verdict and judgment based on consensus. But if there is disagreement in it, then he is to exercise independent reasoning to find the view closest to the [available] evidence, and he is to issue a verdict and a ruling based on it." This is contrary to what is proved by the *ḥadīth* of Mu'ādh, the letter of 'Umar [to Shurayḥ] and the statements of the Companions. (Argument 52)

For Ibn al-Qayyim, *fatāwā* must always be based, and be seen to be based, on scripture. He therefore suggests that *muftīs* should follow the practice of the Prophet, who would often mention proofs for his verdicts, despite the fact that his rulings were themselves a source of law.[169] Similarly, the Companions and the *salaf* would generally mention the primary evidence from the Qur'an and the Sunnah on which they based their rulings. Doing this allows Muslims to recall that it is scripture, not the opinion of a particular *muftī* or scholar, that carries ultimate authority in Islam.[170] A recital of the primary evidence, he argues, keeps the dynamic link between man and God alive in the way that a bare legal *fatwā* simply cannot. Hence, the scriptural evidence is the "spirit" and "ornament" of any *fatwā*.[171]

While *muqallid* scholars dismissed the idea that there could be *madhhab* opinions that were not based on authentic scriptural proofs, Ibn al-Qayyim points out that there are many instances in which the legal schools follow principles that prevent them from acting in accordance with scripture. This formed part of his larger argument, that not every principle acted upon by the legal schools is necessarily correct. Rather, many of these principles are both improperly derived and incorrectly applied—and this is the case whenever they are made the basis for rejecting a clear ruling of the Qur'an and Sunnah.

For Ibn Qayyim, a scholar who resolves to approach the Qur'an and Sunnah free of sectarian and factional biases will be able to find in those sources the answers to all legal and religious questions. It might be thought that this argument is typical of the Salafī circle to which Ibn al-Qayyim and his master belonged, but, as we have seen, *muqallid* scholars such as al-Qarāfī employed virtually the same argument against their critics, that a scholar's factional biases prevent him from upholding the straightforward meaning of scripture. For Ibn Qayyim, a scholar who adopts an unbiased approach would not be forced to maintain contrary propositions in order to defend his *madhhab* as *muqallid* scholars are often forced to do:

> When you imitators find a verse in the Book of God that agrees with your principal, you apparently act according to it, even while your reliance is on what he said, not on the verse itself. And if you find a verse relied on by your opponent that contradicts the opinion of your principal, you do not act according to it. You seek other ways to interpret it, in ways contrary to its apparent meaning, merely because it does not correspond to his view. This is also how you act when it comes to the Sunnah. If you find an authentic *ḥadīth* that agrees with the opinion of your principal, you act according to it, saying, "Our stance is absolutely supported by the words of the Prophet that we choose to rely on." And if you find one hundred *aḥādīth* or more that go against his view, you do not act according to a single one of them. (Argument 18)

Although he presents numerous examples of this approach in his essay on *taqlīd*, Ibn al-Qayyim also devotes a large part of the *I'lām* to an independent study of the jurisprudential principles relied on by the various schools of law. One of the inconsistently followed legal principles that he discusses at length is that calling for a Sunnah that contradicts the Qur'an to be disregarded when it comes to issuing *fatāwā*. In response, Ibn al-Qayyim argues that, because the Qur'an and Sunnah are both forms of revelation from God, any Sunnah that conflicts with the Qur'an should be seen as elaborating the meaning of the Qur'anic text and should be followed as an enactment of the divine command to follow and obey the Prophet.[172] To refuse to accept that the Sunnah can add to the Qur'an would mean opposing the Qur'an itself, which commands obedience to the Prophet and demands that Muslims refer their disputes to God and His Prophet, meaning, Ibn al-Qayyim suggests, the Qur'an and the Sunnah.

Similarly, Ibn al-Qayyim rejects the principle, adhered to by some Mālikī scholars, that, in order to be accepted, a Sunnah must conform to Medinese practice.[173] Ibn al-Qayyim remains committed to the traditionalist principle of al-Shāfi'ī that the Sunnah, as contained in the *aḥādīth*, is to act as arbiter over the actions of a community, and he argues that this Mālikī jurisprudential principle essentially makes the actions of a particular community the arbiter over the Sunnah.[174] Unless the people of Medina are relating, as only they are able to, what the Prophet's Sunnah actually was, there can be no justification for preferring the practice of Medina over the authentically reported Sunnah.[175] Even a solitary Prophetic narration, so long as it is authentic, should be preferred over the practice of the people of Medina that does not find support in the Sunnah.[176] A fortiori, then, there can be no justification for preferring the *ijtihād* of the scholars of Medina over that of other scholars, which, Ibn al-Qayyim reports, is one of the positions upheld in the Mālikī school.[177] Rather, the Sunnah is a higher source of law than *ijtihād*, and all *ijtihād* that opposes the Sunnah is thus necessarily flawed and must not be followed.[178]

Ibn al-Qayyim is also critical of the principle adopted by some schools, such as the Ḥanafīs, that calls for the abandonment of a *ḥadīth* whose narrator issues an opinion conflicting with the *ḥadīth* he narrates.[179] This principle is based on the assumption that the narrator would not have issued a conflicting *fatwā* unless he believed that the *ḥadīth* in question had been abrogated. Ibn al-Qayyim adds that the mere fact of the narrator not acting according to the *ḥadīth* is sometimes used as proof of his corruption, and the *ḥadīth* is then rejected on the grounds that the narrator was an impious individual whose narrations are not reliable.[180] For Ibn al-Qayyim this principle clearly detracts from the supremacy of *ḥadīth* and scripture. After listing numerous instances in which *aḥādīth* have been dropped for this reason, Ibn al-Qayyim demonstrates that *muqallid* scholars from all schools do actually reason on the basis of *aḥādīth*, even when they are contradicted by the *fatāwā* of their narrators. He shows that this is usually done in cases in which the *aḥādīth* in question support the *madhhab* of the *muqallid* scholars themselves.[181] Ibn al-Qayyim argues once again that *muqallid* scholars make *taqlīd* the ultimate legal principle on the basis of which scripture is then forsaken.

### *Scriptural Flexibility*

Ibn al-Qayyim never suggests that accepting the supremacy of scripture will bring an end to all scholarly differences of opinion based on *ijtihād*. On the contrary, his criticism of the regime of *taqlīd* is precisely that it compels obedience to the *ijtihād* of certain scholars, even in matters in which there is no way of establishing, in absolute terms, the superiority of one *ijtihād* over another. In such cases, each scholar should be free to adopt the view that seems best to him and should not be compelled to perform *taqlīd* of another.[182] The view of the early scholars themselves was that nobody had the right to insist on *taqlīd* in matters of *ijtihād*, because *ijtihād* was only possible, in the first place, when the Lawgiver Himself had not given an explicit ruling to be followed on an issue:

> Further, whatever matter is unclear to them [the *muqallid* scholars] is, for them, among the matters subject to *ijtihād*. But, as such, the most that can be said about an opinion issued on such a matter is that following it is permissible. It cannot be said that it is obligatory, nor can anyone be compelled to follow such an opinion. These [early] scholars did not say, "This opinion of mine is the only truth, and that which is contrary to it is not so."

By insisting that even the *ijtihād*-based *fatāwā* of the eponymous Imāms and their followers be upheld and defended, *muqallid* scholars had, in Ibn al-Qayyim's view, destroyed the distinction between *ijtihād* and *ikhtilāf*.[183] Differences in matters of *ijtihād* could arise for any of several reasons, such as a genuine ambiguity in a scriptural text. Here, a *mujtahid* whose *ijtihād* is objectively correct will earn two rewards for his *ijtihād*, but even the *mujtahid* who is incorrect will earn a reward for doing his best to understand what God demanded of him.[184] But it is not the case, Ibn al-Qayyim argues, that every issue over which the scholars hold differing views necessarily falls within the ambit of *ijtihād* in which scripture does not provide a clear ruling. For scholars could have fallen into disagreement even where there was an authentic, clear, and unambiguous scriptural text. Thus, every area of *ijtihād* is one where there is legitimate disagreement (*ikhtilāf*), but the reverse is not true: not every area where *ikhtilāf* has occurred is necessarily one where it is legitimate to carry out *ijtihād*.[185] In areas of legitimate *ijtihād* it is improper to denounce a particular view and insist on one's own *taqlīd*. In areas of *ikhtilāf* where there is no room for *ijtihād* because of the presence of a clear scriptural ruling, *taqlīd* of an incorrect *ijtihād*-based opinion is all the more reprehensible.

Ibn al-Qayyim does anticipate that his legal theory will be attacked for its rigidity and inflexibility in making scripture—both its text and its underlying meaning—the only source of law. He responds to his critics at length and, in doing so, argues that it is actually the rigid *taqlīd* of the *fatāwā* of the Imāms and their schools that brings inflexibility into the law. By contrast, he argues, traditionalists such as Aḥmad b. Ḥanbal and Mālik accept that verdicts and rulings based on scripture do, in fact, change with time, place, and context.[186] *Muftīs* should therefore, as far as possible, issue verdicts in accordance with the local custom of the people, instead of relying on the legal culture and tradition of their own schools.[187] This is particularly true in cases of marriage, oaths, and contracts, in which the custom of people varies with time and place and in which *muqallid* scholars cause great hardship for the people by not updating their legal conventions in accordance with societal change.[188]

Ibn al-Qayyim offers many specific examples of the *sharīʿah* itself changing its specific rules in order to protect its overall objectives. In this context, he discusses the religious obligation to promote righteousness (*al-amr bi-l-maʿrūf*), pointing out that, although this is an obligation, it is at times forbidden, because if carried out it would make matters worse, not better.[189] He also cites the example of the suspension of capital punishment for theft on the battlefield, pointing out that this punishment is suspended because the greater benefit dictates it.[190] Ibn al-Qayyim calls for aims and higher objectives to be considered in the process of legal interpretation not only in interpersonal (civil) law (*muʿāmalāt*) but also in acts of ritual and worship (*ʿibādāt*).[191] Ibn al-Qayyim's discussion of this topic therefore differs from that of many scholars who have addressed the same issue, who would only allow legal objectives to be considered in matters of interpersonal law, not in matters of worship.

## Second Traditionalist Principle: The Harmony of Reason and Revelation

The traditionalists did not only uphold the supremacy of scripture, they also believed in the harmony of scripture and reason.[192] This, too, was a principle that they felt was undermined by the kind of rigid *taqlīd* advocated by the *muqallid* scholars, particularly those influenced by the *ahl al-rā'y* and the speculative theologians. In the traditionalist view, it was the belief of many of the *ahl al-rā'y* that religious rulings are not always rational that compelled them to hold that there can be no scriptural logic by which one legal interpretation or analogy is preferred over another, a position similar to that of the later Ashʿarī scholars discussed previously. Ibn al-Qayyim argues that many *muftīs* who subscribe to the position of the *ahl al-rā'y* presume almost all inferential reasoning based on scripture to be valid and morally neutral, because scripture, according to them, does not provide any objective criterion or rationale on the basis of which one analogy may be preferred over another.[193] The legal and theological culture of the *ahl al-rā'y* therefore pushes scholars to secure legitimacy for a particular legal analogy by fortifying it through the institution of *taqlīd*. For, having rejected the idea that scripture was rational and sought to fulfill certain purposes and objectives, the *ahl al-rā'y* could no longer turn to scripture to justify their (rational) analogies. Instead, the *mujtahid*'s preference (*istiḥsān*) for one of many valid analogies itself becomes, for the *ahl al-rā'y*, a proof of the correctness of that particular analogy and a reason for later scholars to favor it over others. By allowing more unregulated *ijtihād* in the first place, the *ahl al-rā'y* thus end up having to insist on rigid *taqlīd*, to ensure some degree of legal coherence at the level of the school and the legal system. Hence, a jurist working fully within in the legal culture of the *ahl al-rā'y* could not be required to justify his *istiḥsān*, or preference, for a particular analogy on purely rational grounds. Rather, the theological view that God's law was not, or need not be, based on any underlying rationale in the first place meant that such justifications would be regarded as almost impossible. Therefore, a jurist's opinions and his *istiḥsān* would be followed mainly because of one's acceptance of his knowledge, intellect, or even his intuition and spiritual authority, hence the celebration of the spiritual authority of the Imāms. A dictum widely attributed to the *ahl al-rā'y* perfectly captured the solipsism of this position: *al-istiḥsān mā istaḥsan al-mujtahid min 'aqlih*, "istiḥsān is whatever the mujtahid deems as istiḥsān on the basis of his own intellect." The *mujtahid*'s *istiḥsān* could therefore rest on unstated grounds that might be made the subject of *taqlīd*, even if the rationale behind his *istiḥsān* was unclear and apparently opposed to scripture.[194] Thereafter, the more the role of the *mujtahid* is exalted, the more later scholars refuse to depart from his opinions and attribute their own opinions to him to gain legitimacy for them, until *muqallid* scholars such as al-Karkhī eventually adopt a jurisprudential principle stating that every scriptural text that opposes their school's position would have to be reinterpreted until it was in conformity with the same, thereby committing themselves to using scripture to defend opinions that were not evidently rational and that might well have contradicted a scriptural proof.[195]

For traditionalists such as Ibn al-Qayyim, there was a clear link between the theological stance of the *ahl al-rā'y*, their proclivity for *taqlīd*, and the dangerous doctrine that reason and revelation were somehow in conflict. As we have seen, Ibn al-Qayyim was critical of the view that scriptural texts retained a level of inherent interpretive ambiguity which made it impossible to identify an objectively correct opinion on the basis of scripture.[196] For as long as scholars subscribed to this view, they would be driven to derive the authority of a particular legal opinion not from scripture but by linking it with a previous figure or institution of authority. Ibn al-Qayyim thus dismisses *muqallid muftī*s who constantly justify their verdicts by arguing that "such was (*ka dhālik*) the practice of previous authorities" calling them the "'such-was' scholars"![197]

Ibn al-Qayyim also criticizes some of his *muqallid* contemporaries for upholding verdicts and analogies which do not promote the aims of the *sharī'ah*, such as the avoidance of hardship. Instead, Ibn al-Qayyim argues, *muqallid* scholars often uphold verdicts and analogies which undermine these aims. This reinforces the incorrect impression that the law is irrational and inconsistent because religious rulings are seen to be in conflict with the aims and values which the religious law seeks to protect. For Ibn al-Qayyim, a religious ruling that undermines the aims of the *sharī'ah*, for instance by leading to greater hardship, would automatically contradict both scripture and reason. For as the *sharī'ah* exists for the benefit of man, as a means of mercy to him and for the establishment of his welfare, any *fatwā* that does not promote these values automatically falls outside Islam.[198] In fact, such a *fatwā* could have come into the religion only as a result of faulty interpretation or because of a misunderstanding of the rationale underlying God's law.[199] Scripture and reason cannot actually conflict with each other or with themselves.

Ibn al-Qayyim goes on to argue that *muqallid* scholars often, when arguing against a scriptural proof that goes against their *madhhab,* attribute irrationality to scripture and claim that there is a tension between reason and revelation. He suggests that, when viewed free of the partisanship of the *madhhab*, such irrationality tends to disappear. He cites the practice of a group of scholars who, following the principles of their schools, rejected certain *aḥādīth* for being in conflict with reason or with the Qur'an. He cites seventy-three examples of cases in which a group of scholars refused to act on the Sunnah, claiming that the Sunnah being presented contradicted the Qur'an.[200] Ibn al-Qayyim is critical of these scholars, whose loyalty to their schools has led them to hold that Islam (which is built on both authentic scripture, in the form of the Qur'an and Sunnah, and on sound *qiyās* based on these two sources) is self-contradictory and hence irrational. He presents Qur'anic proofs to show that there can be no contradiction in the religion and then presents numerous examples of cases in which these same scholars themselves accept that the Sunnah can restrict the meaning of the Qur'an.[201] Thus, Ibn al-Qayyim attempts to show that it is loyalty to the school that determines when *muqallid* scholars grant the Sunnah the authority to specify the Qur'an and when they do not. Ibn al-Qayyim's argument here echoes that employed by al-Shāfiʿī against Abū Ḥanīfah's student al-Shaybāni (d. 189/805), whom al-Shāfiʿī criticized for following a contradictory approach on the issue of accepting solitary narrations.[202] Instead of starting with the principle of loyalty to their schools—whose positions have to be defended, come what may—Ibn al-Qayyim would prefer that all scholars start with the basic premise that there is no contradiction in anything that comes from God. Human intellect, he argues, should be used to show the strength of revelation by resolving seeming contradictions between the Qur'an, *ḥadīth,* and reason rather than to throw up false contradictions between them for the sake of loyalty to the *madhhab.*[203]

## Third Traditionalist Principle: The Authority of the *Salaf*

Traditionalists such as Ibn al-Qayyim condemned as a blameworthy innovation (*bid'ah*) any religious belief or practice introduced after the era of the *salaf.* This was one of the grounds on which they argued against *muqallid* scholars whom they accused of advocating a form of *taqlīd* that was unknown among the *salaf.* Ibn al-Qayyim makes this the first of his 81 substantive arguments against *taqlīd*:

> We also know as a matter of necessity that during the time of the Companions there was no individual whom everyone followed and imitated in everything, or in favor of whom the views of all others were rejected. We also know necessarily that such a thing did not occur in the times of the Successors and those who followed them. So let the imitators demonstrate that we are liars by producing even a single man who acted according to their pernicious methodology in the generations that were declared meritorious by the Prophet. This innovation appeared in the fourth century, which [period] had already been condemned by the Prophet, may the peace and blessings of God be on him. (Argument 1)

It was thus not *taqlīd* itself but the transformed understanding of the concept advocated by later *muqallid* scholars that traditionalists such as Ibn al-Qayyim rejected. While the *salaf* saw it as acceptable to perform *taqlīd* of a variety of scholars with differing legal opinions, later *muqallid* scholars insisted that everyone adhere to a particular school of law. Early scholars regarded it as acceptable for people to pray behind an *imām* whose prayer they themselves would not regard as valid, as shown by the example of Abū Yūsuf (d. 182/798), the student of Abū Ḥanīfah who regarded his prayer behind the caliph al-Rashīd as valid, even when informed subsequently that al-Rashīd had performed an action that would make his prayer invalid in the Ḥanafī school.[204] By contrast, later scholars would regard as invalid a prayer performed behind someone from a different school.[205] The *salaf* set preconditions for *ijtihād,* which were, by and large, attainable and realistic, but later *muqallid* scholars not only insisted that a *mujtahid* would need to memorize at least 500,000 *aḥādīth* but also set various other preconditions for *ijtihād,* which even the founding Imāms of the four schools could not always be said to have met.[206] Eventually, the transformation in what it means to adhere to the opinions of a scholar or a school becomes so great that we find *muqallid* scholars opining that a person leaving the *madhhab* of these scholars should be given a discretionary punishment (*taʿzīr*), but a person abandoning his own *madhhab* in favor of theirs should not.[207] As for the practice of issuing verdicts, the *salaf,* according to Ibn al-Qayyim, regarded it as prohibited to issue *fatāwā* except on the basis of positive scriptural knowledge. The *muqallid* scholars, by contrast, regard any *fatwā* that is not based on *taqlīd* of a school of law to be invalid. Although *muqallid* scholars did defend their practice on the grounds that their *fatāwā* were mere narrations of the verdicts handed down by earlier scholars, Ibn al-Qayyim dismisses their argument. He points out that a layman, too, has the ability to narrate *fatāwā*, but his inability to carry out scriptural *ijtihād* prevents one from accepting his right to issue them in the first place:

> Now, if this person [the *muqallid*] accepts that issuing verdicts is allowed for the [imitator] who is ignorant of the proofs and of their true meaning, simply because he has memorized the rulings related to trivial matters, he must concede that this right to issue verdicts should also be granted to everyone.

## Innovated *Taqlīd*

By Ibn al-Qayyim's time, *muqallid* scholars had developed a legal culture that allowed a jurist to remain a *muqallid* even while disagreeing entirely with the opinions of the *salaf* from his own school and, occasionally, from all schools.[208] This was done largely by creating elaborate taxonomies of the ranks of jurists that allowed them to be classified as *muqallids*, even when they carried out *ijtihād*.[209] It is no surprise that the scholars most inclined to *taqlīd* also produced the most elaborate typologies of jurists, while critics of *taqlīd* not only had fewer categories of jurists but also insisted that most jurists, regardless of rank, had the right or obligation to carry out *ijtihād*. Ibn al-Qayyim, for instance, recognizes only four categories of jurists.[210] The pro-*taqlīd* Ibn ʿĀbidīn, on the other hand, recognizes as many as seven.[211] This creation of subcategories of *muqallids* and *mujtahids* allowed *muqallid* jurists to pay deference to the principle of *ijtihād* in theory while, in practice, condemning those who did not present their *ijtihād* as a form of *taqlīd*.

The obfuscation of the various subcategories of *ijtihād* and *taqlīd* by *muqallid* scholars was, to some extent, necessary, for only by making these terms genuinely flexible could *muqallid* scholars create the space they needed to exercise their own forms of *ijtihād* under the guise of *taqlīd*. We can see this in the works of Ibn al-Shāṭṭ (d. 723/1323), who, in the course of commenting on al-Qarāfī's *Furūq*, refers to a category of scholars who are "*muqallid-mujtahid*."[212] Similarly, al-Shaʿrānī refers to a form of *ijtihād* that is both absolute and affiliated (*muṭlaq muntasib*), meaning that it is based on scripture but is also affiliated with a particular school of law. In such cases, the oxymoronic nature of the terms being used betrays the underlying confusion surrounding them.[213] It is true that *muqallid* scholars were theoretically not supposed to go beyond the basic jurisprudential principles of their Imāms and schools. However, the fact that *muqallid* scholars were often the ones who created these jurisprudential principles in the first place, as suggested by Shāh Walī Allāh, means that it is at least theoretically possible to rank them higher than the founding Imāms, who rarely clarified their jurisprudential theory. Moreover, jurisprudence was not the only area in which the *muqallid* scholars could be said to have outranked the founding Imāms. The *taqlīd* critic al-Ṣanʿānī points out that later *muqallid* scholars made scriptural interpretations that would have been unknown in the time of the Imāms to whose schools they ascribed themselves.[214] Ibn al-Qayyim also comments on this paradox created by the *muqallid* scholars:

> If the imitator-scholars, whom all the scholars exclude from the category of the people of knowledge, and who themselves admit that they are not so, were the true followers of the principals, then those eminent scholars who relied on proofs could not have been among their adherents. Thus, when it came to following the principals, the ignorant imitator-scholars would end up more felicitous than those scholars who relied on evidence. But this is truly impossible. (Argument 44)

The distinction between *mujtahid* and *muqallid* scholars is further obscured when we consider the ways in which *muqallid* scholars from the various schools of law dealt with *ḥadīth* material when formulating their doctrines and verdicts. The Ḥanbalī school was known to have a long-standing tradition of allowing *muqallid* scholars to base their opinions on authentic *aḥādīth*, even if this meant going against their Imāms. From early scholars, such as Ibn ʿAqīl, to later ones, such as Ibn Taymiyyah, Ḥanbalī jurists often departed from the doctrines of their school on the basis of their understanding of *aḥādīth*, while still claiming to be followers of the Ḥanbalī school.[215] The Shāfiʿīs too, given the legacy of their founding Imām, who had argued for the overarching supremacy of authentic *aḥādīth*, allowed *muqallid* scholars to follow authentic *aḥādīth*, even if these went against the rulings of their Imāms. Several Shāfiʿī scholars would argue that following the authentic *aḥādīth* was itself the primary Shāfiʿī jurisprudential principle and that a scholar who did so was therefore not outside the fold of the *madhhab*. Ibn al-Qayyim records Ibn al-Ṣalāḥ's (d. 643/1245) discussion of an opinion allowing even those Shāfiʿī scholars who do not fulfill all the qualifications of *ijtihād* to follow a *ḥadīth* that contradicted the rulings of their Imām.[216] There was also a trend in favor of this approach in the Ḥanafī school, and many of its scholars issued rulings that a *ḥadīth* that was found to be contrary to the *madhhab* could be acted on by a Ḥanafī scholar. Once again, it was argued that, because following *aḥādīth* was a Ḥanafī jurisprudential principle, the scholar who followed *aḥādīth* in opposition to the rulings of the *madhhab* did not thereby abandon the *madhhab*.[217] Occasionally, Ḥanafī scholars such as Abū Yūsuf even extended this right to lay people.[218]

Calder is therefore wrong in taking the typologies of the ranks of jurists that refer to absolute *mujtahid*s and absolute *muqallids*, such as those presented by al-Nawawī, to be actual representations of the ranks of scholars.[219] In reality, the idea of an absolutely independent *mujtahid*, who consulted nothing but scripture, is an artificial construction, as is the idea of a *muqallid* scholar who does not carry out any *ijtihād*.[220] Ibn al-Qayyim points out that the *mujtahid* Imāms themselves performed *taqlīd* on some issues, even after attaining the rank of *mujtahid*, which makes it difficult to create a strict dichotomy between *muqallid*s and *mujtahid*s. Speaking of the first of his four categories of *muftī*s, who are known for carrying out *ijtihād* based on scripture, Ibn al-Qayyim states that,

> their occasional *taqlīd* of others does not negate their [ability to carry out] *ijtihād*. You will not find a single Imām who did not perform *taqlīd* of someone more knowledgeable than himself on certain issues.[221]

Just as he concedes that a *mujtahid* may sometimes perform *taqlīd*, Ibn al Qayyim also argues that even the layman may occasionally exercise a kind of *ijtihād*, for instance, in his choice of a *muftī*.[222]

Ibn al-Qayyim's comments on this issue set him apart not just from the *muqallid* scholars of his day but also from previous Ḥanbalī authorities such as Ibn ʿAqīl, who had rejected the idea of a *mujtahid* performing *taqlīd*.[223] For Ibn al-Qayyim, while both the *mujtahid* and the layman are allowed to perform *taqlīd*, neither may do so if it means ignoring other, stronger evidence.[224] Any person, scholar or not, who sees that the truth lies with someone other than the one he imitates but continues to imitate him nonetheless, is engaging in a kind of impermissible *taqlīd*. And for Ibn al-Qayyim, no scholar can be excused from the obligation of referring to scripture and the opinions of the *salaf*. It is precisely because *muqallid* scholars devalue these two sources of authority that Ibn al-Qayyim denounces the kind of *taqlīd* they advocate:

> O people of imitation, every sect among you lowers the rank of all the Companions, the Successors, and all the scholars of the community, from the first to the last, to a level where no opinions are to be considered, except for the opinions of the one you imitate. Nor are their verdicts [i.e., of these other scholars] to be looked into, engaged with, or relied upon. Nor is there any point in examining them, except to circumvent them and to sharpen one's mind by exerting oneself in rejecting the views of other scholars, if their opinions contradict the opinions of one's own principals. This is deemed permissible by them in order to refute their rivals. If the opinion of their own principal should go against a clear text of God and His Messenger, they regard it as obligatory to sport with the divine texts and use every artifice to take them out of their proper meaning, circumventing them in every possible way, until the opinion of their principal is proved correct. (Argument 16)

Ibn al-Qayyim rejects the division of labor between *mujtahid* and *muqallid* scholars that makes scriptural *ijtihād* the province of the former to the exclusion of the latter. For, as Ibn al-Qayyim argues repeatedly, there is no real conceptual difference between the work of *mujtahid* and *muqallid* scholars. Once a scholar (of whatever rank) has understood the reason for *ikhtilāf*, he should be able to adopt the view that seems to be correct to him in light of scripture.

## Scriptural *Ijtihād* and *Taqlīd*

The regime of *taqlīd* did indeed allow *muqallid* scholars to use scripture in their legal reasoning but only to prefer one of the existing opinions of a *madhhab* over another. This activity of choosing between existing opinions was known as *tarjīḥ*, and this is precisely where the *muqallid* scholar was supposed to exercise *ijtihād*. *Muqallid* scholars could thus overturn earlier *madhhab* opinions and replace them with their own, claiming all along that they were merely identifying the strongest opinion, known, inter alia, as *rājiḥ*, *ẓāhir*, and *aẓhar*.[225] Furthermore, *muqallid* scholars could displace existing opinions in the *madhhab* by putting forward their own opinion as the predominant opinion (*mashhūr*) of their schools, as al-Ḥajjāwī (d. 968/1560–1561) does throughout his Ḥanbalī handbook, *Zād al-mustaqniʿ*, in which he often substitutes his own opinions for those of the *madhhab* authority Ibn Qudāmah (whose work Ḥajjāwī was summarizing).[226] Scholars who carried out *tarjīḥ* on the basis of scripture were still classified as *muqallids* and partial *mujtahids* (*mujtahid fī l-madhhab*) in their schools, rather than absolute ones.[227] However, basing one's opinions on one's own understanding of scripture is precisely what a *mujtahid* does, and this makes it difficult to see the aforementioned scholars as anything but *mujtahids*.[228] This is the reason some scholars, such as Ibn ʿArabī (d. 637/1240), came out against the use of ambivalent legal terms such as *mashhūr* altogether and argued that a scholar should simply accept the views best substantiated by scripture.[229]

While *muqallid* scholars made much of the difference between *ijtihād* and *tarjīḥ*, critics of *taqlīd* would point out that there was little difference between the *tarjīḥ* of the *muqallid* scholar and the *ijtihād* of a non-*muqallid*. A striking phrase in al-Ṣanʿānī's work on this subject encapsulates the debate on this issue. Addressing his *muqallid* detractors, al-Ṣanʿānī says, "that which the *muqallids* call *tarjīḥ* is in fact *ijtihād muṭlaq*" (*inna hādha alladhī sammāhu tarjīḥan huwa al-ijtihād al-muṭlaq*). Had the contentious scholarly opinion which, under the regime of *taqlīd*, struggles to gain acceptance as an instance of *tarjīḥ*, come forth at an earlier age, it would have been labeled the work of a *mujtahid muṭlaq* and been recognized as an exercise in *ijtihād*.[230] Elsewhere, al-Ṣanʿānī calls *tarjīḥ* "pure opinion," in order to stress the level of personal discretion involved in the process.[231] Ibn ʿAqīl, too, stated that the activity of *tarjīḥ* would involve a *muqallid* choosing between the views of different *mujtahids* by examining them for their compatibility with scripture, which is precisely the activity that marks an absolute *mujtahid*.[232] Ibn al-Qayyim also expresses his dissatisfaction with the *muqallid* scholars who insisted that examining scriptural evidence and proofs was the work of the *mujtahid* but then insisted on doing so themselves:

> The opposite of every religious obligation stands nullified necessarily. If imitation, regarding which there is disagreement, is among the obligations imposed by law, then the nullity of seeking proofs and following evidence is established [because imitation would be

> obligatory, and *ijtihād*, its opposite, would therefore be forbidden]. So, accepting one of these two propositions necessitates the rejection of the other; the veracity of one dictates the nullity of the other. We intend to mention this as evidence and say, "If imitation is part of the religion, then it cannot be permissible to abandon it in favor of ijtihād and the seeking of inferences, because that would necessitate its invalidity." (Argument 74)

Nevertheless, the insistence of the *muqallid* scholars that all *ijtihād* take the form of *tarjīḥ* meant that Ibn al-Qayyim and his peers were not interlocutors in a hypothetical discussion about the possibility of *ijtihād* but a real one, in which many *muqallids* were suggesting that there could no longer be any *ijtihād*, at least *ijtihād* based on scripture.[233] Ibn al-Qayyim presents the views of the *muqallid* scholars in the following terms:

> As the doors of *ijtihād* are shut according to you, and as you closed off the paths leading to it, the only thing that remains as an obligation is imitation. So, leaving it for something the doors to which are closed and the path thereto blocked, is, for you, a sin, and the one who traverses this path is a sinner. (Argument 74)

Scholars who claimed the right to exercise *ijtihād*, such as Ibn Rushd the Grandfather, were strongly criticized by their contemporaries and by later authorities in their own schools for their refusal to perform *taqlīd* of their Imāms, and many of their *ijtihād*-based opinions were marginalized and suppressed by later *muqallid* scholars in their schools.[234] Many of their *muqallid* contemporaries would also deny that scholars, such as the aforementioned Ibn Rushd, who claimed to be *mujtahids*, had actually attained that lofty status. Even al-Suyūṭī's declaration that he was a *mujtahid* makes sense only if we see it in the context of his disagreement with those scholars who held that such a thing was impossible, a fact that also explains the harsh reaction of *muqallid* scholars to his claim. Some critics of *taqlīd* lived in fear for their lives because of their opposition to *taqlīd*, sometimes only revealing their opposition to *taqlīd* on their death beds.[235] By some accounts, al-Shāfiʿī himself was killed by a Mālikī who was outraged at al-Shāfiʿī's insolence in not performing *taqlīd* of his teacher. One may also recall the ordeal of Ibn ʿAqīl, who was pursued through the streets by a Ḥanbalī mob enraged at the fact that he had disagreed with the principles of his school. Similar threats were faced by al-Khaṭīb al-Baghdādī and others. The gates of *ijtihād* might not have closed in reality, but walking through them was a dangerous activity, as critics of *taqlīd* learned.

Ibn al-Qayyim therefore attempts to demolish some of the more abstract distinctions among the degrees of knowledge that were held to be attainable by *mujtahid* and *muqallid* scholars. He defines knowledge as grasping or perceiving something as it is. Since *muqallid* scholars justify their ability to carry out *tarjīḥ* on the basis of their understanding of the legal opinions of their predecessors, Ibn al-Qayyim argues that they are potentially as knowledgeable about those legal opinions as were their predecessors. He also points out that limiting the role of *muqallid* scholars to choosing between preexisting opinions within their schools makes it more difficult for the scripture-based opinions of the *salaf* to be incorporated in the schools of law:

> O you, party of imitation, if some of your scholars from your own school, whom you imitate, issue an opinion that contradicts the opinion of the principal of the school, or if they derive a new opinion based on this, you regard this as acceptable and issue judgments and verdicts according to this new opinion [that comes from your own school]. Yet if an Imām who was a contemporary of your principal or even superior to him in rank has an opinion that contradicts that of your principal, you do not incline towards it, nor is it of any great significance for you. Even though it is well known that just one of the scholars among those who were contemporaries of your principal is more exalted than all the subsequent scholars of your school from beginning to end. So how evil is your division and taxonomy of scholars that it would make the view of the lesser scholar a salient view in the school. By God, this is extraordinary. The verdict or judgment of one who supposedly decides in accordance with one of the scholars of the *madhhab* is more worthy of acceptance than the verdict of one who bases his verdicts on the opinions of the Rightly Guided Caliphs. (Argument 79)

Ibn al-Qayyim also opposes the taxonomies of the ranks of jurists created by the *muqallid* scholars, because these taxonomies often concealed the extent to which later *muqallid* scholars wielded more influence on the schools than did the founding Imāms whom they claimed to imitate. The *muqallid* scholars, in Ibn al-Qayyim's view, claimed to be following their schools, even when they adopted rules that went against the basic foundations on which the school was established. We have already seen that a *muqallid* scholar could gain legitimacy for his views by refusing to acknowledge his own *ijtihād* and attributing it instead to the eponym and the *madhhab*. A *qiyās* made by a Ḥanafī *muqallid*, for instance, could be held to be the actual *qiyās* of Abū Ḥanīfah and, hence, of the *madhhab*, because Abū Ḥanīfah was held to have allowed *qiyās* in principle. According to al-Qārafī, *muqallid* scholars carrying out *tarjīḥ* would also review the appropriateness (*munāsabah*) of a *qiyās* made by earlier authorities, thereby providing the *muqallid* scholar with an opportunity to stamp his own influence on the largest part of law, which was not derived from scripture directly but only through a process of *qiyās*.[236] *Muqallid* scholars could also attribute incorrect jurisprudential principles and even incorrect legal opinions to the Imāms.[237] Some Ḥanafīs, for example, incorrectly attributed to Abū Ḥanīfah the principle that analogy is to be given preference over solitary *ḥadīth* narrations. Ibn al-Qayyim argues that the attribution of this principle to Abu Ḥanīfah is incorrect. He points out that if this had been a principle of Abū Ḥanīfah, he would not have ruled in accordance with a *ḥadīth* that stipulates that a man who laughs in prayer thereby invalidates his state of ritual purity. Despite its weakness, Abū Ḥanīfah preferred this *ḥadīth* over analogy, which would require some common factor or similarity between laughter and other actions that nullify one's ritual ablutions, if they were both going to have the same effect.[238]

Ibn al-Qayyim was correct in commenting on the way in which *muqallid* scholars employed their taxonomies of the ranks of jurists to enhance the authority of the eponymous Imāms and diminish the contributions of later scholars. It is well known, for instance, that Abū Yūsuf and al-Shaybānī both made a greater contribution to the Ḥanafī school than did their Imām, carried out their own scriptural *ijtihād*, and freely rejected many of the doctrines and opinions of their teacher. Yet they would still be classified by later *muqallids* as second-rank *mujtahids*.[239] Later Ḥanafī scholars would explain that all the opinions of scholars belonging to a school could be attributed to the founding Imām, under the assumption that they too were his (unrecorded) opinions.[240] In this way the *muqallid* scholars denied that they made any substantive contribution to the school. Instead, they projected their own opinions back in time, in order to gain authority for them. Similarly, Ibn Ḥanbal's students, who had more to do with the formation of the Ḥanbalī *madhhab* than did Ibn Ḥanbal himself, would always occupy a lower rank than their Imām.[241] In addition, *muqallid* scholars from the various schools of law frequently claimed independent *mujtahids* as *muqallids* of their own schools, thereby attempting to bolster the legitimacy of the latter. Independent scholars who were claimed by *muqallid* scholars for their own schools include Ibn al-Mundhir (d. 318/930) and al-Bukhārī.[242] The latter was even claimed, somewhat fantastically, by the Ḥanafīs, despite the fact that al-Bukhārī was believed to have devoted almost a third of his famous *Ṣaḥīḥ* to refuting the opinions of Abū Ḥanīfah.[243]

For Ibn al-Qayyim, there was little to celebrate in a legal regime that bestowed a false legitimacy on the views of later scholars by attributing them to the *salaf* while actually ignoring the views of the *salaf* themselves:

> The later in time a person is, the more they [the contemporary scholars] adopt his views and the more they abandon (or almost abandon) the views of those who preceded him. This continues until you find that the followers of the Imāms are the ones who most often ignore their opinions. The people of each age deliver judgments and verdicts based on the views of those lower than the Imāms—and lower still—and those closest to them [in time]. As time progresses, the abandonment of the opinions of the earlier times increases, as does the practice of turning away from them. This continues until his [the earlier scholar's] own books almost disappear. The more distant in time he is, the more likely this is to be so. (Argument 72)

Ibn Qayyim's argument here echoes that of other traditionists—such as al-Shāfiʿī, who is said to have made similar criticisms of the ancient schools based on *rāʾy* and local practice—who took their law from "the last generation" of scholars before them rather than from the Prophet himself.[244] *Muqallid* scholars could, as we have seen in the example of the Ḥanafī opinions on the waiting period of deserted wives, accomplish considerable change in the schools without appearing to challenge their doctrines by using marginal secondary sources of law, such as custom or necessity, to displace the opinions of the *madhhab*.[245] Even Calder, who argues that *muqallid* scholars had to follow strict guidelines developed by the *madhhab* to guide the process of issuing verdicts, admits that, practically speaking, the correct version of the *madhhab* for a layman would be the opinion of his *muftī*, which might not represent the widespread opinion adopted by the school.[246] One can see the *muqallid* method on display in the works of Ibn ʿĀbidīn, who insists that scholars in his time are unable to carry out scriptural *ijtihād* but goes on to argue in favor of his opinions on the basis of scriptural proofs and even admits that, if a proof seems weak to scholars of his rank, they would go back and follow scriptural evidence.[247] This, despite the fact that he states that low-ranking jurists, among whom, he modestly hints, he too is included, cannot distinguish "the fat from the lean."[248] Nevertheless, this self-effacing jurist was able—in the nineteenth century, no less—to change some of the fundamental principles on which his *madhhab* had been operating for more than a thousand years, all the while claiming that he did not carry out any *ijtihād*.[249]

It was precisely for such reasons that the preservation of rigid yet illusory hierarchies remained a useful tool for *muqallids* who sought to condemn any call for open *ijtihād*. This was true in Ibn al-Qayyim's time, as scholars violently condemned him for his *ijtihād* on the law relating to the triple divorce. It remains true today, as pro-*taqlīd* scholars attempt to portray Ibn al-Qayyim as a disloyal dissenter from the Islamic legal tradition because of his criticism of a certain kind of *taqlīd*. Timothy Winter (Abdal Hakim Murad) argues against Ibn al-Qayyim:

> The overwhelming majority of the scholars of the past—certainly well over ninety-nine percent of them—have adhered loyally to a *madhhab*. It is true that in the troubled fourteenth century a handful of dissenters appeared, such as Ibn Taymiya and Ibn al Qayyim.[250]

In reality, as Winter himself acknowledges elsewhere, loyal adherence to a *madhhab* never prevented scholars from disagreeing with earlier authorities. Thus, Ibn Taymiyyah and Ibn al-Qayyim, even while disagreeing with previous scholars on occasion, can legitimately be considered loyal Ḥanbalīs, as well as outstanding *mujtahids*.[251]

## A Note on This Text

The text translated in this volume is taken from the printed Arabic edition of the *I'lām* edited by Shaykh Abū 'Ubaydah Mashhūr b. Ḥasan Āl Salmān, which is the best edition of the work to date. It was published in seven volumes by Dār Ibn al Jawzī in 1423/2002. The editor is an avid researcher and *ḥadīth* specialist, so the Arabic edition is heavily annotated with *ḥadīth* references, as well as references to other primary and secondary texts. I have reproduced only those *ḥadīth* references of Mashhūr Ḥasan's that would be well known to an average English-speaking audience and have only occasionally included the editor's own comments.

I have kept the use of Arabic terms to a minimum and have tried to avoid using square brackets to supply missing words, as these tend to obstruct the smooth flow of the text. I do so because I am translating not words but a language and a text. Key Arabic terms are defined in the glossary. Throughout the main text, legal issues mentioned by Ibn al-Qayyim that require some explanation have been discussed in footnotes. The word *taqlīd* has been translated as "imitation" throughout the text. The word "Imām," with initial capital and in roman typeface, refers to the founders of the schools of law or scholars of a school, while *imām,* in lower-case italics, refers to a prayer leader. I have followed Yusuf Ali's translation of the Qur'an but have, at times, taken the liberty of amending his translation where I felt this allowed Ibn al-Qayyim's inference from the verse to become clearer. Citations of the Qur'an are in square brackets and labeled "Q." Throughout the main text, square brackets indicate the page numbers corresponding to the Arabic edition of the text.

# *An Exposition on Imitation*

*In the Name of God, Merciful and Compassionate*

## [3:447] Imitation: Its Three Categories

The Category That Is Forbidden
The Category That Is Obligatory, and
The Category That Is Permissible but Not an Obligation

## That Which Is Forbidden

This [imitation that is forbidden, i.e., the] first category, is of three types:

The imitation that is forbidden is, first, that which involves turning away from what God has revealed, being heedless to it and being content instead with the imitation of one's forbears.

Imitating someone whose status as an authority the imitator is uncertain of is also forbidden.

As is the imitation that is performed in the face of established evidence and after the manifestation of proofs that go against the view of the one who is imitated.

The difference between the first and this last type of forbidden imitation is that, in the former, a person imitates before he is in command of knowledge and evidence. Whereas in the latter, a person imitates even after evidence has appeared before him. The latter, then, is more blameworthy and a greater transgression against God and His Messenger.

God, Glory be to Him, condemned these three categories of imitation on more than one occasion in His Book, as in His, the Most High's, statement,

*When it is said to them, "Follow what God has revealed," They say, "Never! We shall follow the ways of our fathers." What! Even though their fathers were void of wisdom and guidance?* [Q., al-Baqarah, 2:170]. He, the Most High, has also said, *Just in the same way, whenever We sent a warner before you to any people, the wealthy ones among them said, "We found our fathers following a religion, and we shall certainly follow in their footsteps."* [448] *He would say, "What! Even if I brought you better guidance than that which you found your fathers following?"* [Q., al-Zukhruf, 43:23]. The Most High also said, *When it is said to them, "Come to what God has revealed; come to the Messenger," they say, "Enough for us are the ways we found our fathers following."* [Q., al-Māʾidah, 5:104].

This condemnation of the one who turns away from what God has revealed and relies instead on imitation of his forbears is repeated frequently in the Qurʾan.

If it is said, "The one who is condemned is the one who imitates the disbelievers and his ancestors who were devoid of wisdom and guidance, while the one who imitates the rightly guided scholars is not condemned in these verses. Rather, one has been obligated to ask the people of knowledge, these being the scholars. This is exactly what imitating them consists of. For the Most High says: *Ask those who possess the Message, if you know not.*" [Q., al-Naḥl, 16:43]. This is a command directing those who do not have knowledge to imitate those who do.

The response to this is that He, Glory be to Him, condemns whoever turns away from His Revelation toward imitation of his forbears. The pious forefathers [*salaf*] and the four Imāms* were united in their condemnation and prohibition of this type of imitation. As for the imitation which is done by someone who exerts himself in [gaining knowledge in order to] follow what God revealed but despite this some part of knowledge remains concealed from him, so he imitates someone who is more knowledgeable than himself, this is praiseworthy, not condemnable. For this he is rewarded and is not burdened [with a sin]. This will be explained in the forthcoming account dealing with the obligatory and permissible forms of imitation, God willing.

God, The Most High, said, *And pursue not that of which you have no knowledge.* [Q., al-Isrāʾ, 17:36]. Now, imitation is not knowledge by consensus of the scholars, as shall appear shortly. He also said, *Say, "The things that my Lord has indeed forbidden are, shameful deeds, whether open or secret;*

*The four Imāms are Abū Ḥanīfah (d. 150/767), Mālik b. Anas (d. 179/795), al-Shāfiʿī (d. 204/820), and Aḥmad b. Ḥanbal (d. 241/855), after whom the four main surviving schools of law in Sunnī Islam are named.

*sins and trespasses against truth, assigning of partners to God, for which He has given no authority; and saying that about God of which you have no knowledge."* [Q., al-Aʿrāf, 7:33]. He, the Exalted, also said, *Follow the revelation given unto you from your Lord, and follow not, as friends or protectors, other than Him.* [Q., al-Aʿrāf, 7:3].

So God commanded that revelation alone be followed. But the imitator has no possible way of knowing that he is imitating only that which has been revealed. However, if a proof contradicting the opinion of the one he imitates is made apparent to him, then he does at least know that his continued imitation is in opposition to the evidence and thus falls under following something besides revelation. God, the Most High, said, *If you differ in anything among yourselves, refer it to God and His Messenger, if you do believe in God and the Last Day. That is best, and most desirable for the final reckoning.* [Q., al-Nisāʾ, 4:59].

So the Exalted One forbids us from referring to someone other than Him and His Messenger, thus invalidating imitation. God, the Most High, also said, *Or do you think that you shall be abandoned, as though God did not know those among you who have striven hard and fought, and taken none for friends and protectors* [Ar. *walījah*] *except God, His Messenger, and the (community of) Believers?* [Q., al-Tawbah, 9:16]. But there is no *walījah* greater than appointing a specific person [449] to be an arbiter over the Word of God, His Messenger, and the opinions of the entire community [*ummah*]; likewise, to accord precedence to him over all of them, and to discard the Book of God, the Sunnah of His Messenger, and the consensus of the community in favor of that person's opinion. The imitator accepts whatever agrees with the views of his principal, merely because it happens to agree with the former, while he is loath to reject the principal's views, seeking legal stratagems and fictions [to avoid having to reject them]. If this is not *walījah*, then we do not know what else it is! God, the Most High, said, *The Day that their faces will be turned upside down in the Fire, they will say, "Woe to us! If only we had obeyed God and obeyed the Messenger." And they will say, "Our Lord! We obeyed our chiefs and our great ones, and they misled us as to the (right) Path."* [Q., al-Aḥzāb, 33:66–67].

This explicit text nullifies imitation.

If it is said, "The condemnation in this verse applies only to the one who is misguided. As for the one who is rightly guided, how can it be said that this verse condemns him for his imitation [of another]?"

It is to be said, "The answer to this question lies in itself. For a person is not rightly guided until he follows what God has revealed to His Messenger. So this imitator is rightly guided if he has knowledge of this revelation. In this case, he is not an imitator. But if he does not know what God has revealed to His Messenger then, by his own confession, he is ignorant and misguided [and therefore, imitates]. How then can he know that he is rightly guided when the matter relates to his imitation?" This is the answer to every question raised by the supporters of imitation on this topic and also to their argument that if they imitate the righteous, then they themselves are rightly guided.

If it is said, "Because you acknowledge that the scholars who are imitated in the religion are rightly guided, it follows that those who imitate them must also be rightly guided, because they tread in their footsteps."

The response is, "The claim of the imitators, that they tread in the footsteps of the scholars, completely invalidates their imitation of them. For the real way of these scholars was to follow the evidences and to forbid imitation of themselves, as we shall mention when relating their positions on this issue, God willing. Therefore, whoever ignores evidence and does whatever these scholars prohibited—and what God and His Messenger forbade even before that—is not following the path of these scholars at all. Rather, he is among their adversaries. The only one who can be said to be on their path is the one who follows the evidence and submits to proof. Such a person does not appoint a specific individual other than the Messenger whom he honors above the Book and the Sunnah, opposing these on the basis of his opinions. [450]. Therefore, this argument exposes the flaw in the reasoning of the one who posits imitation and following evidence [*ittibāʿ*] as synonymous, thus confusing and muddling up the two. Rather, the imitator is opposed to following. God, His Messenger, and the people of knowledge distinguished between these two categories [i.e., imitating and following], as they are necessarily distinct. Following evidence means adopting the way of the one who is followed and acting the way he does."

## The Difference between Following Evidence [*Ittibāʿ*] and Imitation

In his *al-Jāmiʿ*, Abū ʿUmar [Ibn ʿAbd al-Barr]* wrote a "Chapter on the Corruption of Imitation; Its Rejection and the Difference between This and Following Evidence."

---

* Abū ʿUmar Yūsuf. b. ʿAbd al-Barr al-Namarī (d. 463/1071), a renowned North African traditionist, often referred to as the Bukhārī of the West.

[In it] Abū ʿUmar said, "God condemned imitation at more than one place in His Book, and He said, *They take their priests and their rabbis to be their lords in derogation of God.* [Q., al-Tawbah, 9:31]. It was related from Ḥudhayfah* and others that he said, 'They [i.e., the Jews and Christians] did not worship them alongside God. Rather, the priests and rabbis would declare things permissible and impermissible for them and they would follow them in that.'"[1]

ʿAdī b. Ḥātim† said, "I came to the Messenger of God while there was a cross around my neck. So he said, [451] 'O ʿAdī, remove this symbol of idolatry from your neck,' and I came to him while he was reciting the chapter [of the Qurʾan known as] 'al-Barāʾah,' until he reached this verse: *They take their priests and their rabbis to be their lords in derogation of God.* [Q., al-Tawbah, 9:31]. So I said, 'O Messenger of God, we did not take them as lords.' He said, 'You certainly did. Would they not make permissible for you that which was forbidden [by God], and would you not follow them in deeming it permissible? And would they not also make forbidden for you that which was made permissible [by God], and would you not also follow them in deeming it impermissible?' I said, 'Yes, indeed.' He said, 'This was your worship of them.'"[2]

I say that this *ḥadīth* is in the *Musnad*,‡ and there is a longer version of it in al-Tirmidhī§.

Abū l-Bakhtarī** said (about the Words of the One who is Exalted and Sublime, *They take their priests and their rabbis to be their lords in derogation of God.* [Q., al-Tawbah, 9:31]), "had they commanded the people to worship them alongside God, the people [452] would not have followed them, but they issued commands and declared forbidden that which God made permissible and vice versa. So the people followed them and this was their deification of them."[3]

---

*Ḥudhayfah b. al-Yamān (d. 35/656), a close Companion of the Prophet.

†ʿAdī b. Ḥātim (d. 67/686), a Companion of the Prophet.

‡The collection of *ḥadīth* compiled by Aḥmad b. Ḥanbal and subsequently added to by other members of his family.

§Abū ʿĪsā Muḥammad b. ʿĪsā al-Sulamī al-Tirmidhī (d. 279/892), author of one of the six most reliable collections of *ḥadīth*.

**Wahb b. Wahb b. Kathīr b. ʿAbdallāh b. Zamʿah b. al-ʾAswad b. al-Muṭṭalib b. Asad al-Qurashī (d. 200/815), a famous jurist.

Wakīʿ[*] said, "Sufyān[†] and Aʿmash[‡] both narrated to us from Ḥabīb b. Abī Thābīt[§] from Abī al-Bakhtarī, who said that Ḥudhayfah was asked about the words of God: *They take their priests and their rabbis to be their lords in derogation of God.* [Q., al-Tawbah, 9:31], if this meant that they worship them? He said, 'No. Rather, they would make permissible for them the prohibited and would make prohibited for them the permissible.'"

The Most Exalted One also said, *Just in the same way, whenever We sent a warner before you to a nation, the wealthy ones among them said, "We found our fathers following a religion, and we will certainly follow in their footsteps." The Messenger would say, "What! Even if I brought you better guidance than that which you found your fathers following?"* [Q., al-Zukhruf, 43:23–24]. So their act of following their forefathers [is what] prevented them from accepting guidance. And further, *They said, "For us, we deny that you (Prophets) are sent (on a mission at all)* [Q., al-Saba', 34:34]. It is about these people and their likes that God, the Exalted and Sublime, said, *Then would those who are followed absolve themselves of those who follow (them). They would see the punishment, and all relations between them would be severed. And those who followed would say, "If only we had one more chance, we would absolve ourselves of them, as they have absolved themselves of us." Thus will God show them (the fruits of) their deeds as (nothing but) regrets.* [Q., al-Baqarah, 2:166–167]. The Most High also says, in censure and condemnation of them, *"What are these images, to which you are (so assiduously) devoted?" They said, "We found our fathers worshipping them."* [Q., al-Anbiyā', 21:52–53]. And He says, *And they would say, "Our Lord! We obeyed our chiefs and our great ones, and they misled us as to the (right) Path."* [Q., al-Aḥzāb, 33:67].

There are several examples of this in the Qur'an, that is, of verses pertaining to the condemnation of imitation of ancestors and elders. The scholars argued for the invalidity of imitation based on these verses, and the disbelief of the ones being referred to therein did not prevent them from relying on them [to prove the invalidity of imitation, whether by a Muslim or a disbeliever]. This is because the similarity between the two groups has nothing to do with the disbelief of one and the belief of another.

---

[*] Abū Sufyān Wakīʿ b. al-Jarrāḥ (d. 197/812), a renowned *ḥadīth* scholar from Kufa.

[†] Sufyān b. ʿUyaynah (d. 196/811), one of the leading *ḥadīth* authorities in early Islam.

[‡] Abū Muḥammad Sulaymān b. Mihrān al-Asadī, nicknamed al-Aʿmash (d. 148/796), *ḥadīth* scholar and Qur'an commentator.

[§] Abū Yaḥyā Ḥabīb b. Abī Thābīt al-Qurashī (d. 120/738), renowned *ḥadīth* transmitter.

Rather, the similarity arises between them as both groups imitate without proof. For a person may imitate another and become a disbeliever as a result of his imitation or only commit a sin or merely fall into error in worldly matters. Each instance in which he imitated without proof is condemned. This is because all these examples fall under imitation, and each [453] resembles the other, even if the relative sin attached to each is different. God, the Exalted and Sublime, said, *And God will not mislead a people after He has guided them, so that He may make clear to them what to fear and avoid.* [Q., al-Tawbah, 9:115].

Abū ʿUmar also said, "If imitation is invalidated on account of the arguments we have presented, then what remains is to submit and accept the principle that is obligatory to accept. And that is the supremacy of the Book and the Sunnah and whatever conforms to their true meaning if it is an all-encompassing proof." Then he continued his words, mentioning from the path of Kathīr b. ʿAbdallāh b. ʾAmr b. ʿAwf, from his father, from his grandfather,* who said, "I heard the Messenger of God say, 'I do not fear anything for my community after me except three things.' They said, 'What are they, Messenger of God?' He said, 'I fear for you the mistakes of scholars, the tyrannical ruler, and those vain desires that are followed.'"[4] It is also related from the Prophet, with the same chain of narration, that he said, "I have left two things among you, and you will not stray so long as you hold on to them: the Book of God and the Sunnah of His Messenger."[5]

## Repercussions of the Mistakes of the Scholar

I further add that the authors who wrote about the Sunnah linked the topic of the corruption of imitation and its invalidity to the topic of the mistakes of the scholar, to clarify thus the corruption of imitation, and to illustrate that the scholar sometimes errs, which is inevitable, as he is not infallible. Thus, it is not permissible to accept everything he says and to regard his views as being equal in rank to the views of someone infallible. This is what every scholar in the world has condemned and prohibited. They have condemned those who do so, and this is the real woe and tribulation of the imitators. For they imitate the scholar both when he errs and when he does not. For them, there is nothing to distinguish between these two states. Inevitably, then, they must take the religion adulterated by

---

*ʿAmr b. ʿAwf b. Zayd al-Muzanī (d. 61/680), a Companion of the Prophet.

errors. They thus render permissible what God prohibited and prohibit what He made permissible, and they legislate that which He did not. This must be the case for them as the ones they imitate are not immune from error. [454] They certainly do err. Bayhaqī* and others mentioned this *ḥadīth* of Kathīr from his father from his grandfather directly from the Prophet, "Fear the errors of the scholar and wait for him to recant."[6]

And he mentioned from the *ḥadīth* of Mas'ūd b. Sa'd, from Yazīd b. Abī Ziyād,† from Mujāhid,‡ from Ibn 'Umar,§ who narrated that the Messenger of God said, "The three things I fear most for my community are the errors of the scholar, the hypocrite using the Qur'an in his argument, and [pursuit of] this world, which will [lead you to] smite your [i.e., each others'] throats."[7]

It is well known that the reason for fearing the error of the scholar is that he will be imitated therein. For if there were no imitation, there would be no danger of the scholar's error affecting anyone else.

So, when the imitator knows that what he is following is an error, it is impermissible for him, by the agreement of all Muslims, to follow the scholar in that, for this would be tantamount to following an error deliberately. As for the one who does not know of the error, he is excused. Both of them, however, are transgressing the bounds of their obligations. Sha'bī** said, "'Umar†† said, 'Three things blight the age [in which they are found]: scholars who misguide the people, the hypocrite relying on the Qur'an in argument although the Qur'an itself is truthful, and the errors of the scholar.'"[8] And it has already come earlier [in the *I'lām*] that Mu'ādh‡‡ [455] would not sit in a religious gathering without saying, as he sat, "God is the Just Ruler, and may the people who doubt perish!," and in this narration is also the following, "I warn you of the error of the wise. For Satan sometimes

---

*Abū Bakr Aḥmad b. Ḥuṣayn al-Bayhaqī (d. 458/1066), a renowned *ḥadīth* scholar.

†Abū 'Abdallāh Yazīd b. Abī Ziyād al-Hāshimī (d. 237/852), a junior Successor.

‡Abū al-Ḥajjāj Mujāhid b. Jābir al-Makkī (d. 104/722), a famous Successor and commentator on the Qur'an.

§'Abdallāh b. 'Umar (d. 73/692), a learned Companion and son of the second caliph 'Umar b. al-Khaṭṭāb.

**'Āmir Sharaḥīl b. al-Sha'bī (d. 103/721?) a renowned Successor, who also served as an ambassador in the early Umayyad state.

††'Umar b. al-Khaṭṭāb (d. 23/644), the second caliph after the Prophet.

‡‡Abū 'Abd al-Raḥmān Mu'ādh b. Jabal (d. 18/639), a Companion of the Prophet.

utters a falsehood through the tongue of a wise person. And sometimes the hypocrite utters the truth." The narrator of the report says, "I said to Mu'ādh, 'May God have mercy on you, how would I know if the wise person had uttered falsehood and the hypocrite had spoken a word of truth?' He said to me, 'Stay away from the dubious statements of the wise person, which prompt you to exclaim, What is this? But do not let this turn you away from him, for he might recant his opinion. And you should follow the truth when you hear it, for truth is adorned with light.'"[9]

Al-Bayhaqī mentioned the *ḥadīth* of Ḥammād b. Zayd,[*] from Muthannā b. Sa'īd,[†] from Abī al-'Āliyah,[‡] who said that Ibn 'Abbās[§] said, "Woe to those who follow the slippages of the scholar." It was said, "How can that be, Ibn 'Abbās?" He said, "The scholar says something initially and later hears a *ḥadīth* from the Prophet, so he abandons that which he had held previously"—and in another narration the words are, "of one who is more knowledgeable about the Messenger of God than him, so he informs the scholar of it"—and the scholar recants, while those who follow him continue to rule by what he decided previously.

[456] Tamīm al-Dārī[**] said, "Fear the errors of the scholar." So 'Umar asked what these were. He said, "He errs before the people, and they accept his opinion. It might be that the scholar would later repent, while the people would continue to act according to his incorrect opinion."

Shu'bah[††] said, narrating from 'Amr b. Murrah,[‡‡] from 'Abdallāh b. Salamah,[§§] that he said, "Mu'ādh b. Jabal said, 'O Arabs! What would you do when three things occur? The [pursuit of the] world, which causes you

---

[*] Abū Ismā'īl Ḥammād b. Zayd b. Dirham (d. 179/795), a famous traditionist.

[†] Abū Sa'īd Muthannā b. Sa'īd, a Successor.

[‡] Rafī' b. Mahrān Abī al-'Āliyah al-Riyāḥī, (d. 93/711), a Successor and famed expert on scripture, who was renowned for his piety.

[§] 'Abdallāh b. 'Abbās (d. 68/687?), a Companion and cousin of the Prophet, who is famed for his expertise in *ḥadīth* and scripture.

[**] Abū Ruqayyah Tamīm b. Aws al-Dārī (d. 40/660), a Companion of the Prophet.

[††] Abū Bisṭām Shu'bah b. Ḥajjāj (d. 160/776), a famous traditionist.

[‡‡] Abū Maryam 'Amr b. Murrah al-Juhanī, a Companion who settled in Syria. Most authorities claim that he died during the caliphate of Mu'āwiyah.

[§§] 'Abdallāh b. Salamah al-Hamadānī al-Murādī, a Successor. There is, however, some difference of opinion among traditionists about the identity of the 'Abdallāh b. Salamah from whom 'Amr b. Murrah reports.

to smite your throats, the errors of the scholar, and the hypocrite arguing on the basis of the Qur'an.'" So they were silent, and he said, "As for the scholar, if he is right, then do not imitate him in your religion, and if he is overcome by error, then do not become disheartened, for a believer is sometimes overcome by error, and he then repents. As for the Qur'an, it has lampposts like those you find on the pathways, and these are not concealed from anyone. So do not ask about that which you know. And entrust whatever creates doubts in your minds to the one who knows about it. As for the world, whomever God enriches in his heart has indeed succeeded, and for the one who was not blessed with this, the world is of no benefit."[10]

Abū ʿUmar mentioned the *ḥadīth* of Ḥuṣayn al-Juʿfī,* from Zāʾidah,† from ʿAtāʾ b. al-Sāʾib,‡ from Abī al-Bakhtarī, who said that Salmān§ said, "How would you fare when three things occur: the errors of the scholar, the hypocrite arguing on the basis of the Qur'an, and the world [causing you to] smite your throats? As for the errors of the scholar, if he is right, do not imitate him in your religion. And as for the hypocrite's argument, the Qur'an has lampposts like the ones you find on the pathways, and these are not hidden from anyone. So act on whatever you know and refer what you do not to God. And as for the world [causing you to] smite your throats, avoid this by looking to the one who is worse off than you and not the one who is better off than you."[11]

[459] Abū ʿUmar said, "The error of the scholar can be compared to the capsizing of a vessel. If it sinks, it takes many people with it."

Abū ʿUmar also said, "Since it is true and established that the scholar errs and makes mistakes, it is not permissible for anyone to issue verdicts and to hold something to be part of his religion without knowing its basis."

Yet another author (besides Abū ʿUmar) has said, "As there are three types of judges [*quḍāh*], and two will be in Hell and one in Paradise, so too are there three types of *muftī*s who issue verdicts, and there is no difference between them, except that the judge [*qāḍī*] binds people with his verdicts and the *muftī* does not."

---

* Ḥuṣayn b. ʿAlī b. al-Walīd al-Juʿfī (d. 203/819), a renowned traditionist.

† Abū l-Ṣalt Zāʾidah b. Qudāmah al-Thaqafī (d. 161/777), a *ḥadīth* scholar.

‡ ʿAtāʾ b. al-Sāʾib b. Zayd al-Thaqafī, a Kufan Successor.

§ Salmān al-Fārsī (d. 31/651), a Companion of the Prophet.

Ibn Wahb[*] said, "I heard Sufyān b. ʿUyaynah narrating from ʿĀṣim b. Bahdalah,[†] from Zirr b. Ḥubaysh,[‡] from Ibn Masʿūd,[§] that he was saying, 'Be a scholar or a seeker of knowledge but do not be a freeloader who is neither one nor the other.'" Ibn Wahb said that he asked Sufyān about the freeloader, so he narrated to him from Abī al-Zanād,[**] from Abī al-Aḥwas,[††] from Ibn Masʿūd, that he said, "In the period of ignorance we would define a freeloader as someone who was not invited but who turned up to a meal alongside the one who had been invited. It is the same as the one you refer to as the *muḥaqqib*, the one who follows other people in religion, without proof or evidence."[12] [458]

Abū Zurʿah ʿAbd al-Raḥmān b. ʿAmr al-Naṣrī[‡‡] said that Abū Mushir[§§] narrated to us that Saīʿd b. ʿAbd al-ʿAzīz[***] narrated to us from Ismāʿīl b. ʿUbayd Allāh,[†††] from al-Sāʾib b. Yazīd,[‡‡‡] from the sister of Nimr,[§§§] that he heard ʿUmar b. Khaṭṭāb saying [to the Companions], "Your discourse is the worst of discourses, for you continue to narrate to the people until it is said that some scholars say this and others say that, and the Book of God is abandoned. Whoever among you stands up to speak, let him stand with the Book of God. If not, let him remain seated."[13] This is the instruction of ʿUmar [459] to the best of generations on the face of the earth. How would it fare if he were to learn of how the Book of God, the Sunnah of His

---

[*] Abū Muḥammad ʿAbdallāh b. Wahb, the Egyptian (d. 197/812), a leading Egyptian scholar.

[†] Abū Bakr ʿĀṣim b. Bahdalah al-Asadī (d. 128/745).

[‡] Abū Maryam Zirr b. Ḥubaysh al-Asadī, (d. 83/702, at the age of 120 years), a renowned Successor.

[§] Ibn Masʿūd (d. 32/652), a Companion of the Prophet.

[**] Abū al-Zanād ʿAbdallāh b. Dhakwān al-Qurashī (d. 130/748), a *ḥadīth* expert.

[††] Abū l-Aḥwaṣ Sallām b. Sulaym al-Ḥanafī (d. 179/795), *ḥadīth* transmitter.

[‡‡] Abū Zurʿah ʿAbd al-Raḥmān b. ʾAmr b. ʿAbdallāh b. Ṣafwān b. ʿAmr al-Naṣrī (d. 281/894), a Syrian scholar.

[§§] Abū Mushar ʿAbd al-Aʿlā al-Ghassānī (d. 218/833), a leading traditionist in Syria.

[***] Abū Muḥammad Saīʿd b. ʿAbd al-ʿAzīz al-Tanūkhī (d. 167/783), a *ḥadīth* transmitter.

[†††] Ismāʿīl b. ʿUbaydallāh b. Abī al-Muhājir, the client of Banī Makhzūm (d. 232/846), a renowned traditionist.

[‡‡‡] Sāʾib b. Yazīd b. Saʿīd b. Thamāmah b. al-Aswad b. Ukht al-Nimr al-Kinānī (or al-Kindī) (d. 90/709?). He reportedly accompanied his father to the annual pilgrimage with the Prophet but was only a child of seven at the time.

[§§§] Sister of Nimr, the mother of Sāʾib b. Yazīd.

Messenger and the opinions of his Companions have been abandoned in favor of the opinions of others in our own times? God save us!

## Advice of ʿAlī* to Kumayl b. Ziyād†

Abū ʿUmar said, "ʿAlī b. Abī Ṭālib said to Kumayl b. Ziyād al-Nakhaʿī—and this narration is so well-known [*mashhūr*] among the people of knowledge that its chain need not be mentioned—'O Kumayl, these hearts are vessels. The best of them are those receptive to goodness. And there are three types of people: a scholar devoted to God, a seeker of religious knowledge on the path to salvation, and the commoner who follows anyone who bellows and inclines to every loud-mouthed bawler. Such people are not enlightened with the radiance of knowledge, nor do they stand on firm ground in support of their stance.' Then ʿAlī said, 'Knowledge resides here,' and he pointed with his finger toward his chest. He continued, 'would that I could find those who would acquire it. Rather, I have found only the kind of person who is quick to comprehend but is not reliable. Such a one would use the religion to gain worldly profit, seek victory against the Book of God with His own evidences, and deploy the favors of God in disobeying Him. Or, I have found the kind of person who carries the truth but does not know how to nourish it. Doubt makes his heart quiver as soon as any ambiguity arises. The truth eludes him. Whenever he says something, he errs, and yet remains unaware of it. He is feverishly obsessed with that whose reality is beyond him. He is a tribulation for the one who is influenced by him. The greatest good lies in God bestowing knowledge of His religion upon someone. It suffices to establish the ignorance of such a being that he does not know his own religion.'"

## [460] The Companions Forbade Adopting the Practices of People

Abū ʿUmar mentioned from Abū l-Bakhtarī, who mentioned from ʿAlī, that he said, "I warn you of adopting the practices of others. For a man might be performing the actions of the people of Paradise. Then he might

---

* ʿAlī b. Abī Ṭālib (d. 40/661), cousin and son-in-law of the Prophet who later became the fourth caliph.

† Kumayl b. Ziyād al-Nakhaʿī, (d. 82/701), a renowned Successor.

deviate because of God's pre-knowledge and would then perform the actions of the denizens of the Fire, and so, when he dies, he would become one of them himself. Similarly, a man might be performing the actions of the people of the Fire. Later, he might deviate because of God's pre-knowledge and end up acting like the people of Paradise, and so, when he dies, he would be one of its dwellers. Should you choose to do this [i.e., follow the practices of other people] despite this warning, you [461] ought to adopt the practices of those who are no more, not those who are still alive."[14]

Ibn Mas'ūd said, "No one should imitate another in matters of religion, lest he come to believe as the other believes and disbelieves as the other disbelieves. For evil is never a model to be emulated."[15]

Abū 'Umar said, "It is authentically established from the Prophet that he said, 'The scholars will disappear. Then, people will adopt the ignorant ones as their leaders. They will be asked to deliver verdicts and will do so without knowledge. So they will be misguided and will misguide others.'"[16] Abū 'Umar also said, "All this is said in order to refute imitation and its invalidity is established for the one who understands these proofs and is guided by them."

Then he mentioned from the chain of Yūnus b. 'Abd al-A'lā* that Sufyān b. 'Uyaynah narrated to us that Rabī'ah† once lay down, hanging his head low and crying. It was said to him, "Why do you cry?" He said, "Because of the open display of one's righteous actions and hidden lusts and because people act with their scholars like children with their Imāms. They refrain from whatever these scholars tell them to and perform whatever they command."[17]

[462] 'Abdallāh b. al-Mu'tazz said, "There is no difference between a domesticated animal and a man who imitates."

Then he mentioned from the *Jāmi'* of Ibn Wahb, "Sa'īd b. Abī Ayyūb‡ informed me from Bakr b. 'Amr,§ from 'Amr b. Abī Na'īmah,** from

---

*Abū Mūsā Yūnus b. 'Abd al-A'lā al-Ṣadafī, (d. 264/877), a renowned Egyptian scholar and traditionist.

† Rabī'ah b. Abī 'Abd al-Raḥmān Farrūkh al-Taymī, an early Medinese scholar.

‡ Abū Yaḥyā Sa'īd b. Abī Ayyūb (d. 161/777), a renowned Egyptian traditionist.

§ Bakr b. 'Amr al-Ma'āfirī, the Egyptian (d. after 140/757), the *imām* of the grand Mosque in Cairo.

** 'Amr b. Abī Na'īmah al-Ma'ārifī, an Egyptian scholar whose reliability as a narrator is the subject of some dispute.

Muslim b. Yasār,* from Abū Hurayrah,† that the Messenger said, 'Whoever reports from me something I did not say should choose his place in the Hellfire. And whoever, upon being asked, proffers advice that was against the best interests of his brother, has betrayed him. As for the one who is issued a verdict without a foundation, then the sin of this is on the one who delivers it.'"[18] This *ḥadīth* has preceded, from the narration of Abū Dā'ūd‡.

This contains a proof for the prohibition of issuing verdicts on the basis of imitation, as it is [a form of] doing the former without evidence. By consensus of all people, it is only on the basis of evidence that any ruling is established, as Abū 'Umar has also said.

## An Argument against the One Who Permits Imitation Based on Speculative Proofs

A group of scholars, jurists, and people of erudition argued against the one who would validate imitation by relying on logical reasoning, even after the arguments that have preceded. The best work I have seen in this regard is the opinion of al-Muzanī§, which I present here. He said that it ought to be said to the one who rules in favor of imitation, "Do you have a proof for the judgment you have given on the basis of imitation?" If he answers in the affirmative, his imitation is naturally invalidated, because it is the proof that compelled him to issue that judgment, not imitation. If he says, "I judged this way without proof," it is said to him, "Why did you issue judgments on criminal matters where the shedding of the blood of people is concerned and sexual matters that lead to people's private parts being made permissible [or impermissible] and economic matters wherein, by your verdicts, you destroyed the wealth of the people, while God made all this unlawful, except on the basis of proof. God says, *You*

---

* Abū 'Abdallāh Muslim b. Yāsir, the client of Banū 'Umayyah (d. 100/718), a Successor from Basra.

† Abū Hurayrah al-Dawsi (d. c. 59/679), a Companion of the Prophet and a leading transmitter of *ḥadīth*.

‡ Abū Dāūd Sulaymān b. al-Ash'ath al-Sijistānī (d. 275/888), one of the six leading traditionists and author of the *Sunan* which bears his name.

§ Abū Ibrāhīm Ismā'īl b. Yaḥyā al-Muzanī (d. 264/877), the leading student of al-Shāfi'ī, who spread the teachings of his master in Egypt.

*have no authority for this!* [Q., Yūnus, 10:68] [463], which means, no proof for this."

If he says, "I know that I am correct, even if I do not know the proof, because I have imitated a scholar of high stature, and he does not base his opinion except on a proof that is concealed from me," it is said to him, "If imitation of your teacher is allowed because he gives his opinions on the basis of proofs which are concealed from you, then imitation of your teacher's teacher is preferable. Because he would not have based his opinion on anything other than a proof which was concealed from your teacher, just as the latter would not have said what he said except on the basis of a proof that is concealed from you." If he says, "Yes," he has abandoned imitation of his teacher in favor of that of his teacher's teacher and so on, until he reaches the Companions of the Messenger.

If he does not do this, his claim is self-contradictory. It is then said to him: "How have you declared imitation of the one who is lower in stature and possesses lesser knowledge to be permissible, while you prohibit imitation of one who was higher in stature and more knowledgeable, when this is clearly contradictory?" If he says, "Because my teacher, even if he was of a lower stature, acquired the knowledge of those who were before him. He therefore has more insight about that which he has acquired from them and that which he has not," it is said to him, "Likewise, the one who learnt from your teacher, he too combined his own knowledge and that of those who were before him. So it becomes obligatory on you to imitate him and to abandon imitation of your teacher. Otherwise, you are more worthy of imitation than your teacher, because you have gathered his knowledge and that of those before him." If he calls for his own statement to be imitated, he has rendered the lesser scholars and the ones who narrate from them more worthy of imitation than the Companions of the Messenger. Likewise, he would oblige the Companion to imitate the Successor [*tābiʿī*]*, and the Successor to imitate those lower than him in their analogies. He would also say that those higher in rank should always continue to imitate those who are lower. This much is sufficient to establish the contradiction and corruption of this view.

Abū ʿUmar said, "The people of knowledge and erudition said that the mark of knowledge is clarification and to grasp that which is known just as it is. Therefore, when something is clarified to someone it can be said

---

*A Successor is a disciple of a Companion of the Prophet.

that he knows it." They also said that the imitator has no knowledge. They did not disagree about this. Perhaps it is on the basis of this that al-Bakhtarī said—although God knows best—[464]

*The scholars know your merit in knowledge*
*While the ignorant ones call for imitation*
*And I see mankind agreeing on your merits*
*The masters and their slaves altogether.*

## Imitation and Following [*Ittibāʿ*]

Abū ʿAbdallāh b. Khwāzmandād al-Baṣrī al-Mālikī* said, "Imitation in sacred law [*sharʿ*] means adopting an opinion for which the person who holds it has no evidence. This is disallowed in the sacred law, whereas *ittibāʿ* means doing that for which proof has been established."

Elsewhere in his book he said, "You are an imitator of everyone whose opinion you follow without there being a proof that necessitates that. Imitation in the religion of God is not correct. And you are a follower of the person whose proofs compel you to follow his opinion. Following [*ittibāʿ*] in the religion is allowed and imitation is not."

He also said that Muḥammad b. Ḥārith† said, in the *Akhbār* of Saḥnūn b. Saʿīd‡ from him, that he said that Mālik, ʿAbd al-ʿAzīz b. Salamah§, Muḥammad b. Ibrāhīm b. Dīnār** and others used to refer their disagreements to Ibn Hurmuz††. When Mālik and ʿAbd al-ʿAzīz asked him a question, he answered them. But when Ibn Dīnār and his likes asked him a

---

* Abū Bakr Muḥammad b. Aḥmad b. ʿAbdallāh b. Khwāzmandād al-Baṣrī. A Mālikī scholar, (d. c. 390/1000).

† Muḥammad b. Ḥārith b. Asad al-Khushanī (d. 161/777), a renowned scholar and litterateur.

‡ ʿAbd al-Salām Saḥnūn b. Saʿīd b. Ḥabīb al-Tanūkhī (d. 240/854), the leading Mālikī scholar of his day.

§ ʿAbd al-ʿAzīz b. Salamah b. Dīnār (d. 184/800), a renowned Medinese jurist.

** Abū ʿAbdallāh Muḥammad b. Ibrāhīm b. Dīnār al-Juhanī, (d. 182/798). A Medinese jurist and contemporary of Mālik.

†† Abū Bakr ʿAbdallāh Yazīd b. Hurmuz al-Aṣamm (d. 184/800), one of the leading Successors in Medina.

question, he did not. So Ibn Dīnār came across him one day and said, "O Abū Bakr, why did you do treat me so indecorously?" He [Abū Bakr] said, "My nephew, how is that?" He said, "Mālik and 'Abd al-'Azīz asked you a question, and you answered them, but when my company and I asked a question, you did not." He said, "Did such a thought indeed arise in your heart, nephew?" He said, "Yes." He said, "I am advanced in years, and my bones have grown thin with age, and I am afraid that something similar to what has happened to my body might have happened to my intellect. Mālik and 'Abd al-'Azīz are both knowledgeable jurists. If they hear the correct view from me, they would accept it, and if they hear from me that which is incorrect, they would abandon it. As for you and your peers, you would accept any response I issue." Ibn al-Ḥārith said, "By God, this statement indicates the perfection of the religion [of Ibn Hurmuz ] and a sound, astute intellect, unlike the one who [465] brings forth nonsense and desires his own opinions to be imprinted on the hearts of people as though they were like the Qur'an."

Abū 'Umar wrote the following response to the one who argues for imitation: "Why do you call for it and thus oppose the pious forbears in this, since they never performed imitation?" If he says, "I imitate because I lack complete knowledge about the interpretation of the Book of God and the Sunnah of the Messenger, while the one I imitate knew all of this. So I imitate the one who was more knowledgeable than myself," it is to be said to him, "When the scholars agree on an interpretation of the Book, a report from the Sunnah of the Prophet, or when their opinions on a matter coincide, then that is the indisputable truth. But they disagreed with each other about the matter in which you imitated one of them. So what is your proof for imitating one and not others when all of them are scholars? It might be that the one whose opinion you rejected was more knowledgeable than the one whose opinion you embraced."

If he says, "I imitate him because I know that he was correct," it is then to be said to him, "Do you know this based on evidence from the Book and the Sunnah or from consensus?" If he says, "Yes," then his imitation is nullified, and he is then to be questioned on the basis of the proof he presents. But if he says: "I imitate him because he was more knowledgeable than I am," then it is to be said to him, "Then imitate everyone who was more knowledgeable than you. Surely, you will find many people who fit this description. Do not appoint one individual as the only one you will imitate and no other, if your proof is only that he knows more than you."

If he says, "I imitate him because he was the most knowledgeable of men," it is to be said to him, "Was he, then, more knowledgeable than the Companions?" Such a statement alone is sufficient to establish the reprehensibility of what he says. If the imitator says, "I do [indirectly] imitate some of the Companions," it is to be said to him, "What is your proof for abandoning the views of those whom you do not imitate? It might be that the one whose opinion you have abandoned was more knowledgeable than the one whose opinions you adopted. All this is based on the fact that an opinion is not correct by virtue of its bearer but because of the soundness of the proofs that establish its validity."

Ibn Muzayyin* said, from ʿĪsa b. Dīnār,† that Ibn al-Qāsim‡ said from Mālik, "Not every opinion of a man is to be followed, even if he possesses special merit. For God says, *those who listen to the Word, and follow the best (meaning) in it—those are the ones whom Allah has guided, and those are the ones endued with understanding.* [Q., al-Zumar, 39:18]. If he says [466], "My paucity and lack of knowledge compel me to imitate," it is to be said to him, "The imitation of a scholar about whose knowledge of the revelation everyone is agreed on is excusable, provided that he just transmits that which was narrated to him." This is what he was obliged to do, and he acted as he ought to have, by deriving rulings from revelation in this way. There was no choice available to him but to imitate the scholar where he himself had no knowledge. This is due to the consensus of the Muslims that the blind are to imitate the person whose statement is trusted—to ascertain the direction of the Sacred Mosque when they are praying—because they can do no more than this. But can it be permissible, for the one who is truly in this condition, to issue legal verdicts pertaining to the laws of God's religion, and to direct others through his verdicts to regard as lawful [or not] all kinds of sexual matters, the shedding of blood, enslavement, destruction of property and rendering it to the one to whom it does not belong, all based on a view [i.e., that of his principal] about the truth of which he himself does not know, and for which he has been able to establish no proof? Especially since he acknowledges all along that the

---

* Yaḥyā b. Ibrāhīm b. Muzayyin (d. c. 300/912), an Andalusian scholar, who also commented on Mālik's works.

† Abū Muḥammad ʿĪsa b. Dīnār, (d. 212/827), an Andalusian scholar and student of Ibn al-Qāsim.

‡ Ibn al-Qāsim (d. 191/806), a leading disciple of Mālik.

one whose opinion he follows did make mistakes on some occasions and was correct on others and that the one who disagreed with him in this particular matter is perhaps the one who is more correct therein. Now, if this person accepts that issuing verdicts is allowed for the [imitator] who is ignorant of the proofs and of their true meaning, simply because he has memorized the rulings related to trivial matters, he must concede that this right to issue verdicts should also be granted to everyone. Such an outcome is sufficient to establish the nullity of such a view and its opposition to the Qur'an. God, the Most High says, *And pursue not that of which you have no knowledge* [al-Isrā', 36], and He says *Do you say that about God which you know not?* [Q., Yūnus, 10:68].

The scholars are agreed that whatever is unclear and does not give rise to certainty is not knowledge—rather, it is mere conjecture, and conjecture cannot be a substitute for the truth. Then he mentioned the *ḥadīth* of Ibn 'Abbās (in both its *marfū'*[*] and *mawqūf*[†] forms): "Whoever issues a verdict relating to something of which he has no knowledge shall bear the sin of it."[19] He also said, "It is established that the Prophet, may the peace and blessings of God be on him, said, 'Beware of conjecture, for conjecture is the most untruthful type of speech.'"[20] [467]

He also said that there is no dispute between the scholars of the provinces about the nullity of imitation. Then he mentioned, from the path of Ibn Wahb, "Yūnus narrated to me from Ibn Shahāb that Abū 'Uthmān b. Sannah[‡] informed me that the Messenger of God, may the peace and blessings of God be on him, said, 'Knowledge began as something strange, and it shall return to being something strange, as it began. So there are glad tidings for the estranged.'"[21] He also narrated from the path of Kathīr b. 'Abdallāh,[§] from his father, from his grandfather, that the Prophet, may the peace and blessings of God be on him, said, "Islam began as something strange, and it shall return to being something strange, as it began. So there are glad tidings for the estranged." He was asked, "O Messenger

[*] A *ḥadīth* whose chain is "elevated" all the way to the Prophet himself.

[†] A *ḥadīth* whose chain stops at a Companion.

[‡] Abū 'Uthmān b. Sannah al Khuzā'ī. While some authorities claim he was a Companion who accepted Islam toward the end of the Prophet's life, Ibn Ḥajar and others regard him as a Successor only.

[§] Kathīr b. 'Abdallāh b. 'Amr b. 'Awf, who narrated around the middle of the second Islamic century (the end of the eighth century CE).

of God, who are the estranged?" He said, "The ones who revive my Sunnah and teach it to the people."[22]

It was said [468] that the scholars are the estranged ones because of the prevalence of those who are ignorant. Then he narrated from Mālik b. Zayd b. Aslam his interpretation of the Words of the Most Exalted One, *We raise whom We will, degree after degree* [Q., al-An'ām, 6:83], that this was "because of knowledge." Ibn 'Abbās said, interpreting the Words of God, the Exalted, *God will raise, to (suitable) ranks (and degrees), those of you who believe and who have been granted knowledge* [Q., al-Mujādalah, 58:11], that this means, "God elevates those Believers who have been granted knowledge above those who have not, by degrees." [469]

Hishām b. Sa'd* narrated from Zayd b. Aslam† about the interpretation of His Words, *Those Messengers! We preferred some of them to others* [Q., al-Baqarah, 2:253], that this was by virtue of their knowledge. So, if the imitator is not among the knowledgeable ones, which he is not by agreement of the scholars, then he does not fall under these texts. God alone grants success.

## The Principals of the Four Schools Forbade Imitation of Themselves

It is established that the four Imāms proscribed imitation of themselves and condemned those who adopted their rulings without understanding the reasons behind them. As al-Shāfi'ī said, "The similitude of the one who seeks knowledge without understanding is that of the woodcutter who works during the night. He carries a load of sticks, and in them there could be a snake that could strike him without his knowledge." Al-Bayhaqī mentioned this statement.

Ismā'īl b. Yaḥyā al-Muzanī says, in the first part of his *Mukhtaṣar*, "I have summarized what follows from the knowledge of al-Shāfi'ī, and the import of what he says is that he will share this knowledge with the

* Hishām b. Sa'd al-Qurashī (d. 160/777), a traditionist who died in the first year of the caliph al-Mahdī.

† Abū 'Abdallāh Zayd b. Aslam al-'Umarī, (d. 136/754), a highly regarded traditionist who used to lecture in the Prophet's mosque.

one who wants it, while also narrating al-Shāfiʿī's well-known prohibition of imitation of himself and others, so that everyone can gain knowledge to save his religion and protect himself [by acquisition of this knowledge]."

Abū Dāʾūd said, "I asked Aḥmad, 'Does al-Awzāʿī* deserve to be followed more than Mālik?' He said, 'Do not imitate anyone among them in matters of the religion. Rather, take that which comes from the Prophet and his Companions and then the Successors. After them, one has the option to accept or reject the opinion of everyone else.'"

Aḥmad did, however, insist on the difference between imitation and following. Abū Dāʾūd says that he heard Aḥmad say, "*Ittibāʿ* is that a person follows what is related from the Prophet and his Companions. After that, it is his right to choose from among the Successors." Aḥmad also said, "Do not imitate me, Mālik, al-Thawrī†, or al-Awzāʿī. Rather, take knowledge from where they took it." [470] He also said, "It is among the signs of a man's lack of wisdom that he follows others in matters of religion."

Bishr b. al-Walīd‡ said that Abū Yūsuf§ said, "It is not permissible for anyone to say what we have said without knowing the reasons why we said so."[23]

Mālik said explicitly that the one who abandons a ruling of ʿUmar b. al-Khaṭṭāb in favor of a ruling of Ibrāhīm al-Nakhāʿī** should repent for doing so. But then, what about the one who abandons the command of God and His Messenger in favor of someone who is not even of the rank of Ibrāhīm or others [among the Successors] who were equal to him?

Jaʿfar al-Firyābī†† said that Aḥmad b. Ibrāhīm al-Dawraqī‡‡ narrated to him that al-Haytham b. Jamīl§§ narrated to him that he said to Mālik b.

---

*Abū ʿAmr ʿAbd al-Raḥmān b. ʿAmr al-Awzāʿī (d. 157/774), a renowned jurist from Syria.

†Sufyān b. Saʿīd al-Thawrī (d. 161/778), renowned traditionist and scholar.

‡Abū l-Walīd Bishr b. al-Walīd b. Khālid al-Kindī (d. 238/853), a renowned Ḥanafī scholar and disciple of Abū Yūsuf.

§Abū Yūsuf Yaʿqūb b. Ibrāhīm (d. 182/798), the foremost disciple of Abū Ḥanīfah.

**Abū ʿImrān Ibrāhīm b. Yazīd al-Nakhāʿī (d. 96/715), renowned jurist from Iraq.

††Jaʿfar al-Firyābī (d. 301/914), a judge and traditionist, who died at the age of ninety-four.

‡‡Abū ʿAbdallāh Aḥmad b. Ibrāhīm al-Dawraqī (d. c. 248/862), a traditionist.

§§Abū Sahl al-Haytham b. Jamīl (d. 214/829), a scholar who narrates from Sufyān b. ʿUyaynah and Mālik, among others.

Anas, "O father of ʿAbdallāh, there are people among us who have put aside the study of books, saying instead, 'so-and-so narrates that ʿUmar b. al Khaṭṭāb said thus,' and another one of them says that 'Ibrāhīm said thus, and we act according to the stance of Ibrāhīm.'" Mālik asked, "Has the statement of ʿUmar been established as authentic by them?" I said, "It is a report as authentic to them as that of Ibrāhīm." Mālik delivered his ruling, saying, "These people must repent."[24] And God, the Most High, knows best.

# *A Disputation between an Imitator and His Adversary*

AN ACCOUNT OF a debate between an imitator and one who submits to proofs wherever they may be:

1. The imitator says, "We are the party of imitation, acting by the command of God to *Ask the people of knowledge if you are ignorant.* [Q., al-Naḥl, 16:43]. God, the exalted, Himself commands those who do not know to ask those who are more knowledgeable than them. This is the clear text of the Qur'an, upon which we base our actions."
2. The Prophet, may God's peace and blessings be on him, directed the one who did not know to ask someone who did. As he said in the *ḥadīth* [known as the *ḥadīth*] of *Shajjah*, "Why did you not ask if you did not know? Indeed the cure of [471] ignorance is to ask."[1]
3. The father of the laborer who had committed *zinā*[*] with the wife of his employer said, "I asked the people [472] of knowledge [about the punishment due to my son], and they informed me that my son was to be awarded a hundred lashes and was to be exiled for a year and that the woman with whom he had committed illegal intercourse was to be stoned."[2] We see that he was not prevented from imitating those who were more knowledgeable than him.[†]

---

[*] Unlawful sexual intercourse, which refers to all sexual activity outside a valid marriage.

[†] The reason for the difference in punishment is the difference in the marital status of the two parties. A married person who commits *zinā* is stoned, while the unmarried offender receives one hundred lashes.

4. Another example is that of ʿUmar, who is among the most knowledgeable people on earth, yet he imitated Abū Bakr*. For Shuʿbah relates, on the authority of ʿĀṣim, from al-Shaʿbī, that Abū Bakr issued a ruling about the inheritance of the one who dies in the state known as *al-kalālah*, saying, "I have given a ruling in this case. If it is correct, then that is from God, and if it is wrong, then that is from me and from the devil, and God is free of it. As for *kalālah*, it is when a person dies without a father or a son."† Now ʿUmar b. al Khaṭṭāb said, "I would be belittled in the sight of God if I were to oppose a ruling of Abū Bakr."[3] It is also authentically reported from him that he said, about Abū Bakr, "Our judgment is in obedience to yours." [473]
5. It is also reported authentically, from Ibn Masʿūd, that he used to adopt the rulings of ʿUmar.
6. Al-Shaʿbī reports from Masrūq‡, "Six of the Companions of the Prophet used to issue legal rulings to the people, Ibn Masʿūd, ʿUmar b. al-Khaṭṭāb, ʿAlī, Zayd b. Thābit§, ʿUbayy b. Kaʿb,** and Abū Mūsā††. Out of these, three would abandon their own rulings for the rulings of three others: ʿAbdallāh [i.e., Ibn Masʿūd] would abandon his own rulings for those of ʿUmar, Abū Mūsa for those of ʿAlī, and Zayd for those of ʿUbayy b. Kaʿb."[4] Jundub‡‡ said, "I would not abandon a ruling delivered by Ibn Masʿūd for the ruling of anyone else."
7. The Prophet, may the peace and blessings of God be on him, [474] said, "Muʿādh has established a practice for you, so do as he does."[5] He said this about the case of a delayed prayer, of which the part which was not prayed with the *imām* is prayed after the *imām* has finished his prayer, whereas the practice before Muʿādh's action was for the people to pray what they had missed first and then commence prayer with the *imām*. The imitator [continues his argument], "God, the most

---

* Abū Bakr al-Ṣiddīq (d. 13/634), the "truthful one," the closest Companion of the Prophet and the first caliph.

† *Kalālah* is the state of a person who dies without ascendants or descendants who may inherit from him.

‡ Abū ʿĀʾishah Masrūq b. al-Ajdaʿ al-Hamadānī (d. c. 63/683), a Successor.

§ Zayd b. Thābit al-Ḍaḥḥāk al-Anṣārī (d. c, 45/666), a Companion who was instrumental in the compilation of the Qurʾan.

** ʿUbayy b. Kaʿb (d. 28/649), a renowned Companion.

†† Abū Mūsā ʿAbdallāh b. Qays al-Ashʿarī (d. c. 42/662), a famous Companion.

‡‡ Jundub (d. c. 70/689), a Companion of the Prophet.

High, has commanded obedience to Himself, to His Messenger and to those in authority, by which is meant the religious scholars, or the religious scholars and the rulers. So obedience to them lies in imitating them in their religious verdicts, for if there was no imitation, there could be no obedience specifically to them."

9. God, the most High says, *The foremost of those to embrace Islam of those who forsook (their homes) and of those who gave them aid, and (also) those who follow them in (all) good deeds, well-pleased is God with them, as are they with Him* [Q., al-Tawbah, 9:100], and imitation of them is the fulfillment of the command to follow them, so those whom God Himself is pleased with should be imitated. The well known *ḥadīth*, "My Companions are like the stars—whichever of them you follow, you will be guided,"[6] is sufficient proof of this view. [475–477].
10. ʿAbdallāh b. Masʿūd said, "Whoever performs a religious act, let it be in accordance with the practice of those who have already passed away. For the living can never be secure from error. The ones who should be followed are the Companions of Muḥammad, who have the most righteous hearts of this community. They have the most insight and knowledge, and are the least affected of them. They are a people whom God chose for companionship of His Prophet and for the establishment of His religion. Hold on to their guidance and recognize their merits, for they are upon the straight, right path." [478].
11. It is authentically reported from the Prophet, may the peace and blessings of God be on him, that he said, "Follow my Sunnah and the Sunnah of the righteous Caliphs after me,"[7] and also that he, may the peace and blessings of God be on him, said, "Judge according to the ones after me, Abū Bakr and ʿUmar, and receive guidance [479] from ʿAmmār,* and hold fast to the oath of ʿAbdallāh."
12. Further, ʿUmar wrote to Shurayḥ† that he was to judge according to what was in the Book of God, and if a solution was not be found in it, then it was to be sought from the Sunnah of the Messenger of God, may the peace and blessings of God be on him, and if a solution was not be found in this either, then he was to judge according to the decisions of the righteous ones.[8]

---

* ʿAmmār b. Yāsir al-ʿAnsī, (d. 37/657), a Companion who died in battle, at the age of ninety-three.

† Shurayḥ b. Ḥārith b. Jahm al-Kindī (d. c. 78/697), a Successor who gained fame as a judge.

13. ʿUmar forbade the sale of slave women who had borne children to their masters,[9] and the Companions followed him in this, and he enforced the triple divorce [as an irrevocable divorce],[10] and the Companions followed him in this also.* Once, when he had a wet dream, ʿAmr b. al-ʿĀṣ† told him to put on another garment,‡ but he replied that if he did so, it would become a *sunnah*.[11]
14. ʿUbayy b. Kaʿb and other [480] Companions used to say, "Act according to that which is clear to you, and entrust whatever seems ambiguous to you to the one who knows about it."[12]
15. The Companions also used to deliver legal verdicts while the Prophet, may the peace and blessings of God be on him, was still alive. These verdicts were accepted purely on the basis of imitation, because their own verdicts had no legal standing during the life of the Prophet, may the peace and blessings of God be on him.
16. And God, the most High, says, *Nor should the Believers all go forth together, if a contingent from every expedition remained behind, they could devote themselves to studies in religion, and admonish the people when they return to them, that thus they (may learn) to guard themselves (against evil)*. [Q., al-Tawbah, 9:122]. So He obligated this party of Believers to accept whatever they were warned with when they returned to them. This amounts to imitation of the scholars among the Companions.
17. It is authentically reported from Ibn al-Zubayr§ that he was asked about the inheritance share of the grandfather existing alongside the brothers of the deceased. He said, "As for the one about whom the Messenger, may the peace and blessings of God be on him, said, 'If I were to take a friend among the people of the earth, I would take him as a friend'"[13]; he [Abū Bakr] treated the grandfather like the father.** This is blatant imitation of him.

---

*An irrevocable divorce is one that is issued thrice over a period of three menstrual cycles. ʿUmar enforced a triple divorce issued in a single sitting.

†Abū ʿAbdallāh ʿAmr b. al-ʿĀṣ al-Sahmī (d. c. 42/663), a Companion who conquered and subsequently served as the governor of Egypt.

‡Having a wet dream nullifies one's state of ritual purity and requires that one's body and clothes be purified.

§ʿAbdallāh b. al-Zubayr b. ʿAwwām (d. 73/629), grandson of the caliph Abū Bakr who established a rival caliphate in Mecca, during the reign of the Umayyads.

**The Companions held various views on whether or not a grandfather acted like a father in blocking collateral relatives such as brothers and sisters from inheriting their shares of inheritance. Abū Bakr held the view that he did. Out of the four schools, only the Ḥanafīs rule according to the opinion of Abū Bakr. Ibn al-Qayyim also defends this view in the *Iʿlām*.

18. God, the Most Perfect, [also] commanded that the testimony of the witness be accepted and this also involves imitating the witness.
19. The sacred law dictates acceptance of the one who estimates quantities of foodstuff, the one who tracks footsteps, and the one who traces the genealogy of people by examining their visages. The law also dictates accepting the judgment of the one who divides items for sale, quantifies damages in [481] foodstuffs and other goods, and the two people who decide on the likeness of an animal in awarding compensation for [the sin of] hunting in a state of ritual consecration [*iḥrām*].* All this is pure imitation.
20. The community is agreed on the permissibility of accepting the statement of a translator, a messenger, a genealogist, and the regulator, even if they disagreed about whether or not reliance could be placed on just one of them. This is pure imitation of them.
21. The community also agreed on the permissibility of buying different types of meat, garments, edibles, and other things without asking questions about their permissibility or impermissibility, and this is done in imitation of the owners of these things.
22. If everyone were obligated to perform *ijtihād* and be exceptional scholars, man's well-being would come to an end, and material progress and commerce would be suspended. It is possible neither in sacred law nor in the divine will [*qadr*] (which prevents such a thing from occurring), for everyone to become a *mujtahid*.
23. People are agreed that the groom imitates [i.e., he is led by] the women who direct him to his wife, and his having intercourse with her is permissible in imitation [of their indication to him] that she is his wife.
24. Everyone also agrees that in the matter of facing the Holy Mosque for ritual prayers, a blind man imitates the one who can see; likewise everyone agrees that the prayer leaders are imitated in matters of purification and recitation of the Opening Chapter of the Qur'an and all those acts of prayer wherein it is proper for them to be followed. Likewise the wife (whether or not she is Muslim), is imitated about the acceptance of the fact that her menstruation has ceased, and restoration of permissible sexual relations with her is based on imitation of her. Similarly, it is permissible for a guardian to marry his female

---

*The killing of any creature by a person in a state of ritual consecration is prohibited. A person who hunts in this state must offer penance by sacrificing an animal that has been judged by two people to be a suitable offering.

ward once he accepts, having imitated her, that her waiting period is over, and this too is done by imitating her.

25. Similarly, everyone agrees on the permissibility of people performing imitation of the muezzin about the commencement of the times of prayer. Here too, *ijtihād* is not compulsory on the people, nor is it compulsory for them to know the signs that indicate the time of prayer.
26. A dark-skinned woman said to ʿUqbah b. al-Ḥārith*, "I breast-fed both you and your wife."† So the Prophet, may the peace and blessings of God be on him, ordered ʿUqbah to separate from his wife and ordered him to imitate the woman by accepting the information she had conveyed to him.[14]
27. The scholars were explicit about the permissibility of imitation. Ḥafṣ b. Ghiyāth‡ said, "I heard Sufyān say, 'If you see a man performing an act whose permissibility is uncertain, then do not stop him, even if you believe his act to be forbidden.'" [482] Muḥammad b. Ḥasan§ said, "It is permissible for the scholar to imitate one who is more knowledgeable than him, but it is impermissible for him to imitate one who is his equal in knowledge."
28. Al-Shāfiʿī, too, explicitly maintained the permissibility of imitation, when he issued a ruling regarding the rib bone broken [as a result of assault], that the compensation for it was a camel and added that he had said this imitating ʿUmar. He said, about the matter of selling an animal with the claim that it is free of defects, that he had said this imitating ʿUthmān**. He also said, regarding the matter of the grandfather inheriting alongside the brothers of the deceased, that he [i.e., the grandfather] shares with them [i.e., the brothers]. Then he said, "I have said this because of the opinion of Zayd, and it is from him that we get most of our knowledge of the law of inheritance." In yet another place in his later writings he said, "I said this imitating ʿAṭāʾ††."

---

*Abū Sarwaʿah ʿUqbah b. al-Ḥārith b. ʿĀmir b. Nawfal b. ʿAbd Manāf b. Quṣayy, a Companion who died during the caliphate of Ibn al-Zubayr.

†Marriage is prohibited between two individuals who, as children, were breast-fed by the same woman.

‡Abū ʿUmar Ḥafṣ b. Ghiyāth al-Nakhaʿī al-Tamīmī (d. 194/810), a judge.

§Muḥammad b. Ḥasan b. Farqad al-Shaybānī (d. 189/804),a student of Abū Ḥanīfah.

**ʿUthmān b. ʿAffān (d. 35/656), a Companion and the third caliph after the Prophet.

††ʿAṭāʾ b. Abī Rabāḥ (d. 114/732), a renowned early Successor.

29. Here, [consider also] Abū Ḥanīfah, may God have mercy on him, about his opinion on the legal issues related to [the purification of] wells*. He has no support for his view in this matter, except that which is based on imitation of what the predecessors among the Successors had said about it. Neither did Mālik depart from the practice of the people of Medina. He also said clearly in his book *The Well Trodden Path* [*al-Mawaṭṭa'*] that he "found this to be the practice" and that "this was what was done by the people of knowledge in our city." He said, on more than one occasion, "I have not seen anyone whom I follow acting thus." If we were to gather all the examples of this from his works, it would become too lengthy. Furthermore, al-Shāfi'ī said, regarding the Companions, "Their views are preferable to us over our own views." Similarly, we [the proponents of imitation] affirm that the views of al-Shāfi'ī and the scholars around him are dearer to us than our own views.
30. [Further, the imitator argues,] "God, glory be to Him, created in the minds of his servants a natural disposition to imitate their teachers and scholars. This is something common to all disciplines and professions, and it enables a great social benefit to be achieved."
31. God, glory be to Him, has also distinguished between the mental abilities of people, just as He has distinguished between their physical abilities. He, in His wisdom, justice, and mercy, does not desire to make it obligatory on all His creation to know the truth or to respond to that which opposes it in every matter, minor and major, based on evidence. If He had decreed this, each and every man would have been a scholar. Rather, God makes one person a scholar, another a seeker of knowledge, and yet another a follower of a scholar, just as the worshipper follows the *imām* in prayer, and one person follows the path of another. Has God prohibited the ignorant one from being a follower of a scholar (whom he imitates), doing whatever the scholar does? God, the Most Perfect, knows that new matters always arise before people. Has He therefore specifically obligated everyone to derive a legal ruling relating to a new matter from the divine proofs (according to all the proper procedures and conditions)? Is this even possible, let alone a requirement of the law?

---

*This refers to the issue of how to purify a well that has been contaminated with an impure substance, such as an animal carcass.

32. Consider the Companions of the Prophet, may the peace and blessings of God be on him, who conquered new lands wherein those who had recently embraced Islam would seek verdicts from them. [483]. They would issue these verdicts and would not refuse to do so by saying, "You must seek the truth in this verdict through examination of the evidence." This is not reported from a single one of them. So is imitation, then, anything other than a necessary accompaniment to moral obligation and responsibility, and a concomitant of existence? It is indeed a necessity that flows from the law and from divine decree. Those who deny it are themselves forced to accept it. This is what came earlier [*in the I'lām*] in the discussion on rulings and elsewhere.

33. [The imitator continues,] "We say to the one who seeks to prove the invalidity of imitation, 'For every narration that you use as proof for your argument, you rely on its chain of narrators, and thus you imitate them. In the absence of any clear proof of their truthfulness, you have no option but to imitate the narrator. Similarly the adjudicator has no option but to imitate a witness, and so too, the ordinary man has no option but to imitate a scholar. So what makes it permissible for you to imitate the narrator and the witness while preventing us from imitating a scholar? Just as the former hears with his ears that which he narrates, so too the latter understands with his heart that which he hears. The former then recounts what he heard and the latter what he understood, as is obligatory upon them both. Thus, whoever is not of their rank must accept what both of them convey.'"

34. [The imitator ends,] "Then it is said to those who warn against imitation, 'You only forbid it because of the fear that the one who imitates will fall into error, if the one whom he imitates has erred in his verdicts. But then you oblige him to consider and evaluate evidence in search of the truth. There can be no doubt, however, that the likelihood of his being right is greater if he imitates a scholar than if he makes *ijtihād* for himself. This is like the case of someone who wishes to buy an item of which he has no knowledge, so if he imitates someone who is knowledgeable about that item and who, in addition, is trustworthy and sincere in giving advice, then he is more likely to achieve exactly what he desires than if he relies on his own reasoning. This is something on which all right-minded people agree.'"

# A Refutation of the Arguments of the Proponents of Imitation

The interlocutor who favors reliance on proofs says, "How eccentric you are, O people of imitation. You yourselves, and the people of knowledge, all bear witness that the imitators are not in the community of the learned and are not counted among that group. Your entire approach [of using proofs to justify your stance] is invalidated by [your earlier] stance [regarding imitation]." For how does the imitator come to be concerned with proofs at all? How can the position of the imitator even be compared to that of the one who relies on proofs? All the proofs you have presented are, in effect, robes usurped from the one who is reliant on proofs, and by wearing them you bedizen yourselves in flamboyant garments before the people. By doing this, you appear to be that which you are not. You speak of knowledge that you acknowledge you do not have! This is an ill-fitting cloak you have chosen to wear—it is a station you have usurped without being entitled to it. So tell us, do you incline toward imitation because of a proof that leads you [484] to it or an evidence guiding you to it, so that it might be said that this proof led you somewhere close to the point where you would rely on it (although because of imitation you were far away from this very point?). Or, it might be that you chose this path by chance, or that, in reality, you search for something other than proof. There is no other option for you. Whichever of the two [alternatives you adopt], it would be decisive in nullifying imitation. So it is obligatory to return to the method of reliance on proofs.

When we speak to you with evidence, you respond, "We are not party to this approach." Whereas if we address you with the rulings of the scholars, relating to imitation, there is no sense in considering all these proofs [you have previously presented in support of your position].

It is strange that every group and community claims that it is on the right path, except the party of imitation, who do not make this claim. If they were to make it, they would be in error. For they have acknowledged that they hold these opinions neither because of a proof leading them to these opinions nor because of some evidence that guides them to the same. Rather, their approach is pure imitation, and the imitator does not know truth from falsehood or the sound from the unsound.

Even stranger is the fact that their scholars forbade imitation of themselves, but the imitators opposed them, revolting against the scholars themselves. They claimed to be following their schools, even when they adopted rules that went against the basic foundations on which the school was established, for the positions of the principals of the schools were built on evidence. They forbade imitation and advised their followers that, whenever new evidence became apparent to them, they were to abandon their statements and follow the evidence the imitators opposed them in all of this, and still they claim that they follow them. They are deluded. No one follows them, except the one who adopts their approach both in basic principles and secondary issues.

Stranger still than all of this is that they have declared the nullity and prohibition of imitation explicitly in their books and that it is not permissible to rule on its basis in the religion of God. Some of them also declared that, if the ruler were to appoint a judge under the condition that he render decisions according to a specific school, the condition and the appointment of the judge is void (although some of them validated the appointment and nullified only the condition).

Similarly, it is prohibited by consensus of the people for a *muftī* to render an opinion on the basis of something of whose authenticity he has no knowledge. Now the imitator lacks knowledge about the validity or nullity of a statement, as this path is out of bounds to him. Further, each imitator knows that he is an imitator of his principal, so he does not abandon the statement of his principal and leaves everything that contradicts it, even if it be from the Qur'an, the Sunnah, the statements of a Companion, or the statement of a scholar who is more knowledgeable than his principal or of one who is his equal. This is absolutely bewildering.

## Responses to the Arguments of the Imitators

### The first argument:

We also know that during, the time of the Companions, there was no individual whom everyone followed and imitated in everything, or in whose favor the views of all others [485] were rejected. We also know that such a thing did not occur in the times of the Successors and those who followed them. So let the imitators demonstrate that we are liars by producing even a single man who acted according to their pernicious methodology in the generations that were declared meritorious by the Prophet. This innovation appeared in the fourth century, [a period] that had already been condemned by the Prophet, may the peace and blessings of God be on him. The imitators, following their principals, rendered permissible the shedding of blood and the violation of property, and, then following them elsewhere, they forbade these same things, without knowing whether any of this was right or not. This path of theirs was a very dangerous one. They shall have a heavy reckoning before God, whence it will become apparent that those who spoke about Him without knowledge were upon mere nothingness.

Similarly, we say to everyone who imitates a specific person in preference to others, "What is it that makes your principal more worthy of being imitated than all others?" If he says, "Because he was the most knowledgeable person of his time" (and perhaps they would even elevate him over those who went before him because of their erroneous conviction that no one more knowledgeable followed him), it should be said to him, "How do you know that this person was the most knowledgeable of the community in his time when you are not knowledgeable (as you acknowledge yourself)?" Such a thing can be known only by one who knows the schools and their evidences, their stronger and weaker positions. How can a blind man count dirhams? This is yet another instance of speaking about God without knowledge.

## The second argument:

Abū Bakr, ʿUmar, ʿUthmān, ʿAlī, Ibn Masʿūd, ʿUbayy b. Kaʿb, Muʿādh b. Jabal, ʿĀʾishah*, Ibn ʿAbbās, and Ibn ʿUmar are all, without a doubt, more knowledgeable than your principal. So why not abandon him and imitate them? Even Saʿīd b. al-Muṣayyib, al-Shaʿbī, ʿAtāʾ, Ṭāʾūs, and their like were undoubtedly more knowledgeable and superior than your principal, so why did you abandon imitation of one who is superior in knowledge, and the one who possessed the greater share of the means of blessings, knowledge, and religion? Why did you turn away from the statements and schools of these toward those who are inferior to them?

If the imitator replies, "Because my principal and the one I imitate have more knowledge of the early scholars than I do, so my imitation of him obliged me to oppose the statement of the earlier scholar in favor of his own statement. Moreover, the wide knowledge of my principal and his excellence in religion prevent him from opposing a scholar who is his superior and is more knowledgeable than him, except on the basis

*ʿĀʾishah (d. 58/678), the daughter of Abū Bakr and the wife of the Prophet.

of an evidence he relies upon, this evidence being preferable to everyone else's statements."

Then it is to be said to him, "How have you come to know that the evidence adopted by your principal—the one you assume to be your principal—is preferable to the evidence adopted by the one who is more knowledgeable or better than him, or even his equal? These statements, taken together, are contradictory and cannot be correct. Rather, only one of them is correct. It is known that the one who is more knowledgeable is more likely to arrive at the correct view than the one who is his inferior."

If you [i.e., the imitator] reply, "I came to know of this on the basis of evidence," [486] you have turned from the path of imitation to that of seeking proofs and in doing so, have nullified imitation.

## The third argument:

This principle of yours will not benefit you at all whenever there is disagreement, as there is between the one you imitate and the one imitated by others. When the one who is imitated by others has adopted the view of Abū Bakr, ʿUmar, ʿAli, Ibn ʿAbbās, or ʿĀʾishah or others excluding your principal, why do you not follow your own advice and act on your own understanding of righteousness by saying, "Both of them are eminent scholars, and any one of them who mentions the Companions (as his proof) is worthier of being imitated by me."

## As a result it will be said to him:

4. One scholar is the equal of another, and the statement of a Companion is to be accepted [above all, as he is superior] and is more deserving of imitation. It will also be said:
5. Because you have accepted that your principal can attain knowledge that had eluded ʿUmar b. al-Khaṭṭāb, ʿAlī b. Abī Ṭālib, ʿAbdallāh b. Masʿūd, and their companions, it is certainly true and possible that his contemporaries and those who come after him can also attain the knowledge that eluded the principal. For there is far greater similarity between your principal and his contemporaries than between your principal and the Companions. The truth is more likely to remain concealed from your principal than it is from them.
6. You have allowed yourself to oppose the better and more knowledgeable person in favor of an inferior one. Why not instead allow yourself

to oppose the inferior one in favor of the one who is more knowledgeable? Did you not do the exact opposite of what was proper and necessary?

7. In imitating your principal and legalizing marriages, shedding blood, and transferring the wealth of people from its owners to others are you acting in accord with the command of God, His Messenger, the consensus of his community, or the statement of any one of his Companions? If he replies, "Yes," he is saying something whose invalidity is known to God, His Messenger and all scholars. If he says, "No," his intellectual paucity is sufficient for us, as he has made God, His Messenger, and the people of knowledge testify against himself.
8. Imitating your principal itself prohibits you from imitating him, for he forbade imitation and said that it was not [487] allowed for anyone to rule on its basis, unless he knew the rationale of his rulings. He forbade you from imitating him and other scholars, so if you are truly a complete imitator of his school, this too is from it. Why will you not imitate him in this?
9. Are you sure or unsure that your principal is more correct than everyone else from the earlier and later generations, whose opinions you have abandoned? If the imitator replies, "I have insight," he says something which he knows to be void. If he says, "I do not have insight" (and this is the truth), it will be said to him, "What will your excuse be tomorrow, when your principal will be able neither to benefit you with a single good deed in front of God nor take away a single sin from you. When you then render decisions and verdicts among people on the basis of this uncertainty about your principal being correct, is this right or wrong?"
10. "Do you assert the infallibility of your principal, or do you concede that he could make errors?" The first proposition is impossible. In fact, you concur on its nullity. Therefore, the second proposition must be correct. Then, when it is possible for him to err, how do you legalize the shedding of blood, contracts of marriage, transfers of property, and the infliction of corporal punishments on the people? How do you legalize, prohibit, and create obligations for others, based on the statement of the one you acknowledge could have been in error.
11. When you render a verdict or a decision according to the statement of your principal, do you say, "This is the religion of God, which He revealed to His Messenger and in His Book. And this is the Law He decreed for mankind, there being no religion that comes from Him

except this?" Or do you say, "The religion of God, which He legislated for mankind, is against this?" Or do you say, "I do not know?" You would have to respond with one of these statements.

You certainly cannot respond with the first statement, for it is not permissible to oppose the religion of God—which is the only true religion—while you deem it permissible to oppose the religion by allowing opposition to your principal. The least that can be said about the one who opposes the true religion is that he is a sinner. Nor do you respond with the second statement. As a result, you have no choice but to respond with the third. By God, this is strange—that marriages, the shedding of blood, transfers of rights and property, and general legal permissibility and prohibition should all proceed on the basis of something, about which the best that can be said is, "I do not know."

If you do not know, that is an affliction.
If you do know, the affliction is but greater.

12. What did the people do before the birth of the founders of the schools, whom you imitate and whose statements you equate with the texts of the Lawgiver? If only you had stopped here. Instead, you have preferred to follow them rather than the explicit texts of the Lawgiver. Were the people who were alive before the existence of your principals on [488] the right path or not? You must respond that they were. Then it is to be said to them, "What were they doing, other than following the Qur'an, the Sunnah, and the practices of the Companions and preferring these over everything that contradicted them. Were they doing anything other than referring to these for judgment over the statements and opinions of others? When this is the right path, what is left after this except misguidance? How then can you be so misguided?"

If every sect among the imitators were to say—and they already do—"Our principal remained firm on the path of earlier scholars, and followed their methodology," it will be said to them, "Did other scholars share this trait with your principal, or was he the only one following the early scholars, while others were deprived of this ability?"

One of these two propositions must apply. If they go for the second, they are even more misguided than cattle. If they go for the first, it will be asked, "How could you agree to accept all the statements of your principal and to reject all the statements of his equal or even those of the one more knowledgeable than him?"

You do not reject any opinion of one of the scholars [i.e., your own principal], and you do not accept any opinion of the other. You do this until it seems that the truth was a trust endowed to your principal and error to the one who opposed him.

Because of this, it is as if you are advocates appointed to support him in everything he says and to reject everyone who opposes him. And this is also how the other scholars' faction regards you.

## What Is Said Regarding the Scholars' Proscription of Imitation of Themselves

13. Those scholars whom you imitate actually prohibited you from doing so. Therefore, you are their foremost opponents.

Al-Shāfiʿī said, "The similitude of the one who seeks knowledge without evidence is that of the one who is collecting wood at night. He carries a load of sticks, but in them there might be a snake who could bite him while he is still unaware." Abū Ḥanīfah and Abū Yūsuf said, "It is not permissible for anyone to say what we have said, unless he knows the basis on which we have said it." Aḥmad [b. Ḥanbal] said, "Do not imitate anyone in your religion."

## Another Argument with the Proponents of Imitation

14. It is said to the imitators, "Do you believe that tomorrow you shall be standing before God, and He shall ask you [not only] about the judgments you issued, as a result of which the blood of His people was shed, their private parts declared lawful to each other, corporal punishment inflicted on them, and their wealth pronounced permissible or forbidden, [but] also [about] the verdicts you issued [489] in His religion, declaring things lawful, permissible, and obligatory?"

As for the ones who say, "Yes, we believe in that," it is to be said to them, "If you are asked, 'How could you say this? How would you respond?'" They would say, "Our response will be that we rendered things permissible and forbidden and issued judgments according to what was narrated in the book *al-ʾAṣl* by Muḥammad b. Ḥasan from the opinions and selected rulings of Abū Ḥanīfah and Abū Yūsuf, according to *al-Mudawwanah* from the narration by Saḥnūn of Ibn al-Qāsim's opinions and selected rulings, according to what was in *al-Umm* from the narration of the opinions and selected rulings of Rabīʿ and according to the responses of others that contain the same." Had you but stopped there. If only you had gone so far and no further. If only your strength had failed you here. Rather, your response is far beneath even this. So, if you are asked by God, "Did you act so out of obedience to Me or My Messenger?," at that time, what will your response be? If it is possible for you to say then, "We did what You and Your Messenger commanded," you will have succeeded and concluded the matter, but if you are not able to say this, then you must say, "Neither You nor Your Messenger nor our scholars commanded us to do this." You must offer one of these two responses. It does seem that the second answer is the one you will profess.

15. It is also to be said, when Jesus the son of Mary descends as a fair Imām, a just ruler, and a judge, according to whose school will he decide? According to whose opinions will he rule? It is known that he will not rule or judge with anything other than the law of our Prophet, which God legislated for His creation. So it is preferable to rule with this law, by which he too will rule. It is obligatory on you to follow and to rule by the one who is closer to Jesus the son of Mary than all others [i.e., the Prophet Muḥammad]. It is not at all permissible for anyone to follow or to issue verdicts according to any other authority. If you say, "We both agree on this issue," it is to be said, "Yes, but our responses before God will differ."

For we shall say, "Our Lord! You know that we did not appoint any individual scholar an arbiter over Your Word or the word of Your Messenger. Nor did we refer to such a person to resolve our disagreements. Nor did we hold the opinion of a scholar to be the arbiter, nor did we accord precedence to his opinions over Your Words, those of Your Messenger and his Companions. We deemed all of creation too unworthy for its words and views to be awarded precedence over Your revelation. Rather, we ruled according to what we found in Your Book, what reached us from the Sunnah of Your Messenger, and what was ruled by his Companions. If we ever turned away from this, it was an unintentional error. Nor did we take an ally [Ar. *walījah*], other than You, Your Messenger, or the Believers. Never did we split up our religion and become divided into sects.

"We did not break up our religion into pieces nor take our scholars as our absolute authorities and intermediaries between us and Your Messenger in what they related to us about him. Nor did we follow and imitate them in all those [matters that they narrated], for You and Your Messenger [490] commanded us to hear from the scholars and to accept what they convey from both of you, so we heard and accepted this out of obedience to Your command and in fulfillment of it. We did not take the scholars as lords on the basis of whom we argued and by whose rulings we judged. Nor did we call and invite people to this. Rather, we presented their opinions before Your Book and the Sunnah of Your Messenger and accepted whatever was in agreement with them, rejecting and turning away from whatever was not. We did this even if they were more knowledgeable than us about You and Your Messenger, for the one whose opinion matches the view of Your Messenger in a particular issue is the one who has the most knowledge of him in it."

This is our response. And we ask you by the right of God over you, "Are you also in a similar state, so that it would be possible for you to give this response in front of the One whose Word does not change and before whom falsehood does not stand?"

16. O people of imitation, every sect among you lowers the rank of all the Companions, the Successors, and all the scholars of the community, from the first to the last, to a level where no opinions are to be considered, except for the opinions of the one you imitate. Nor are their verdicts [i.e., of these other scholars] to be looked into, engaged with or relied upon. Nor is there any point in examining them, except to circumvent them and to sharpen one's mind by exerting oneself in rejecting the views of other scholars, if their opinions contradict the opinions of one's own principals. This is deemed permissible by them in order to refute their rivals. If the opinion of their own principal should go against a clear text of God and His Messenger, they regard it as obligatory to sport with the divine texts and use every artifice to take them out of their proper meaning, circumventing them in every possible way until the opinion of their principal is proved correct. By God, what would have become of His religion, His Book and His

Messenger's Sunnah when faced with an innovation that, if successful, would almost ruin the throne of faith and destroy its pillar? For they would have succeeded if God had not guaranteed that there would always be someone in this religion who would speak with its signs and protect the religion from deviance through them. As for the person who does not turn toward the opinion of a single one of the Companions nor toward their verdicts but only turns toward the verdicts of his principal, whom he has taken as an ally other than God and His Messenger, nobody has cast worse disrepute on the Companions, the Successors, and on all the Muslim scholars than him. Nobody is worse in belittling their rights and a greater denier of what is their due. Nobody demeans them more than this person.

17. It is also to be said, "O imitators, the most puzzling part of your affair is that you have acknowledged and conceded that you yourselves are incapable of recognizing the truth based on its evidence from the Word of God and the word of His Messenger, despite its ease, its proximity as a source, its being comprised of the clearest, most eloquent expression, and the impossibility of contradiction and conflict [491] therein." Furthermore, it is authentically reported from the infallible transmitter.

God has established clear evidence for truth and has made lucid for mankind what they should be conscious of. However, you claim an incapacity to recognize that for which He has established evidence and for the eloquent expression of which He has taken responsibility. Then you allege that you know, based on evidence, that your principal is more worthy of being imitated than others, the most knowledgeable one in the community and the most highly ranked in his own age.

The extremists from all your sects obligate imitation of their own principal and prohibit imitation of everyone else, as is stated in your books on jurisprudence.

It is truly astounding for the person who is unable to see the right path for which God has established evidence and who cannot be guided to it, to be guided somehow to the knowledge that his principal is more correct and more likely to arrive at the truth than anyone else. This is something for which God never established any evidence.

18. It is to be said, "It is even more astounding that when you imitators find a verse in the Book of God that agrees with your principal, you

apparently act according to it, even while your reliance is on what he said, not on the verse itself. And if you find a verse relied on by your opponent that contradicts the opinion of your principal, you do not act according to it. You seek other ways to interpret it, in ways contrary to its clear meaning, merely because it does not correspond to his view. This is also how you act when it comes to the Sunnah. If you find an authentic *ḥadīth* that agrees with the opinion of your principal, you act according to it, saying, 'Our stance is absolutely supported by the words of the Prophet that we choose to rely on.' And if you find one hundred *aḥādīth* or more which go against his view, you do not act according to a single one of them. All this time you do not even have a single *ḥadīth* that supports you, allowing you to say: 'We follow the Prophet in such and such a way.' If you find a *mursal ḥadīth*[*] that agrees with the opinion of your principal, you act according to it, presenting it as a proof. However, if you find one hundred *mursal āḥādīth* which go against his view, you leave them all in their entirety. And you [then] say, 'We do not act according to the *mursal* traditions.'"

## The Position of the Imitators Regarding *Ḥadīth* and Examples Thereof

19. It is to be said, that, even stranger than all of this is that, when you do accept a *ḥādīth* (whether it be *mursal* or *musnad*),[†] because of its agreement with the opinion of your principal, and you then find a ruling in it which goes against another opinion of his, you do not act according to it, even though the same *ḥadīth* that contains both rulings. It is as if the *ḥadīth* is a proof to the extent that it agrees with the view of the person you imitate and is devoid of proof to the extent that it goes against his view.

We shall mention examples of this, for it is the most bizarre part of their affair. [492]

---

[*] A *mursal ḥadīth* is one that is reported by a Successor without naming the Companion from whom he narrates.

[†] A *musnad ḥadīth* is one whose chain of transmission is connected to the Prophet.

# A Section on the Straying and Wavering of the Imitator in Adopting Some of the Sunnah and Abandoning Other Parts of It

A group of them argued for the inability of water that has already been used in ritual purification to remove a state of impurity, based on the report that the Prophet forbade a man from performing ablution (*wuḍū'*) with the excess water left over by a woman after performing ablution; and he also forbade a woman from performing ablution with the excess water left over by a man.[15] They said, "That which is 'left over' is the water that drips from their limbs after ablution." Then they went against the *ḥadīth*, allowing each to perform ablution with the excess pure water left by the other, even though the prohibition of the excess water is the main import of the *ḥadīth*. It forbids a man from performing ablution with the excess water left by the woman if she performed ablution in private, but her being in private has no significance for these imitators. Nor is there any significance attached to the fact that the water is left over by a woman. So they went against the *ḥadīth* on which they themselves relied, interpreting it out of context. For the excess water of ablution is certainly that which is left over [in the vessel containing the water], not that with which ablutions are actually performed. For this latter is not called excess. Therefore, they used the *ḥadīth* to rely on something to which it does not pertain. And it is deemed invalid by them to argue on its basis for that which it indicates. [493]

Similar is their view on water becoming impure by contact with an impurity, even if the water does not change as a result, relying on the fact that the Prophet, may the peace and blessings of God be on him, prohibited that standing water be urinated in.[16] But then they said, "If he does urinate in standing water, it does not become impure, unless it is less than [that held by] two large containers [*qullatayn*]."

They also relied, in proving its impurity, on the Prophet's words, "When one of you rises from his sleep, let him not immerse his hands in the water container until he washes them thrice."[17] But then they said, "If he does immerse his hands before this, it does not render the water impure, nor is it obligatory on him to wash them, and if he wishes to immerse them before they are washed, he is free to do that."

In this issue, they also relied on the fact that the Prophet commanded the earth on which someone had urinated to be dug up and its soil to be taken out. But then they said, "It is not necessary to dig it up.[18] Rather, if it is left until it becomes dry by the sun and the wind, it will be purified." [494]

They argued that water that had already been used for ablution could not be re-used, based on the words of the Prophet, may the peace and blessings of God be on him, to Banī ʿAbd al-Muṭṭalib*: "God dislikes that you use that with which people have purified their hands [Ar. *zakāt*].† What the Prophet meant was the *zakāt* [i.e., the wealth tax]. But they then said, "*Zakāt* is not forbidden for the Banī ʿAbd al-Muṭṭalib."

They also argued that dead floating fish, as opposed to other dead sea animals, do not pollute the water, based on the words of the Prophet about the sea, "Its water is pure, and its dead animals are lawful for consumption."[19] But then they [495] went against this report and said, "Dead fish in the sea are not lawful. Nor, as a matter of principle, is it permissible to eat anything other than fish."

The *ahl al-rāʾy* relied on the words of the Prophet: "If a dog licks a bowl belonging to one of you, let him wash it seven times,"[20] to prove the impurity of a dog and its saliva. But then they said, "It is not necessary to wash it seven times. Rather, it can be washed once." And some of them said, "Thrice."

They argued for the distinction between a major impurity, which was the size of a dirham coin, and that which was not, based on a *ḥadīth* (which is not authentic) from the chain of Ghuṭayf, from Zuhrī, from Abī Salamah,‡ from Abū Hurayrah in *marfūʿ* form, "Repeat the prayers, because of the impurity that is the size of a dirham."[21] But then they said, "The prayer is not to be repeated on account of an impurity of this size." [496]

They relied on the *ḥadīth* of ʿAlī b. Abū Ṭālib, about *zakāt* on surplus camels numbering more than 120, to say that the *zakāt* here returns to the original amount, that is, one goat is offered for every five camels.[22] But then they disagree with twelve other points in this narration. They relied also on the *ḥadīth* of ʿAmr b. Ḥazm: "There is no *zakāt* on whatever exceeds 200 dirhams, until it reaches 40, and then there is a dirham to be paid as *zakāt*."[23] But they went against the explicit parts of the same *ḥadīth* [497] in no less than 15 areas.

---

* Banī ʿAbd al-Muṭṭalib refers to the clan of the Prophet, descendants of his grandfather, ʿAbd al-Muṭṭalib.

† The Arabic word *zakāt* literally means purification but is also used to refer to the specific legal tax imposed by Islamic law on accumulated wealth.

‡ Abī Salamah b. ʿAbd al-Raḥmān al-Qurashī (d. 94/713), a renowned Medinese traditionist.

They argued that the option of rescission* is not for a period of more than three days, based on the *ḥadīth* of the *Muṣarrāt*.[24] This is absurd, for they are the staunchest rejecters of this *ḥadīth*.† They do not rule according to it, so, if it is correct, then it is obligatory to follow it in its entirety. And if it is not correct, it is not permissible to rely on it for the purpose only of ascertaining the three-day period. Besides, there is no contradiction between this *ḥadīth* and the option of rescission. So they reject what the *ḥadīth* is actually about and what it indicates, while it offers no proof of the argument for which they relied on it.

They also relied, in this matter, on the *khabar*‡ of Ḥabbān b. Munqidh,§ who was being cheated in contracts of sale. So the Prophet gave him a period of three days to rescind the sale.[25] They go against the entire report. They do not affirm the right [498] of rescission for being cheated, even if what the buyer has bought is worth ten times less than what he has spent. Likewise, they do not affirm the right of rescission, whether or not the buyer says beforehand, "Do not deceive me," and whether he was deceived about a large amount of money or a small one—none of this creates a right of rescission [according to them].

They argued for the obligation of atonement for the one who breaks his fast during the day of Ramaḍān,** as some of the words of the *ḥadīth* say that a man broke his fast, so the Prophet commanded him to atone for it.[26] But then they go against these very words and say, "If he inhales flour or incense he has thereby broken his fast but there is no atonement due on him."

They argued for the necessity of making up the fast later for the one who intentionally vomits, based on the *ḥadīth* of Abū Hurayrah,[27] but then

---

* An option of rescission allows a person to nullify a contract of sale within a certain period, normally three days, for those who accept the doctrine in the first place, which the Ḥanafīs do not.

† The *ḥadīth* of *muṣarrāt* states that a person who unknowingly buys an animal which has not been milked for several days (thus giving a false impression about the amount of milk it would normally yield) may return that animal with a measure of dates to compensate for the milk consumed by the buyer. The *ḥadīth* is not acted upon by the Ḥanafīs, who argue that, because there is no equivalence between milk and dates, the *ḥadīth* goes against the rational principles that underlie the law of sales.

‡ A *khabar* is normally a report about a Companion that does not purport to be a *ḥadīth*.

§ Ḥabbān b. Munqidh b. ʿAmr al-Anṣārī al-Māzinī, a Companion who died during the caliphate of ʿUthmān.

** Ramaḍān, the Muslim month of fasting.

they go against this very *ḥadīth* and say, "If he vomits less than a mouthful, there is no obligation on him to make up the fast."

They argued for the existence of a limit regarding the travel that allows one to avail oneself of the dispensation of not fasting and of combining the ritual prayers based on the Prophet's words, "It is not permissible for a [Muslim] woman who believes in God and the Last Day to travel a distance of three days, except with her husband or her non-marriageable kin."[28] They say this [499] despite the fact that there is no evidence here for what they claim. Nevertheless, they still go against it saying, "It is permissible for a slave woman, the *mukātibah* slave,* and the *umm al-walad*† to travel without a husband and non-marriageable kin."

They argued for the prohibition of the person in a state of ritual consecration [*iḥrām*] covering his face, based on the *ḥadīth* of Ibn ʿAbbās about the one whose she-camel threw him off while he was in a state of ritual consecration, and he died. So the Prophet said, "Do not cover his head or his face, for he will be raised on the Day of Judgment reciting the *talbiyah*.‡ This is strange, for they are the ones who say, "If a person in a state of ritual consecration dies, it is permissible to cover his head and his face, and his state of ritual consecration is nullified."

They argued for the obligation of compensation for the one who kills a hyena in a state of ritual consecration, based on the *ḥadīth* of Jābir,§ in which he ruled that the hyena be eaten and that the killer pay a sum of money. He attributed this to the Messenger of God. Then they go against the *ḥadīth* itself and say, "It is not permissible to eat it."

They argued, regarding the one who was liable to pay a one-year-old female camel [in *zakāt*] and who offers two-thirds of a two-year-old female to equal the one year-old female (or a donkey that is equal in value to it), that this will be sufficient for him, based on the authentic *ḥadīth* of Anas**, which contains the words: "Whoever is liable to pay a one-year-old female

---

*The *mukātibah* is a slave woman who is contracted to be freed upon payment of an agreed sum to her owner.

†A slave woman who has borne children to her master and who thus may not be bought or sold.

‡The words "Here I am, at your service Lord, here I am," which are uttered by the pilgrim who enters *iḥrām*.

§Abū ʿAbdallāh Jābir b. ʿAbdallāh b. ʿAmr al-Salami al-Anṣārī (d. 78/697), a famous Companion of the Prophet.

**Abū Ḥamzah Anas b. Mālik (d. 93/712), a Companion of the Prophet.

and does not have one but does have a two-year-old female, then this will be taken from him, and the collector will return two goats or twenty dirhams to him."[29] This is strange, as they do not rule according to what the *ḥadīth* indicates about this form of paying *zakāt*. And they argue on the basis of it for something that it does not indicate in any way whatsoever, and for what was not even intended by it.

They argued that the corporal punishments [*ḥudūd*, sing. *ḥadd*] mentioned in the Qur'an and the Sunnah are suspended in the abode of war, even if the Muslim acts in a way that would require their implementation, based on the *ḥadīth*, "Do not amputate hands during war." In another narration the words are, "during travel."[30] But they do not rule according to [500] this *ḥadīth*, for, according to them, neither travel nor battle has anything to do with suspension of *ḥudūd* punishments.

They argued for the obligation of slaughtering an animal after the major pilgrimage, based on the *ḥadīth* that the Prophet commanded that animals be slaughtered and that one's neighbors and the needy be fed from them. They say, "It is not obligatory to feed the neighbor, nor the needy."

They argued for the permissibility of the slaughter done by the one who has usurped or stolen an animal, based on the report in which the Messenger was invited to a meal, along with a group of his Companions. When he took a morsel he said, "I believe this goat was taken unlawfully." So the woman who had invited him said, "I took it from another woman without the knowledge of her husband." So the Prophet commanded that the non-Muslim prisoners be fed with it.[31] They go against this *ḥadīth* and say, "The slaughter carried out by a usurper is lawful, and that meat is not prohibited for the Muslims." [501]

They argued for the termination of compensation for wounding livestock, based on another *ḥadīth*: "The wounds caused by an animal are not to be considered when determining compensation."[32] Then they oppose it, in what it indicates and what is meant by it, saying, "Whoever rides an animal, leads it, or directs it, he is liable to the one whom the animal bites with its mouth, and there is no compensation on him for what the animal damages with his feet."

They argue for delaying financial compensation for injury until the victim recovers from the same, based on the well-known *ḥadīth* that a man struck another in his knee with a horn and thereby demanded compensation. The Messenger of God told him to wait until he recovered, but he refused,[33] so he arranged for the payment to be made to him before his recovery. They went against what the *ḥadīth* relates about blood money [*qiṣās*] for stabbing and maintained that there is no *qiṣās* in that.

They argue for the suspension of *ḥadd* on the one who commits adultery with the slave woman of his son or with the slave who is his child's mother, based on the words of the Prophet: "You and what you own belong to your father." But they go against what is indicated in this by saying, "The father does not have any right over what his son owns. And it is not permissible for him to take from his son's wealth so much as a twig from an arak tree [a species of palm], or even less than that." They even obligate imprisoning the father for a debt to his son and for return of the security for a loan which the father handed over to him. [502]

They argue that the *imām* says, "God is Great," when the one pronouncing the second call to prayer [*iqāmah*]* says, "The prayer has been established," based on the *ḥadīth* of Bilāl†, in which he said to the Messenger of God, "Do not precede me in saying 'Amen.'"[34] And based also on an identical statement of Abū Hurayrah to Marwān‡, "Do not precede me in saying Amen." Then they go openly against this report and say, "Neither the *imām* nor the one praying behind him is to say 'Amen.'"

They argue for the obligation of wiping one-fourth of the head in ablution, based on the *ḥadīth* of Mughīrah b. Shuʿbah§ that the Messenger of God wiped his forelock and turban.[35] Then they go against that which it indicates and say, "Wiping on the turban is not permissible [503] and no purification is achieved by wiping over it." In their view, the obligation is fulfilled only by wiping the forelock, and wiping the turban is neither obligatory nor preferable.

They argue for the preferability of performing the actions of prayer alongside the *imām* [instead of immediately after him], based on the Prophet's words: "The *imām* is there to be followed."[36] They say, "Following him requires that one act exactly as the *imām* acts." Then they go against what this *ḥadīth* conveys, for it also contains the following: "When

---

*The first call to prayer, the *adhān*, signals the beginning of the time for each of the five daily prayers. The second call, the *iqāmah*, signals the start of the congregational prayer, which is to be performed during that time.

† Bilāl b. Rabāḥ (d. 20/641), a Companion of the Prophet, who served as muezzin during the latter's lifetime.

‡ Marwā b. al-Ḥakam (d. 65/685), the fourth Umayyad caliph.

§ Abū ʿAbdallāh Mughīrah b. Shuʿbah al-Thaqafī (d. 50/670), a Companion of the Prophet.

the *imām* proclaims *takbīr**, proclaim *takbīr*, when he bows, bow, and when he says, 'God hears those who praise Him,' say, 'Our Lord, and Yours is all praise.' If he prays sitting down, then all of you are also to pray sitting down."

They argue that the recitation of the Opening Chapter of the Qur'an is not specified as an obligatory part of the prayer, based on the *ḥadīth* regarding the one who made errors in his prayer, when the Prophet said to him, "Recite whatever is easy from that which you have memorized."[37] Then they go against what it explicitly conveys in its words, "Then bow until you are at rest in your bowing, rise until you are at rest standing, and then prostrate yourself until you are at rest prostrating." [They also go against] his words, "Go back and pray, for you have not prayed," for they said, "Whoever neglects to be at rest has still prayed validly, and the order commanding this [the repetition of prayer] was not meant to convey a necessary obligation," despite the fact that both the command to do this and that regarding recitation of the Opening Chapter were conveyed in the same grammatical form [i.e., as an imperative] in the same *ḥadīth*.

They argue for the suspension of the practice of sitting for a rest when rising from prostration during the ritual prayer, based on the *ḥadīth* of Abī Ḥamīd[38] as he did not mention [504] doing so in it.† But they opposed the practice of raising the hands at the time of bowing and rising, which was also mentioned in it.

They argue for the suspension of the obligation of delivering prayers on the Prophet and the salutation [*salām*] in the ritual prayer, based on the *ḥadīth* of Ibn Mas'ūd: "If you say this much, your prayer is complete." Then they opposed it over this very thing [505] and said, "His prayer is complete whether he said this or not."

They argue for the permissibility of speaking while the *imām* gives the sermon at the pulpit on Friday, based on the words of the Prophet to the one who entered the mosque while the Prophet was delivering his sermon: "Did you pray before you sat down?" The man replied in the negative, so the Prophet said, "Arise and offer two units of prayer [*rak'āt*]."[39] They oppose it, regarding whatever else it conveys by saying, "Whoever enters while the *imām* is delivering his sermon is to sit down and is not to pray."

---

* *Takbīr*, the recitation of "God is the greatest," a formula repeated upon each bodily movement during the ritual prayer.

† 'Abd al-Raḥmān b. Sa'd (or b. 'Amr) b. al-Mundhir Abū Ḥamīd al-Sā'idī, a Companion of the Prophet, who died toward the end of the caliphate of Mu'āwiyah I.

They argue for the reprehensibility of raising the hands before and after bowing in prayer, based on the words of the Prophet: "What is wrong with them that they raise their hands as if they were the tails of stubborn horses?"[40] Then they oppose it, regarding everything else it conveys, for it also contains the words, "It is sufficient for one of you [at the end of the ritual prayer] to offer the salutation of peace to his brother to his right and then to his left saying both times, 'May peace be with you and the blessings of God.'"[41] They said that this is not needed, and something other than this which ends the prayer will be sufficient for him.

They argue for moving the *imām* back in the congregation if he breaks wind, based on the authentic report that the Messenger of God went out while Abū Bakr was leading the people in prayer, so he moved back and the Prophet stepped forward, leading the people in prayer.[42] [506] Then they go against it, regarding whatever else it indicates. They say, "The prayer of him who does this is invalidated." Thus, they invalidate the prayer of one who acts like the Prophet, Abū Bakr and those Companions who were present. So they argue, on the basis of the *ḥadīth,* for something which it does not indicate, while invalidating the act mandated by it.

They argue that if the *imām* prays the ritual prayer sitting down because of an illness, the follower praying behind him is to pray standing up, based on the authentic report from the Prophet, that he went out and found Abū Bakr leading the people in prayer while standing. So the Prophet went ahead of him and sat down and led the people in prayer, and Abū Bakr stepped back.[43] Then they go against the *ḥadīth,* regarding the very thing it conveys and say, "If the *imām* steps back without having broken wind and another person precedes him, the prayer of both *imāms* and the whole congregation is nullified."

They argue for the nullity of the fast of the one who eats, thinking it is nighttime when it is in fact daytime, based on the words of the Prophet: "Bilāl delivers the call to prayer at night, so continue to eat and drink until Ibn Umm Maktūm* does so."[44] Then they go against the *ḥadīth,* regarding everything else it indicates and say, "It is not permissible to give the call to the pre-dawn prayer during the night in Ramaḍān or at any other time." [507] They go against it from another perspective, too, for the same *ḥadīth* says, "Ibn Umm Maktūm was a blind man who would not give the call to

---

* 'Ātikah bt. 'Abdallāh b. Umm Maktūm, although various names are given for this Companion, including 'Abdallāh b. Zā'idah and 'Amr b. Qays, the authorities agree that he was the blind muezzin.

prayer until it was said to him repeatedly: 'It is morning.'"[45] According to them, the fast of the one who eats at this time is invalidated.

They argue for the impermissibility of facing the *qiblah*[*] or turning one's back toward it when answering the call of nature, based on the words of the Prophet: "Do not face the *qiblah* while you are answering the call of nature nor when urinating, and do not turn your backs to it."[46] They went against the same *ḥadīth* and allowed one to face it and to turn one's back to it when urinating.

They argue that it is not a condition of *iʿtikāf*[†] that one be fasting, based on the authentic *ḥadīth* from ʿUmar that he vowed, in the period of ignorance, that he would perform *iʿtikāf* in the Sacred Mosque, so the Messenger of God, may the peace and blessings of God be on him, commanded him to fulfill his vow.[47] They do not rule according to the *ḥadīth*, for in their view, a vow made by a disbeliever does not have to be fulfilled after he accepts Islam.

They argue for the doctrine of *radd*,[‡] based on the *ḥadīth*, "The woman acquires three types of inheritance. From the one she set free [508], from the one who is her foundling, and from her son, who was the subject of a vow of imprecation [*liʿān*]."[48] However, they do not rule according to the *ḥadīth* when it comes to her acquisition of the wealth of her foundling, even though ʿUmar b. Khaṭṭāb ruled according to the *ḥadīth*, as did Isḥāq b. Rāhawayh[§], and this is the correct position.

They argue that the distant kindred inherit from the wealth of the deceased, based on the report in which the Prophet said, "Seek an heir or a relative for him from among the distant kindred." But, when the Companions were unable to find any, he said, "Give it to the oldest from the tribe of Khuzāʿah."[49] They do not rule according to this [509], in its provision that the wealth of the one who does not have an heir is given to the oldest member of his tribe.

They argue for the prohibition of the killer inheriting from the wealth of the one he kills, based on the report of ʿAmr b. Shuʿayb, from his father,

---

[*] The direction of Mecca, which Muslims face when offering ritual prayer.

[†] *Iʿtikāf* is the practice of secluding oneself in the mosque for a period of time, as an act of devotion.

[‡] The doctrine of *radd* calls for returning the inheritance of the deceased to his Qurʾanic heirs, if there is a residual amount left but no residuary left to inherit it.

[§] Abū Yaʿqūb Isḥāq b. Rāhawayh (d. 238/853), a renowned traditionist scholar and associate of Aḥmad b. Ḥanbal.

from his grandfather:* "The killer does not inherit. Nor is a believer killed [in retaliation for killing] for a disbeliever."[50] So they only rule in accordance with the first part of the *ḥadīth* and not the second [510], as they hold that a believer is killed for killing a disbeliever.

They argue for the permissibility of performing purification with clean earth [*tayammum*] for the funeral prayer performed in a residential area (if it is feared that one might miss the prayer), even if water is actually available, based on the *ḥadīth* of Abī Jahm b. al-Ḥārith, regarding the *tayammum* of the Prophet, may the peace and blessings of God be on him, for returning the greeting of peace.[51] Then they go against it, about what it implies in two ways:

First, [saying] that the Prophet performed *tayammum* with his face and hands and not his arms.

Second, they do not dislike it for one who has broken wind to return the greeting, nor do they approve of *tayammum* for that.

They argue for the permissibility of reducing the required quantity of stones in cleansing one's self after defecation [*istinjā*] to just two stones, based on the *ḥadīth* of Ibn Masʿūd, that the Messenger of God, may the peace and blessings of God be on him, went to answer the call of nature and said to him, "Fetch me some stones." So he brought him two stones and some dried dung. The Prophet took the stones and cast away the dried dung saying, "This is unclean."[52] Then they disagree with that which it is explicit about, for they allowed the one who is cleaning himself with dry material [*istijmār*] to do so with dried dung. They also relied on it to justify that for which there is no proof therein, that is, regarding two stones being sufficient to achieve purification.†

They argue that touching a woman does not invalidate the ablution [*wuḍūʾ*] based on the prayer of the Prophet, may the peace and blessings of God be on him, while he was carrying ʿAmāmah bt. Abī al-ʿĀṣ b. al-Rabīʿ‡. When he stood, he carried her on his back, and when he bowed or prostrated, he would put her down. Then they said, "The

---

*Abū Ibrāhīm ʿAmr b. Shuʿayb b. Muḥammad b. ʿAbdallāh b. ʿAmr b. al-ʿĀṣ, a renowned traditionist from the generation after the Successors.

† *Istinjā* and *istijmār* are two methods of cleansing one's self after answering the call of nature. The first is to wash oneself with water, and the second involves cleaning oneself with stones or other dry material.

‡ Umm Yaḥyā ʿAmāmah bt. Abī al-ʿĀṣ b. al-Rabīʿ b. ʿAbd al-ʿUzzā, the granddaughter of the Prophet.

prayer of whoever prays like this is invalid, as is that of the one who prays behind him."

Some people of knowledge said, "It is bizarre that they invalidate this prayer while they regard the prayer [described below] as valid:" A prayer in which a person recites only the verse, *Dark-green in colour (from plentiful watering)* [Ar. *mudhāmmatān*; Q., al-Raḥmān, 55:64] in Persian. Then he bows only for as long as a single breath, rises only to the extent of the sharp edge of a sword or does not even rise that far. Rather, he falls, as he is, into prostration and does not place his hands or his feet on the ground. And if it is not possible for him to place his knees or his forehead on the ground, it would suffice if he were to place the tip of his nose on the ground for as long as a single breath. Then he sits for as long as the prescribed period of sitting after the prostrations, and then he performs an act that nullifies prayer, such as breaking wind silently or loudly, or laughing, or any such thing.*

They argue for the prohibition of having intercourse with a female prisoner or the slave before they are established to be without child, based on the words of the Prophet, may the peace and blessings of God be on him: [511] "Do not have intercourse with a pregnant woman until she casts forth her child nor with one who has not been pregnant for a long period, until she is established to be free of child by the arrival of her period." Then they go against its manifest part, saying, "If he set her free and married her, it is permissible for the husband to have intercourse with her on the wedding night."

They argue about affirmation of the right of guardianship for the maternal aunt, based on the report of the daughter of Ḥamzah and on the fact that the Messenger decided that her maternal aunt would have custody of her.[53] Then they disagreed with it and said, "If the maternal aunt marries with a person who is not in the prohibited degrees of kinship with the ward, such as her cousin, her right of custody is suspended."

They argue for the prohibition of separating brothers who are both slaves, based on the *ḥadīth* of ʿAlī, which prohibits this.[54] [512] Then they go against it and say, "The slave who is sold is not returned even if this occurs," while the *ḥadīth* contains an order that the slave who is sold be returned.

*The whole prayer described here is a veiled criticism of those Ḥanafīs who allow all these actions, including the recitation of the Qur'an in Persian, during prayer.

They argue for the application of retribution [*qiṣāṣ*] between a Muslim and a person belonging to a religious minority which is protected by the Islamic state [*dhimmī*], based on the report that the Prophet, may the peace and blessings of God be on him, gave a Jew compensation after having taken it from the Muslim who slapped him.[55] Then they went against the same and said, "There is no retaliation for a slap or for beating, neither between two Muslims nor between a Muslim and a disbeliever." [513]

They argue that there is no *qiṣāṣ* between a slave and his master, based on the words of the Prophet, "Whoever slaps his slave, then the slave is free."[56] Then they go against it and say, "He is not freed by this." They also argue based on the *ḥadīth* that contains the words, "The slave is freed from the one who tortures him." They say, "He is not obliged to pay compensation." Then they add, "He is not freed from him."

They argue, based on the *ḥadīth* of ʿAmr b. Shuʿayb, from his father, from his grandfather: "For the eye, [the compensation to be paid is] half of the blood money [for homicide]."[57] Then they oppose it in various ways, among them in the statement of the Prophet, "and for the eye that remains firm in its place, [the compensation is] a third of the blood money."[58] They also oppose his statement, "For the blackened tooth, [the compensation is] a third of the blood money."

They argue for the permissibility of favoring some children over others [in the distribution of gifts], based on the *ḥadīth* of Nuʿmān b. Bashīr,* in which the Prophet said, "Let someone else be a witness over it."[59] Then they went against it explicitly. For the *ḥadīth* itself contains the words, "This is not right." And, in another wording, "I do not bear witness over injustice." They said, "Rather, [514] this is meritorious and not unjust. Everyone ought to be a witness over it."

They argue for the position that impurities can be removed without the use of running water, based on the *ḥadīth*, "If one of you tramples over filth with his shoes then the earth is a purifier for them."[60] Then they oppose it and say, "If dung or fecal matter clings [515] to his sandals, the earth does not purify them."

They argue for the permissibility of wiping over a bandage, based on the *ḥadīth* of the one who was wounded. Then they go against it explicitly and say, "It is not permissible to combine purification with water with purification with earth. Rather, such a person is to wash the sound parts

---

*Nuʿmān b. Bashīr b. Saʿd al-Khazrajī (d. 64/684), a Companion of the Prophet.

of the body, if they are more than the wounded ones, and he is not to perform *tayammum*. Rather, he only performs *tayammum* if the wounded part is greater, and, in this case, he is not to wash that part of the body that is sound."

They argue for the permissibility of appointing a succession of leaders and rulers or setting out an order by which two people will succeed the leader, one after the other, based on the words of the Prophet, may the peace and blessings of God be on him, "Your leader is Zayd,* and if Zayd is killed, then Jaʿfar,† and if he is killed, then ʿAbdallāh b. Rawāḥah.‡"[61] Then they went against the *ḥadīth* and said, "It is not permissible to make leadership dependent on a condition." But we bear witness with God that this appointment was the best one on the face of the earth and that it was more correct than all the ones made by the imitators, from start to finish.

They argue for holding the one who damages property liable for what he damaged, and they also hold that he is entitled to its possession, based on the *ḥadīth* about the borrowed bowl that one of the Wives of the Prophet broke. So the Prophet returned another bowl to the one who owned it. Then they opposed it explicitly and said, "He is to be held liable to pay dirhams and dinars and is not to compensate with another item like it."

They also argue for this based on the report that contains an account of the goat that was slaughtered without the consent of its owner. The Prophet, may the peace and blessings of God be on him, did not return it to its owner. Then they went against it explicitly. For the Prophet, may the peace and blessings of God be on him, did not declare the one who killed that animal as its owner. Rather, he commanded that it be fed to the disbelieving prisoners.

They argue for suspending the amputation of the hand for theft of fruit and that item which is about to rot, based on the report, "There is to be no amputation of hands for dates nor for the surplus amount."[62] Then they opposed the *ḥadīth* in several ways:

First [517], it also contains the words, "If he takes it to a storehouse, then the punishment of amputation does apply to it, if it is stolen."[63] Whereas for them, there is never to be any amputation in this case, whether the thief takes it to the storehouse or not.

---

* Zayd b. Ḥārithah (d. 8/629), the adopted son of the Prophet.

† Jaʿfar b. Abī Ṭālib (d. 8/629), the cousin of the Prophet.

‡ ʿAbdallāh b. Rawāḥah al-Khazrajī (d. 8/629), a Companion of the Prophet.

Second, the Prophet said, "If it reaches the value of a shield, then the hand is to be amputated as a punishment for theft."[64] And in the *Ṣaḥīḥ*,* it is found that the value of the shield [518] is three dirhams,[65] whereas in their view, the thief's hands are not to be amputated for this amount.

Third, they said, "A storehouse is not a place of safety, therefore, if he steals a dry date from it when there was no one guarding it, then his hands are not to be amputated."

They argue that the person who brings back a runaway slave is entitled to forty dirhams, based on the report that contains the words, "Whoever brings back a runaway slave from outside the sacred precincts is entitled to ten dirhams or dinars."[66] But they opposed it openly and held it obligatory that he be paid forty. [519]

They argued that the option in preemption arises only immediately after the preemptor learns of the sale, based on the *ḥadīth* of Ibn al-Baylmānī,† "Preemption is like the loosening of the cord, and there is no preemption for the minor nor for the one who is absent,[67] and whoever tortures his slave, then the slave is freed." Then they went against all of this, except his statement, "Preemption is like the loosening of the cord."

They argued for the prohibition of retaliation between the father and son and the master and slave, based on the *ḥadīth*, "The father is not retaliated against for [killing] his son, nor the master for [killing] his slave."[68] [520] Then they went against the *ḥadīth* itself, for it also contains the words, "Whoever tortures his slave, then the slave is freed."

They argued that the illegitimate child is attributed to the master of the bed [i.e., the adulterer] and not the adulteress, based on the *ḥadīth* of Ibn Walīdah Zamʿah,‡ which says, "The child is for the [master of the] bed." Then they went against the *ḥadīth* explicitly and said, "The slave-woman is not [associated with] the bed," even though this ruling was given regarding the case of the slave-woman herself. It is strange that they say that if a man contracts a marriage with his mother or his daughter or his sister, he will not be given a *ḥadd* punishment, because of the existence of a doubt that renders the punishment invalid, and this woman [who is his relative] will become associated with the bed, even with this void and prohibited

---

* *Ṣaḥīḥ*, the authentic collections of *ḥadīth*, most often referring to those of al-Bukhārī and Muslim.

† ʿAbd al-Raḥmān b. Abī Zayd Ibn al-Baylmānī, a Successor from Yemen.

‡ ʿAbd al-Raḥmān b. Zamʿah al-Qurashī al-ʿĀmirī, the child who was the subject of the aforementioned *ḥadīth* that bears his name.

contract. On the other hand, the slave woman who has borne him a child and is the mother of his children and with whom he has intercourse day and night will not become associated with his bed.

Among the truly outrageous matters is that they argue for the permissibility of fasting in Ramaḍān, when one only formed the intention to do so before midday on the day of the fast itself, based on the *ḥadīth* of ʿĀʾishah that the Prophet, may the peace and blessings of God be on him, used to come to her and ask if there was anything for lunch. She would reply in the negative. So he would then say, "In that case I am fasting."[69] Then they said, "If a person does this in a voluntary fast, his fast would not be valid." Whereas the *ḥadīth* relates to the voluntary fast itself. [521]

They argue for the prohibition of the sale of the *mudabbar** slave because one of the causes of freedom is already present in him and his sale would nullify this. They responded to the argument that the Prophet sold a *mudabbar*,[70] by saying that he sold his service. Then they said, "It is not even permissible to sell the service of a *mudabbar*."

They argue for the obligation of including trees in the contract for the sale of land, based on his statement [i.e., the statement of the narrator who related this tradition that], the Messenger of God decreed that preemption be applied in every share of a building and wall. Then they went against the explicit meaning of the same *ḥadīth*, for it also contains the words, "It is not permissible for him to sell until he informs his partner. If he sells it without informing him, then the partner is more entitled to it." Then [the Shāfiʿīs] said, "It is permissible for him to sell it before his consent." And [the Ḥanafīs said], "It is permissible for him to circumvent the preemption by using legal fictions." And [most of the scholars among the imitators say], "If he sells it after the consent of his partner, then the partner is still more entitled to preemption. And his giving consent or withholding it is irrelevant, as far as his right to preemption is concerned."

They argue for the prohibition of the sale of olive oil in exchange for olives, except after one knows that the amount of oil within the olives is less than the olive oil [being offered in exchange]. They based this argument on the *ḥadīth* that has in it a prohibition on the sale of meat in exchange for animals. Then they went against it and said, "It is permissible to sell meat in exchange for animals, whether the meat comes from that same type of animal or from a different one."

---

* A *mudabbar* slave is one who is to be freed upon his master's death.

They argue that the unconditional gift of a patient [suffering from a terminal illness], such as a bequest, is not upheld, except to the value of a third of the gift, based on the *ḥadīth* of ʿImrān b. Ḥuṣayn* that a man freed six slaves at the time of his death and had no wealth except for them. So the Prophet, may the peace and blessings of God be on him, divided them into three groups, and he cast lots between them, freed two, and kept the other four as slaves.[71] Then they went against it in two ways: They said, "No lots are to be cast between them." They also said, "Each one of them is freed to the value of one-sixth." [522]

There are numerous examples of this. The point to consider is that imitation commands you to act thus. In fact, it forcefully compels you to it. If you had accorded precedence to following evidence over imitation, you would not be in such a predicament. If these traditions are true, it is obligatory to submit to them and to uphold whatever lies therein. If they are not authentic, then nothing [in terms of rulings] can be derived from them. As for authenticating and accepting that part of them that agrees with what the principal of your school said, while falsifying and rejecting them if they go against the statement of the principal, or interpreting them in contrived ways, this is the gravest of errors and contradictions.

You sometimes say the traditions that we oppose are contradicted by stronger ones, whereas what we act on is not opposed by something [which would necessitate] that it be abandoned or rejected.

In response, it is said, "These and all other traditions like them must either be abrogated or operative. If they are abrogated, then indeed, no proof can be sought from that which is abrogated. If they are operative, then it is not allowed to oppose any part thereof."

If it is said that they are abrogated to the extent that we oppose them and operative to the extent that we agree with them, then it is to be said, "This, as well as being manifestly wrong, connotes that the one who makes this claim has no knowledge about it. He says something for which there is no evidence. The least that can be said about this is that, if the opponent [i.e., an imitator from another school] is dealt a similar argument as this [i.e., that a *ḥadīth* is operative insofar as it agrees with the views of his principal or school], that claim would be the same as this one, and there would be no difference between the two. Both of them would therefore claim something that cannot be proved. The obligation is to

*ʿImrān b. Ḥuṣayn b. ʿUbayd al-Khuzāʿī al-Kaʿbī (d. 52/672), a Companion, who died in Basra.

follow the Sunnah of the Messenger of God, may the peace and blessings of God be on him, to judge by it and to refer to it, until decisive evidence is established about the abrogation of the relevant part thereof. Or, until the whole community agrees to act contrary to what is in it. And this second option is absolutely impossible. For the community—and God be praised—did not agree to abandon practicing a single Sunnah, except in favor of one whose abrogation was well known to the community. In such a case the community agreed to act on the abrogating *ḥadīth* or Sunnah, and not the abrogated. As for abandoning a Sunnah because of the opinion of an individual, this can never happen, no matter who that individual is." Only God grants success.

## The Imitator Opposes the Command of God, His Messenger, and His Own Scholars

20. The party of imitation has adopted the path of opposition to the Command of God, His Messenger, the guidance of the Companions and the norms of their own scholars. They tread a path never taken by the people of knowledge. As for the Command of God, He decreed that whatever the Muslims disagree over be referred to Him and His Messenger, while the imitators say, "We will refer what we disagree on [523] to the ones we imitate." According to the command of His Messenger, may the peace and blessings of God be on him, in cases of dispute, he, his Sunnah, and the Sunnah of the Rightly Guided Caliphs must be adopted. He commanded that it be grasped and held on to firmly, while the imitators say, "Rather, when in dispute, we hold on to the view of the one we imitate. We prefer it over everything that opposes it."

As for the guidance of the Companions, it is known as a matter of necessity that there was not among them a single one who imitated another individual in everything the latter said, opposing all the other Companions by not rejecting anything from this person's opinions and not adopting anything from theirs. To do this is among the greatest of innovations and the most disgusting of novelties.

As for their opposition to their own scholars, it arises because the scholars forbade imitation of themselves and warned against it, as can be gathered from some of their narrations that have already been mentioned.

As for their adopting a path other than that of the people of knowledge, this is because their way is to seek the opinions of the scholars and to preserve them, look into them, and match these with the Qur'an, the confirmed Sunnah from the Messenger of God, and the statements of the righteous caliphs. So, whatever from these two sources [i.e., the Qur'an and the Sunnah], conforms to that which their own scholars have said, they adopt it and follow God by following it, issuing judgments, and delivering verdicts according to it. Whatever part of the two sources, the Qur'an and the Sunnah, opposes this opinion of their own scholars, they do not turn to. Instead they reject them.

Further, whatever matter is unclear to them is, for them, among the matters subject to *ijtihād*. But, as such, the most that can be said about an opinion issued on such a matter is that following it is permissible. It cannot be said that it is obligatory, nor can anyone be compelled to follow such an opinion. These [early] scholars did not say, "This opinion of mine is the only truth, and that which is contrary to it is not so." This is the path of the people of knowledge followed by the predecessors and the later generations of scholars.

## The Later Generations Changed the Condition of the Religion

As for these later imitator-scholars, they took the opposite path and changed the condition of the religion. They falsified the Book of God, the Sunnah of His Messenger, and the opinions of all his Companions and the Successors. They matched these with the opinions of the ones they imitated. So, whatever part [of the Book, the Sunnah, and the opinions of the Successors and Companions] agreed with the view of the one they imitated, they said, "We accept this." They submitted and yielded completely to this part thereof. Whatever opposed the opinions of their principals, they said, "Another person argued against this," so they neither accepted nor adopted the Book, the Sunnah, and the opinions of the Successors and Companions.

Their experts used every technique to reject the Book, the Sunnah, and the opinions of the Successors and Companions, where these contradicted the opinions of their principal—in every possible way. They sought every stratagem by which they could reject these sources, even if these same sources conformed to their schools in another area of law. They denounced their rivals for rejecting these sources, even if the same techniques for rejecting them were well established in their own schools. They also denounced the rejection of the sources by their opponents, even though the arguments of their opponents would be exactly those that they themselves employed. But in their own case they say, "Such arguments are not sufficient to warrant rejection of the texts."

The one who hopes to enjoy the sublime approval of God and seeks His help [524] in defending the truth with which He sent His Messenger, wherever and with whomever it is to be found, is unhappy with himself for arguing thus, which is a sign of an inverted and blameworthy disposition.

## God's Condemnation of Those Who Split His Religion

21. God, the Most Exalted, condemned those who instigate division in the religion and split up into sects: *Each sect rejoicing in that which is with itself!* [Q., al-Rūm, 30:32].

These are none other than the people of imitation, as opposed to the people of knowledge. For the people of knowledge, even if they disagree, neither create divisions in the religion nor become sects. Rather, they are one group agreed on the necessity of seeking the truth, and they agree that it is accorded favor over all else, and is preferred over everything else, when it becomes apparent. They are one group whose aspirations and path are united. The path and aim they share is one, but the imitators are the exact opposite of this. Their aims are different and their paths divergent, and neither in the means nor in the ends to those means are they with the scholars.

## God's Condemnation of Those Who Split the Unity of Their Religion into Pieces

22. God, the Most High, condemned the ones who split their religion into sects [*zubur*]: *Each party rejoicing in that which is with itself!* [Q., al-Rūm, 30:32]. *Zubur* are the written books that people are pleased to follow over the Book of God and over what He sent His Messenger with. The Most Exalted One says, *O Apostles! Enjoy (all) things good and pure and perform righteousness, for I am well-acquainted with (all) that you do. And verily this community of yours is a single community, and I am your Lord and Cherisher, therefore fear Me (and no other). But they have cut off their affair (of religion) between them into sects, each sect rejoicing in that which is with itself.* [Q., al-Muʾminūn, 23:51–53].

So [God], the Most High, imposed the same obligation on the Prophets as on their nations: to consume pure things, to act righteously, to worship Him alone, to obey only His command, and to refrain from splitting up in religious matters. The Messengers and their followers continued on this path, obeying the Command of God, receiving His Mercy until disagreements emerged that occasioned splits between them, every sect rejoicing over what it had. So whosoever reflects on these verses and applies them to contemporary times will learn the reality of the matter and will learn which of the two parties he hails from. And God is the Helper.

23. God, the Most High, said, *Let there arise out of you a group of people inviting to all that is good, enjoining what is right, and forbidding what is wrong. They are the ones to attain felicity.* [Q., Āl-ʿImrān, 3:104]. He specified these people as the successful ones, to the exclusion of all others. The ones who call to righteousness are those who call to the Book of God and the Sunnah of His Messenger, not the ones who call to the opinions of others.

## [525] God's Condemnation of Those Who Refuse to Refer All Disputes to His Authority

24. God, the Most High, condemned the one who, when he is called to turn to God and to His Messenger, turns away and is content to judge by something else. This is the quality of the people of imitation. The Most High said, *When it is said to them, "Come to what God has revealed, and to the Messenger," you see the hypocrites avert their faces from you in disgust.* [Q., al-Nisāʾ, 4:61].

So, whosoever turns away from the one who calls him to that which God and His Messenger brought, toward something other than that, will bear this condemnation, some to a great extent, others less so.

## Truth Lies in One Opinion

25. It is to be said to the party of imitation, "The religion of God is one, and it is to be found in the opinion of your principal and also in a contradictory opinion that opposes it. So, are all these contradictory

and conflicting opinions, which nullify and go against each other, the religion of God?" If they respond, "Yes, these contradictory and conflicting opinions, some of which oppose each other, are all the religion of God," they have opposed the statements of their own scholars. For all of them were agreed that the truth can lie only in one opinion out of many. Just as the correct direction of prayer can be only one among all possible directions. Thus they depart from the Qur'an, the Sunnah, sound reasoning, and common sense. By saying this they make the religion of God subservient to the opinions of men. If they respond, "The undeniable truth is that the religion of God is one and that is what God revealed in His Book and sent His Messengers with and which He chose for His creation, just as the Prophet of this religion is one, and their direction of prayer is one, so whoever conforms to this is correct and has two rewards, and whoever is mistaken has one reward for his mistaken *ijtihād*," then it is to be said to them, "The obligation then is to seek out the truth, to exert one's reasoning and effort in attaining it to the greatest degree possible, because God, the Most High, obliged His creation to fear Him to the extent of their abilities. Fearing Him means complying with His commands and abandoning what He forbids. Therefore, the believer must know what he has been commanded with in order to act upon it, what he has been prohibited from so as to stay away from it, and what is permissible for him in order to be able to carry it out. None of this knowledge will come about, except with a kind of *ijtihād* and search for the truth." If he does not do this, then he has been given a responsibility, and he will meet God without having fulfilled that which he was entrusted with.

## [526] The Call of the Messenger Was General

26. The call of the Messenger of God, may the peace and blessings of God be on him, was general, for the one who was alive in his time and for the one who would come later, and this message is to last until the Day of Resurrection. So the obligation on those who come after the Companions is exactly the same, even if the attributes and qualities of this obligation have changed with the passage of time. It is known as a matter of necessity that the Companions would not match what they heard from him, may the peace and blessings of God be on him, against the opinions of their own scholars. Rather, their scholars had

no opinions other than the opinions of the Messenger. Not a single one of the Companions would pause before accepting what he heard from another in order to establish its conformity with the views of yet another scholar or of anyone else whose opinion was worthy of being followed. This, then, is the obligation without which faith is not complete. This is precisely what is obligatory on us and on all those subject to the law until the Day of Resurrection. It is known that this obligation was not abrogated after his death, nor was it limited to his Companions. So whoever departs from this approach has opposed that religious obligation itself.

## On the Multiplicity of Legal Opinions and the Fallibility of Those Who Issue Them

27. The opinions of the scholars and their views cannot be collected or bound. Further, it cannot be guaranteed that these opinions are free of error, except where they do not differ, for their agreement can be nothing but the truth. It is also impossible that God and His Messenger directed us to fulfill an obligation that is boundless. He did not guarantee that the opinions of the scholars would be immune from error. Nor has any evidence been established for us that, in a dispute between two parties, the opinion of one of them is to be preferred over the other's, let alone that the opinion of one should be rejected completely and that of the other accepted entirely. It is impossible that God would legislate such a thing or that He would be satisfied with it, except if one of the two parties to the dispute were a Messenger and the other was a dissimulator lying against God, for only in such a case would the obligation be to act as these imitators do with their principals and opponents.

## Knowledge Must Decrease

28. The Prophet, may the peace and blessings of God be on him, said, "Islam began as something strange and it shall return to being something strange as when it began." He thus informed us that knowledge would decrease. Now, what the truthful one informed us about must occur. But it is known that the books of the imitators appeared in the East and West, and never were they more prevalent than they are now.

We see them multiplying every year. The imitators memorize from them whatever they are able to, word for word. Further, these manuals and books are not unknown among the people. Rather, they are very popular in their midst. Indeed they, and nothing else, are all that is known. If this were the knowledge that God sent His Messenger with, [527] the religion would always be gaining prominence, it would be on the rise, and knowledge would be popular and manifest. This would be contrary to what the truthful one [the Prophet] informed us would happen.

29. There is much disagreement in the books of the imitators and in their opinions, but there is no contradiction in that which is from God. Rather, it is the truth, and each part of it reinforces the other. Each testifies to [the truth of] the rest. The Most High said, *Had it been from other than God, they would surely have found therein much contradiction.* [Q., al-Nisāʾ, 4:82].
30. It is not obligatory that a person imitate A (Zayd) instead of B (ʿUmar). Rather, according to the imitators, it is permissible for him to turn from one to the other. But if the opinion of the one he followed first was more correct than that of the second, then you have allowed him to turn from the truth to its opposite. This would be perverse. If, however, the second is the only one who is correct, then you have allowed persistence in error [by allowing him to continue imitation of the first]. If you respond, "Both contradictory opposing opinions are correct," this is entirely impossible. You have no choice but to uphold one of these three responses.
31. It is to be said to the imitator, "How did you come to know that the truth is with the one you imitate and not with the one you do not?" If he says, "I know this based on evidence," then he is not an imitator. And if it is said, "I know this by imitating him, for he issued this verdict and believed in it, and his knowledge, his piety, and the community's high opinion of him all prevent him from saying anything other than the truth," it is to be said to him, "Was he infallible, according to you, or could he commit an error?" If he says that he was infallible, he has erred.

If he concedes that he was not infallible, then it is to be said to him, "How can you be so sure that he did not err in those things in which you imitate him and in which he opposed someone else?" If he says, "Even if he erred, he is rewarded," it is to be said, "Certainly he is rewarded for his *ijtihād*, while you are not, for you did not come up with the [*ijtihād* that was the] cause of this reward. Rather, you fell short of the obligatory following [of the Prophet], in which case you are blameworthy." If he says, "How is it possible that God would reward him for his verdict, praise him for it, and condemn the seeker of the verdict for accepting it? How can this possibly make sense?," then it is to be said to him, "If the seeker fell short and was neglectful of his duty of seeking the truth despite his ability to do so, blame and punishment would rightly fall on him. But if he exerted himself and did not fall short in what he had been commanded with, and if he feared God as much as he was able, he will be duly rewarded. As for the partisan who considers the opinion of his principal the arbiter of the Qur'an, the Sunnah, and the opinions of the Companions, weighing all these against the former, adopting whatever matches the opinion of his principal, rejecting what does not—such a one is more deserving of criticism and condemnation than of reward and recompense." If it is said, as is the case when such an argument is presented, "I follow and imitate him, and I do not know whether he is correct in his verdict [528] or not, so the responsibility is on the one who delivered it, and I merely narrate his statements," it is to be said to him, "By doing this, have you absolved yourself from being questioned by God about how you ruled between the people and about the verdicts you issued to them?" By God, there exists for the judges and *muftīs* an especially high standard of questioning, and none shall overcome it, except the one who knew the truth, then judged and issued verdicts according to it. As for the one who does not know the truth and does not give verdicts according to it, he shall know when the matter is unveiled [on the Day of Judgment] that he has no ground to stand on.

## The Reason for Preferring One Opinion over Another

32. We say, "Did you adopt the opinion of so-and-so because he commanded this or because the Messenger of God, may God's peace and blessings be upon him, ordered this?" If you say, "Because of the former," you have made the opinion of a mere individual a legal proof. This is manifest error. And if you were to say, "Because the Messenger of God, may the peace and blessings of God be upon him, said so," this would be yet more grave and repulsive. For this involves both lying about the Messenger of God and attributing to him something

> that he did not say. It also involves false attribution to the principal, who never said that this ruling of his was the ruling of God's Messenger, may the peace and blessings of God be on him. So your view revolves around two possibilities with no option of a third. Either you make the opinion of a fallible person a proof in the religion, or you falsely attribute to a sinless person something that he did not say. One of these must be the case.

If you respond to this by saying that a choice between these two is not necessary and, in fact, a third option remains, which is to say that, "We say this because the Messenger of God, may God's peace and blessings be on him, commanded us to follow those who were more knowledgeable than us. He also commanded us to ask the people of knowledge when we do not know, and to refer what we do not know to them as they can infer legal rulings. So we are following the command issued to us by our Prophet." To this it is to be said, "Have we been crooning [Ar. *nudandin*] about anything other than the necessity of following the commands of the Prophet, may the peace and blessings of God be on him? So come and agree to this principle without which a person's faith and religion cannot be considered complete. We ask you, by the right of the One who sent the Prophet, when his command appears and the ruling of the one you imitate stands in contradiction to it, would you abandon the latter's opinion in favor of the opinion of the Prophet, may the peace and blessings of God be on him, and throw the former's opinion against a wall? Would you prohibit reliance on his opinion and continue on this course, until obedience to the Messenger has been truly attained as you claim? Or would you still adopt your principal's opinion and consign the command of the Messenger, may the peace and blessings of God be on him, to God? Would you say, 'He was more knowledgeable about the Messenger of God, may the peace and blessings of God be on him, than us, and he would not have opposed this *ḥadīth* had he not had knowledge of another *ḥadīth* that abrogated this or contradicted this and that was a stronger *ḥadīth*, or the *ḥadīth* which goes against his view must have been deemed inauthentic by him?' Would you then consider the statement of the principal decisive [*muḥkam*] and the statement of the Messenger merely ambiguous [*mujmal*]? If you had truly been following your principal because the Messenger commanded you to adopt his opinion, you would have accorded precedence to the opinion of the Messenger at all times." [529]

33. Where did the Messenger command you to adopt the opinion of one of the scholars entirely and to abandon the opinions of his contemporaries and those who were more knowledgeable and closer to him? Is this anything but attributing a command to the Messenger of God, when, in reality, he never issued such a command at all?
34. What you have mentioned is, in itself, evidence against you. For God, Exalted be He, has commanded, asking the people of remembrance. And remembrance [*dhikr*] means the Qur'an and the *ḥadīth* that God, in His statement, commanded the Wives of His Prophet to recite: *And remember what is recited to you in your homes, of the Signs of God and His Wisdom.* [Q., al-Aḥzāb, 33:34]. This, then, is the knowledge that God commanded us to follow. He commanded the one who does not have knowledge to ask those who possess it. This is what is obligatory on this person who has no knowledge, namely, to ask the people who do know what God revealed to His Messenger, so that they can inform him about it. Once they have done so, he cannot but follow that which is revealed. This was the way of the scholars among the people of knowledge. They did not have a specific person whom they would imitate in everything he said. ʿAbdallāh b. ʿAbbās would ask the Companions about the words, actions, and practices of the Messenger of God, may the peace and blessings of God be on him, and he would not ask them about anything else. Likewise, the Companions would ask the Wives of the Prophet, especially ʿĀʾishah, about the actions of the Messenger of God, may the peace and blessings of God be on him, in his house. Likewise, the Successors would only ask the Companions about the affairs of their Prophet. Similar to this were the scholars of law. As al-Shāfiʿī said to Aḥmad, "O Abū ʿAbdallāh, you are more knowledgeable about *ḥadīth* than I am. So if you deem a *ḥadīth* to be authentic, inform me, whether it is from Syria, Kufa, or Basra, so that I may act according to it." Not a single one of the people of knowledge ever asked about the opinions of any individual and his school with a view to adopting only this and opposing everything besides it.
35. The Prophet, may the peace and blessings of God be on him, guided the ones who sought a verdict for the man who was afflicted with a wound to ask only about his ruling and Sunnah. He said, "They killed him, may God destroy them." He made this invocation against them because they issued a verdict without knowledge. This demonstrates the impermissibility of issuing a verdict based on imitation. For imitation is not considered to be knowledge by agreement of the people. If

the Messenger of God, may the peace and blessings of God be on him, supplicated against him, that is a sign that the action of that individual who issued a verdict without real knowledge was forbidden. This is one of the proofs that indicate the impermissibility of imitation, so what the imitators rely on is one of the strongest evidences against them. And God is the Helper.

Similar to this incident is that of the laborer who committed *zinā* with the wife of the one who hired him, and his father asked the people of knowledge about the punishment to be inflicted on his son. When they informed him about the Sunnah of the Messenger of God, may the peace and blessings of God be on him, about the punishment to be given to the virgin who commits *zinā*, the father of the laborer accepted this and did not depart from their views [530]. He did not question them about their own views and their affiliations to schools.

## Regarding the *Ḥadīth* of *Kalālah* and the Attitude of Abū Bakr and ʿUmar

36. As for their statement, "ʿUmar said about the issue of *kalālah*, 'I would feel embarrassed to disagree with Abū Bakr,' and this can be regarded as ʿUmar's imitation of Abū Bakr," there are five responses to this.

### ʿUmar Did Not Imitate Abū Bakr

First, they have presented only an abridged form of the *ḥadīth* and have concealed the part that invalidates their inference from it. However, we shall mention it in its entirety: Shuʿbah said, from ʿĀṣim al-Aḥwal*, from al-Shaʿbī, that Abū Bakr said about *kalālah*, "I shall render judgment on it according to my own view. If it is correct, it is a favor of God, and if it is incorrect, it is from myself and the devil, and God is absolved of it. [*Kalālah*] is when an individual dies without a child or a parent." So ʿUmar b. Khaṭṭāb, may God be pleased with him, said, "I would feel embarrassed to disagree with Abū Bakr." [This shows that] ʿUmar was too embarrassed to oppose Abū Bakr, when the latter himself had admitted

*Abū ʿAbd al-Raḥmān ʿĀṣim b. Sulaymān al-Tamīmī al-Baṣrī (d. 140/757), a renowned traditionist.

the possibility of his making an error and acknowledged that not all his opinions were correct and infallible. This is also demonstrated by the fact that ʿUmar b. Khaṭṭāb acknowledged, at the time of his own death, that he had not issued a judgment on *kalālah* at all and that he had not understood the issue.[72]

## Matters in Which ʿUmar Opposed Abū Bakr

Second, the issues on which ʿUmar disagreed with Abū Bakr are too well known to require repetition. He opposed him, for instance, on the issue of the prisoners of the apostates captured by the Muslims. Abū Bakr imprisoned them, while ʿUmar opposed him. His disagreement reached the extent that he sent them back to their families as free women, except those among them who gave birth to children from their masters. So he quashed Abū Bakr's ruling.[73] Among these women was Khawlah al-Ḥanafīyyah Umm Muḥammad b. ʿAlī.* So how does this compare to the way the imitators act in relation to their principals?

He also disagreed with Abū Bakr about the land that was gained after victory in battle. Abū Bakr divided this among the fighters, and ʿUmar established it as a trust [*waqf*].[74] He also disagreed with him about preferential shares in issuing stipends,† in which Abū Bakr favored equal treatment of all the Companions of the Prophet, and ʿUmar favored preferential shares.[75] Among these issues was that of appointing a political successor, about which ʿUmar said explicitly, "If I were to appoint a successor, Abū Bakr too has done so, and if I were not to appoint a successor, then the Messenger of God, may the peace and blessings of God be on him, also did not appoint a successor." Ibn ʿUmar said, "By God, as soon as he mentioned the Messenger, I realized that he would not appoint a successor."[76] This is how the people of knowledge act when a Sunnah of the Messenger of God, may the peace and blessings of God be on him, seems to them to contradict the opinion of someone else. They do not equate the Sunnah with anything else, as opposed to the imitators, whose position is contrary to this, as they explicitly acknowledge. Also well known

* Khawlah al-Ḥanafīyyah Umm Muḥammad b. ʿAlī, the mother of Muḥammad, the son of the fourth caliph, ʿAlī.

† The disagreement related to whether those who had participated in the first of the Prophet's battles with him should be given a preferential share.

under this topic is ʿUmar's disagreement with Abū Bakr about the inheritance shares of the true grandfather and the brothers of the deceased when inheriting together.[77] [532]

## Returning to a Refutation of the Imitators, Based on the Practice of ʿUmar

Third, even if one supposes that ʿUmar imitated Abū Bakr in everything he said, this would not give any respite to the imitators of those who came after the Companions and the Successors, who do not come close to or anywhere near the Companions in merit. So if, as you claim, ʿUmar's example is a fair one, you should follow it and imitate Abū Bakr and abandon imitation of everyone besides him. God and His Messenger and all of His creation would praise you for this imitation in a way that they would not praise you for imitating someone other than Abū Bakr.

Fourth, when it comes to their own scholars, the imitators do not feel embarrassed about disagreeing with them, as ʿUmar felt embarrassed over disagreeing with Abū Bakr. This is because they oppose the rulings of Abū Bakr—and of ʿUmar alongside him—and are not embarrassed to do so, in favor of the opinion of the scholars they imitate. Rather, some of their extreme partisans have explicitly stated in some of their books of jurisprudence that it is not permissible to imitate Abū Bakr and ʿUmar, but it is obligatory to imitate al-Shāfiʿī. By God! How ludicrous it would be for God to command that al-Shāfiʿī be imitated and for Him to forbid you from imitating Abū Bakr and ʿUmar. As for us, we call God as a witness over us, and He shall ask about this on the day we meet Him, that if an opinion is authentically reported from the rightly guided Caliphs, the ones whom the Messenger of God, may the peace and blessings of God be on him, commanded us to obey and to follow, then, even if all the people of the earth were to gather against this, we would not turn toward the opinion of any one of them. We praise God that He saved us from that which afflicted the one who forbade imitation of Abū Bakr and ʿUmar and obligated imitation of his own principal among the scholars.

In summary, even if ʿUmar's imitation of Abū Bakr were to be accepted, there would be no relief to be gained in this by the ones who imitate those whom God and His Messenger have not obligated imitation of. God never made such a person a standard by which to judge the Book and Sunnah of His Messenger, nor would this person ever claim this for himself.

Fifth, the most that can be said about Abū Bakr and ʿUmar is that ʿUmar followed Abū Bakr in a particular issue. Does this prove the permissibility of adopting all of the opinions of a specific individual and giving them the same rank as the explicit texts [*nuṣūs*] of the Lawgiver, and referring to no one other than that person, not even to the texts of the Lawgiver, unless they agree with what he has said? By God, the whole community is agreed on the impermissibility of this. Nor did this appear in the community until after the passing away of the blessed generations. [533]

## Arguments Invalidating Imitation

37. As for your statement, "'Umar said to Abū Bakr, 'our opinion follows yours'." It seems that the one who advances this as an argument for imitation has heard the people uttering a statement that is [in its brief form] sufficient for the intelligent folk, but he restricts the *ḥadīth* in which these words are to be found to just these words and is content with that. However, this *ḥadīth* is among the greatest nullifiers of his position. It is found in the *Ṣaḥīḥ* of al-Bukhārī,* from Ṭāriq b. Shihāb,† who said, "A delegation of Buzākhah, from the Asad and Ghaṭfān tribes, came, asking Abū Bakr for a truce. He presented them with a choice between a war leading to exile and an ignominious [*mukhziyah*] peace. They said, 'We understand the war that, if lost, would lead to exile, but what is this ignominious peace?' He said, 'We shall take your weapons, fighting horses, and possessions as booty, and you shall return to us our possessions that you took from us. You must also pay us compensation for our dead, while your dead, being in the fire of Hell, will not be compensated for. You will also dissociate from the people who are obsessed with agriculture, until God makes the successor of His Prophet [i.e., Abū Bakr, the caliph] and the Migrants accept an excuse for your actions.' So Abū Bakr presented this decision of his before the people. 'Umar then rose and said, 'You have an opinion, and we shall advise you about it. What you have said about the war leading to exile is well said, as is what you have said about the truce of ignominy. And what you have said about us taking what we got from them and them not taking what they got from us, this too is well said. As for what you said about them compensating us for our dead and their own dead being in the fire, since our fallen ones fought and were killed in

---

*Muḥammad b. Ismā'īl al-Bukhārī (d. 256/870), author of the most renowned work of *ḥadīth*, the *Ṣaḥīḥ* that bears his name.

†Abū 'Abdallāh Ṭāriq b. Shihāb b. 'Abd Shams al-Bajalī (d. 82/701), a Kufan narrator.

obedience to God, their reward is with God, and there is no compensation to be offered for them.' So the people agreed with what 'Umar had said." In some versions of this *ḥadīth* are mentioned the words, "You have an opinion, and our opinion follows yours."[78] So, is there any succor in this narration for the party of imitation? [534]

## Ibn Masʿūd Would Not Imitate ʿUmar

38. As for their statement, "Ibn Masʿūd adopted the views of 'Umar," the disagreements of Ibn Masʿūd with 'Umar are too well known to require citation. He agreed with him as one scholar agrees with another. Even if he adopted the opinions of 'Umar in imitation of him, this was only in approximately four issues, which we shall state. Consider also that he was one of his functionaries, and 'Umar was the sovereign Commander of the Believers. As for his disagreements with him, these occurred in approximately one hundred areas. Among these issues in which they disagreed are the following: it has been authentically reported from Ibn Masʿūd that he would free the slave woman who bears children to her master, in proportion to the share of inheritance of her child in his father's inheritance.[79] Ibn Masʿūd also placed his hands between his knees when bowing in ritual prayer until his death,[80] while 'Umar, when bowing, was accustomed to place his hands on his knees.[81] Ibn Masʿūd said about a man's pronouncement that his wife was forbidden to him, that this was like an oath that had to be atoned for if violated,[82] while 'Umar [535] said that this counted as a [536] single pronouncement of divorce.[83] Ibn Masʿūd prohibited the marriage of an adulteress to an adulterer forever,[84] whereas 'Umar would ask them to repent and marry one another.[85] Ibn Masʿūd would view the sale of a slave woman as her divorce,[86] [537] while 'Umar held that she would not be divorced by this.[87] There are numerous examples of such divergences in their views.

## The Pre-eminence of Ibn Masʿūd Among the Companions, Based on His Knowledge

It is strange that those who rely on this argument approve neither of imitating Ibn Masʿūd nor of imitating 'Umar, while imitation of Mālik, Abū Ḥanīfah, and al-Shāfiʿī is dearer to them and more prevalent among them.

Furthermore, how can they equate their imitation of men [who are beneath Ibn Masʿūd in rank] to Ibn Masʿūd's imitation, when he was the one who said, "The Companions of the Messenger of God, may the peace and blessings of God be on him, knew that I was the most learned of them regarding His Book. If I were to learn that someone else is more knowledgeable than I am, I would undertake a journey to learn from him." Shaqīq said, "I sat in the circles of the Companions of the Messenger of God, and I did not hear a single one of them deny this."[88] Ibn Masʿūd also used to say, "I swear by the One besides whom there is no other God, there is no chapter of the Qurʾan but that I am the most knowledgeable about where it was revealed, and there is no verse but that I am the most knowledgeable about the reason it was revealed. If I were to learn of anyone who was more learned in the Book of God than I am, I would journey to meet him so long as camels could take me to him."[89] Abū Mūsā l-Ashʿarī* said, "For a while we would regard Ibn Masʿūd and his mother as belonging to the household of the Prophet, may the peace and blessings of God be on him, because of their frequent visits there and their being attached to them."[90] Abū Masʿūd al-Badrī† said, [538] while ʿAbdallāh b. Masʿūd was standing nearby, "I do not know of anyone left by the Messenger of God, may the peace and blessings of God be on him, after his death, who is more knowledgeable regarding what God has revealed than this man who is standing." Abū Musā said, "He would be present with the Messenger, while we would be absent, and he would be allowed to enter into his presence, while we would be refused permission."[91] ʿUmar wrote thus to the inhabitants of Kufa, "I am sending ʿAmmār‡ among you as your governor, and ʿAbdallāh b. Masʿūd as your teacher and advisor, and they are among the most outstanding of the Companions of the Messenger of God, may the peace and blessings of God be on him, from among the Companions who participated in the Battle of Badr. So learn from them, and follow them, for by giving you ʿAbdallāh [b. Masʿūd], I have preferred you over myself."[92] It is also authentically reported from him, that he asked for the verdict of Ibn Masʿūd regarding the irrevocable divorce and acted according to it.[93] But

---

*Abū Mūsā ʿAbdallāh b. Qays b. Salīm al-Ashʿarī (d. 44/664), a Companion of the Prophet.

†Abū Masʿūd ʿUqbah b. ʿAmr b. Thaʿlabah al-Anṣārī, a renowned Companion, who witnessed the battle of Badr and died circa 40/660, according to some reports.

‡ʿAmmār b. Yāsir al-ʿAnsī (d. 37/657), a Companion of the Prophet, who witnessed the battle of Badr.

this was not done in imitation of Ibn Masʿūd. Rather, it was after he had heard that which convinced him of its truth. This is how some Companions used to act, when basing their actions on the opinions of others. It is also authentically reported from Ibn Masʿūd that he said, "Be a scholar or a student, but do not be a freeloader." So he excluded the freeloader—and this is the imitator—from the company of scholars and teachers. The truth is as he stated it, may God be pleased with him. Truly, such a person is not with the scholars nor with those who learn with knowledge and evidence, as should be clear to whoever reflects on this.

## The Companions Did Not Imitate Each Other

39. As for their statement, "ʿAbdallāh b. Masʿūd abandoned his own view for that of ʿUmar, and Abū Mūsā abandoned his own view for that of ʿAlī, and Zayd abandoned his view for that of ʿUbayy b. Kaʿb." The response to this is, "They did not abandon what they knew of the Sunnah in imitation of these three, as is the practice of the people of imitation. Rather, the one who reflects on the lives of these people sees that, when a Sunnah became known to them, they would not [539] abandon it for the statement of anyone else, no matter who he was." Ibn ʿUmar abandoned the opinion of ʿUmar, when the Sunnah became apparent to him. Ibn ʿAbbās denounced the one who countered the report in the Sunnah that had reached him by saying, "but Abū Bakr and ʿUmar said [the opposite]." Ibn ʿAbbās would say [when he heard someone countering the Sunnah with the opinion of someone else], "I fear that stones from the sky will be sent down upon you [as a punishment]. For I say that the Messenger of God, may the peace and blessings of God be on him said this, and you respond, 'But Abū Bakr and ʿUmar said something to the contrary.'"[94] May God have mercy on Ibn ʿAbbās, and may He be well pleased with him. By God, imagine if he had witnessed these later generations, to whom, when it is said, "The Messenger of God, may the peace and blessings of God be on him, said this," they respond, "But other people said something different"—and this too for someone who is not of the same rank as the Companions—rather he is far beneath that. The Companions would abandon their opinions in favor of those of other Companions because they recognized that their opinions and those of others were equal. So, when the evidence supported the view of others, they would accept that and abandon their own

views. This is exactly what the people of knowledge did, and Ibn ʿAbbās was more beloved to them than he is to these later scholars. This is, however, the exact opposite of the manner of the people of imitation in every way.

This is the correct way to respond to their citing as evidence of their view the statement of Masrūq, "I would not abandon the view of Ibn Masʿūd for the view of anyone else."

## The Real Import Behind the Messenger's Order to Follow Muʿādh

40. As for their statement, "The Prophet, may the peace and blessings of God be on him, said, 'Muʿādh* has set a practice for you so follow him'." Strange is the one who argues for the validity of imitation of an individual in the religion of God on the basis of this *ḥadīth*. The Sunnah of Muʿādh was not established as a valid practice to be followed except by the words of the Prophet, may the peace and blessings of God be on him, "Follow him." This is just like the call to prayer that became a Sunnah only after the Prophet commanded that it be given, approved of it, and legislated it as part of the law.[95] It did not happen by the occurrence of the dream [of the Companion who, before this, saw the call to prayer being delivered in his dream]. [540]

If it is said, "what then is the meaning of the *ḥadīth*," it is to be said, "It means that God legislated Muʿādh's action as a Sunnah for you." It became a Sunnah for us when the Prophet, may the peace and blessings of God be on him, commanded us to do it, not because of Muʿādh's performing it. It is authentically reported from Muʿādh that he said, "How would you fare when three things occur: the pursuit of this world which will lead you to smite each others' throats, the mistakes of the scholar, and the hypocrite using the Qur'an in disputation? As for the scholar, if he is rightly guided, do not imitate him in matters of religion, and if he is overcome by error, then do not become disheartened, for a believer is sometimes overcome by error, [from which] he then repents. As for the Qur'an, it has lampposts

---

*Abū ʿAbd al-Raḥmān Muʿādh b. Jabal (d. 18/639), a Companion of the Prophet who died of the plague in Palestine.

like the ones you find on the pathways, which are not concealed from anyone. So do not ask about that which you know. And whatever causes doubts within you, then entrust it to the one who knows about it. As for the world, whoever God enriches in his heart has indeed succeeded, and for the one who was not blessed with this, the world is of no benefit to him." So Muʿādh, may God be pleased with him, disclosed the truth and forbade imitation in everything. He further commanded that the clear meaning (*ẓāhir*) of the Qurʾan be followed and that one ought to ignore whoever opposes this, and he commanded suspending one's view wherever there was a difficulty. All of this is contrary to the way of the imitators. God is the One who grants ability. [541]

## Obedience to Those in Authority

41. As for your statement, "God, the Exalted, commands obedience to those in authority, which is a reference to the scholars, and obedience to them is imitating them in their legal opinions." The response to this is that it has been said by some that the people of authority are the rulers and by others that they are the scholars. Both of these views are narrated from Imām Aḥmad. The truth is that the verse includes both groups, and obedience to them is part of obedience to the Messenger. But the imitators have not understood that these people are to be obeyed only in submission to God, if they command that which was ordered by God and His Messenger. The scholars are the ones who disseminate and proclaim the orders of the Messenger, and the rulers are the ones who enforce his orders. As such, obedience to them rests on submission to God and His Messenger. Is there any proof in this verse for preferring the views of men over the Sunnah of the Messenger of God, may the peace and blessings of God be on him and preferring imitation [of men] over the Sunnah?
42. This verse is one of the most cogent proofs against you. It is also among the strongest ones invalidating imitation. This is for several reasons.

First, the verse contains a command to obey God which means to do what He orders and abstain from what He prohibits.

Second, the verse commands obedience to His Messenger. But a person cannot obey the Messenger until he is aware of the commands of God and His Messenger. As for the one who confirms that he is not among the people who have knowledge of the commands of God and His Messenger and that, when it comes to knowing about them, he imitates the people of knowledge, it is impossible for him to verify what this obedience to God and His Messenger entails.

Third, the people of authority have prohibited imitation of themselves, as has been authentically reported from Muʿādh b. Jabal, ʿAbdallāh b. Masʿūd, ʿAbdallāh b. ʿUmar, ʿAbdallāh b. ʿAbbās and others among the Companions. We mentioned explicit statements about this from the four Imāms and others besides them. As such, if obedience to them in this is necessary, that itself would invalidate imitation [because they themselves prohibited imitation, and this prohibition would also have to be obeyed]. If, however, it is not obligatory, then the inference drawn from this verse by the imitators is incorrect.

Fourth, God, the Exalted, said in the same verse, *If you differ in anything among yourselves, refer it to God and His Messenger, if you do believe in God and the Last Day* [Q., al-Nisāʾ, 4:59], which is clear in nullifying the validity of imitation. What is prohibited here is for the disputant to return to mere opinion, to a school, or to imitation.

If it is said, "Then what is this obedience that is owed especially to them? For if they are obeyed regarding the knowledge concerning God and His Messenger that they convey to us, then our obedience is to God and His Messenger and not to them."

It is to be said, "This, indeed, is the truth. They are obeyed out of obedience to God and His Messenger. They are not obeyed independently of that. This is why God linked obedience to them to that of the Messenger, and He did not repeat this command ['obey!'] when it came to the people of authority. However, he did issue the command ['obey!'] independently a second time when mentioning the Messenger so that it would not be mistakenly [542] assumed that the Messenger is being followed out of obedience to someone else, as is the case with those in authority. For this is not the case at all. Rather, obedience to the Messenger is an independent obligation, regardless of whether or not his commands and prohibitions are present in the Qurʾan."

## Merits of the Successors and How They Qualify As Such

43. As for their statement, "God, the Perfect and Majestic, praised the first predecessors among the Immigrants and the Helpers who invited the Prophet to reside in Medina and those who followed them with sincerity. And this is precisely what imitation is."

How true is the first part of this proposition, how false the second! Rather, the verse is one of the strongest proofs against the party of imitation, for following the scholars means adopting their path and methodology. But they forbade imitation and being a freeloader. They also told us that a person with this quality lacked true insight.

There was not a single one among them (and all praise is due to God) who was on the same path as these imitators. God saved and protected them from what happened to the one who rejected the texts in favor of imitation of the opinions of mere men. The imitators tread on a path never taken by the people of knowledge. Therein lies their opposition to them. The ones who truly follow them with sincerity are the people of knowledge and insight who do not prefer any view, analogy, reasoned argument, or the opinion of any scholar over the Book of God and the Sunnah of His Messenger. Nor do they make the school of one person the arbiter of the Qur'an and the Sunnah. These, then, are their true followers. May God, by His Grace and Mercy, include us among them.

## Who Are the True Followers of the Scholars?

44. If the imitator-scholars, whom all the scholars exclude from the category of the people of knowledge, and who admit themselves that they are not so, were the true followers of the principals, then those eminent scholars who relied on proofs could not have been among their adherents. Thus, when it came to following the principals, the ignorant imitator-scholars would end up more felicitous than those scholars who relied on evidence. But this is truly impossible.

Rather, it is the one who opposes a single one of them on the basis of evidence who is truly a follower of that scholar, not the one who accepts his statement without evidence. The former is the stance adopted by the true followers of the Imāms. I seek the refuge of God if these imitators, who treat the statements of the scholars as they do the clear texts [of the Qur'an and the Sunnah]—who, in fact, reject the scriptural texts in favor of the statements of their principals—are the true followers of the Imāms. They are not the true adherents of their scholars at all. The only ones who are so are those actually on their path, pursuing their methodology.

Some imitators objected to the teaching of the Shaykh al-Islam [Ibn Taymiyyah] in the Ibn al-Ḥanbalī seminary, which was established as a trust for the Ḥanbalīs themselves, while the scholar who performs *ijtihād* is necessarily not one of them. So he said to them, "Whatever I took from the school of Aḥmad, I took on the basis of my knowledge of it, not in imitation of it."

These imitators cannot be acting [534] according to the schools of their principals, as opposed to the contemporaries of those scholars who would never imitate them.

Thus the people who most often followed Mālik are Ibn Wahb and his contemporaries, who judge only on the basis of evidence, submitting to proofs wherever found.

Similarly, Abū Yūsuf and Muḥammad, despite their frequent opposition to him, followed Abū Ḥanīfah more than the imitators.

Likewise al-Bukhārī, Muslim*, Abū Dā'ūd, Athram,† and this class from the companions of Aḥmad follow him more closely than the ones who merely imitate him and ascribe themselves to him [i.e., his school].

Therefore, in the same vein, an endowment of a trust for the followers of the Imāms, who are people of knowledge and who follow evidence, is preferable to an endowment for the imitators.

## A Brief Statement on the *Ḥadīth*, "My Companions Are Like the Stars"

45. As for their statement that the famous *ḥadīth*, "My Companions are like stars, whomever among them you follow, you will be guided," is sufficient to prove the validity of imitation, there are several responses.

First, that this *ḥadīth* was narrated by way of A'mash, from Abū Sufyān,‡ from Jābir, and from the *ḥadīth* of Sa'īd b. al-Muṣayyib,§ from 'Umar, and by way of Ḥamzah al-Jazarī,** from Nāfi',†† from Ibn 'Umar. However,

---

*Abū l-Ḥuṣayn Muslim b. al-Ḥajjāj al-Nīsābūrī al-Qushayrī d. (261/875), author of the renowned *Ṣaḥīḥ* collection that bears his name.

†Abū Bakr Aḥmad b. Muḥammad b. Hāni' al-Athram (d. after 260/873), a disciple of Aḥmad b. Ḥanbal and a traditionist.

‡Abū Sufyān Ṭalḥah b. Nāfi' al-Iskāf, a Successor who claims to report from some of the Companions.

§Abū Muḥammad Sa'īd b. al-Muṣayyib al-Makhzūmī (d. 140/757), a renowned Successor.

**Ḥamzah b. Abī Ḥamzah al-Jazarī, a *ḥadīth* narrator, who has been discredited by leading traditionists, such as al-Bukhārī.

††Abū 'Abdallāh Nāfi' (d. 117/735), client of 'Abdallāh b. 'Umar and a renowned traditionist.

nothing about it is conclusive. Ibn ʿAbd al-Barr said that Muḥammad b. Ibrāhīm b. Saʿīd narrated to us that Abū ʿAbdallāh b. Mufriḥ told them that Muḥammad b. Ayyūb al-Ṣamūt narrated to them that al-Bazzār* said to us, "As for what was related from the Prophet, may the peace and blessings of God be upon him, 'My Companions are like stars, whomever among them you follow, you will be guided,' this is not authentically attributed to him."

Second, it is said to these imitators, "How, then, did you come to abandon imitation of those stars by whom you were to be guided? [544] How did you then end up imitating those who were far beneath them [in rank]? Do you not prefer the imitation of Mālik, al-Shāfiʿī, Abū Ḥanīfah, and Aḥmad to that of imitation of Abū Bakr, ʿUmar, ʿUthmān, and ʿAlī?" You thus contradicted the clear import of the *ḥadīth*. You used the *ḥadīth* to argue for the validity of imitating those with whom the *ḥadīth* was not at all concerned.

Third, this *ḥadīth* should obligate you to imitate those Companions who allow the grandfather to receive a share of inheritance alongside the siblings of the deceased[96] and of those Companions who forbid the grandfather a share in a similar scenario. Likewise, you would have to imitate the Companion who says that a man's oath to stay away from his wife is just an oath [which can be atoned for if it is violated][97] and the Companion who says that this counts as a divorce.[98] And you ought to imitate the Companion who forbids having intercourse with two slaves who are sisters[99] and the one who regards this as permissible.[100] Likewise, you would imitate the Companion who allows the fasting person to eat snow[101] [545] and the one who forbids this for him.[102] And [similarly] imitate the Companion who says that a widow is in a waiting period for the lesser of two terms[103] and the one who says she is to wait until delivery of the child.[104] [And you would have to] imitate the Companion who prohibits the one in a state of ritual consecration from using incense[105] and the one who allows this.[106] You would also have to imitate the Companion who permits the sale of one dirham for two dirhams[107] [546] and the one who considers this to be forbidden[108] and also the Companion who regards a bath as obligatory [upon a man who has sexual intercourse] even if there was no emission [of semen][109] [547] and the one who says a

*Abū Bakr Aḥmad b. ʿAmr b. ʿAbd al-Khāliq al-Bazzār, d. 292/904, a renowned Basran *ḥadīth* compiler.

bath is not obligatory in such a case.[110] You must also imitate the one who allows a share of inheritance for the distant kindred[111] [548] and of the one who excludes them from receiving a share.[112] In the same way, you would be compelled to imitate the Companion who holds that marriage becomes unlawful by either adult having been breast-fed by the close relative of the other,[113] and the one who does not agree with this.[114] Furthermore, would you [not have to] imitate [549] the [Companion] who prohibits ritual purification with dust for the one who is in a state of impurity[115] and also of the one who regards this as obligatory?[116] And [would you not also have to] imitate the Companion who regards the triple pronouncement of divorce as one[117] and the one who regards this as three separate pronouncements?[118] [550] And [the same would apply in the case of] the one who regards it as obligatory to transform the nullified major pilgrimage into a minor pilgrimage[119] and the one who ruled against this[120]—that is, you would have to imitate them both. And [you would be imitating] the Companion who permits consumption of the meat of domesticated donkeys[121] and of the one who forbids this. And also of the Companion who holds that ablution is nullified by touching the private parts[122] [551] and the one who does not regard this to be the case.[123] [553] And you would have to imitate the Companion who regards the sale of a slave woman as her divorce[124] and the one who does not.[125] And also the Companion who holds that the one who fulfilled his vow to abstain from sexual relations with his wife is to be stopped at the end of the period of his vow [from resuming sexual relations with her] [554] and the one who would not stop him after this period.[126]

There are many, many examples of such disagreement between the Companions of the Messenger of God, may the peace and blessings of God be upon him. So if you accept this, you should not seek to establish the superiority of one opinion over another through evidences, nor the superiority of one school over another. Rather, you should provide a person the option to adopt whichever opinion he desires. You should not object to the one who belongs to another school and accepts the opinion of one of the Companions. If you do not allow all this, then you are truly the people who nullify this *ḥadīth* by opposing it and saying something that is against its import. You cannot free yourself from this contradiction.

Fourth, following the Companions is [to be interpreted as] following the Qur'an and the Sunnah, and everyone who invites [people] to these sources is obeyed. So, following them is what renders imitation impermissible for you, and it necessitates seeking evidences and judging only by them, as was the practice of the Companions themselves, may God be pleased with them. Thus, the *ḥadīth* is among the strongest arguments against you, and God is the one who grants strength.

## The Companions Are the Ones Whose Practices We Have Been Commanded to Follow

46. As for your statement, "'Abdallāh b. Mas'ūd said, 'Whoever among you adopts a Sunnah, let him adopt the Sunnah of the ones who exist no more. These are the Companions of Muḥammad.'" This is one of the most convincing evidences against you, for many reasons. This statement prohibits adopting the Sunnah of those who are alive while you imitate them and those who exist no more.

[555] Second, 'Abdallāh b. Mas'ūd specified those who were to be followed, and they were the best of creation, and the most righteous, the most learned of the community of Muslims—the Companions—may God be pleased with them, while you imitators do not approve of imitating or following them, but you approve of doing so for those far beneath them in rank.

Third, adopting their Sunnah means following them, which means that the follower acts as they acted, and this itself violates the principle of not accepting the opinion of anyone without evidence, which the Companions never did.

Fourth, the impermissibility of imitation is authentically reported from Ibn Mas'ūd himself, who referred to the imitator as a freeloader having no real intellect. Thus it is learned that by the word "following," he cannot have meant "imitation."

47. As for your statement, "It is authentically reported that the Prophet, may the peace and blessings of God be upon him, said, 'Follow my Sunnah and the Sunnah of the rightly guided Caliphs after me,' and also his statement, 'Follow the two who come after me, Abū Bakr and 'Umar.'" These are the strongest evidences we have in establishing the evil of the imitation you practice, for it is against the practice of the Rightly Guided Caliphs. It is known as a matter of necessity that none of them would abandon the Sunnah, once it became apparent, in order to adopt the opinion of someone else, no matter who that other

person was. Nor would any one of them hold a contradictory opinion himself alongside the Sunnah. But the practice of the people of imitation is quite unlike this.

48. Further, the Prophet, may the peace and blessings of God be upon him, [in his words,] bound his Sunnah to that of his Companions. So adopting their Sunnah does not entail imitating them. Rather, it constitutes following the Sunnah of the Messenger of God, may the peace and blessings of God be upon him, just as the call to prayer is not delivered in imitation of the one who saw this in his dream, and performing what one missed of one's ritual prayer in congregation after the *imām* has made the salutation of peace is not done in imitation of Muʿādh. Rather, all this is done in obedience to the [Prophet, who was the] one who commanded us to act so. Is the imitation that you perform similar to this?

## The Later Generations Do Not Adopt the Sunnah nor Do They Decide According to the Judgments of the Companions

49. Further, you are among the foremost opponents of the command of these two *aḥādīth*. For you do not regard adopting the Sunnah of the Rightly Guided Caliphs (or of Abū Bakr and ʿUmar) or deciding by their actions, to be obligatory. Their opinions constitute no proof for you [556]. Some of your misguided partisans have explicitly forbidden performing imitation of them, while imitation of al-Shāfiʿī is still regarded as obligatory by them. So it is most peculiar that you should deploy as proof something that you are foremost in opposing. And God grants success.

50. The *ḥadīth* is a proof against you in every way. For it commands, in all cases of frequent disagreement, that recourse be made to the Sunnah of the Messenger and of the caliphs, whereas you command that the view of a particular scholar and his school be followed. Second, it warns of newly invented matters in the religion. It also informs us that every such matter is an innovation, which is misguidance. Now, it is known, as a matter of necessity, that the imitation you practice, for which you abandoned the Qur'an and Sunnah of the Messenger (and against which you weighed the Qur'an and Sunnah and which you rendered a criterion by which they are to be

judged) is among the most blameworthy of innovations, from which God protected the first generations whom He honored and chose over all others. In conclusion, whatever was established by the righteous caliphs for the community, is a proof which it is not permissible to turn away from. How does this compare to what the people of imitation say: that their sunnah is not a proof and that imitation of them is not permissible?

## The Messenger Predicted that There Would Be Much Dispute in His Community

51. The Messenger, may the peace and blessings of God be on him, said in the same *ḥadīth*, "So whoever among you lives after me will see much disagreement." This is a condemnation of those who disagree. It is also a warning against adopting their path. Certainly disagreement has arisen and worsened because of imitation and its proponents. They are the ones who divided the religion into factions, each one glorifying and turning to its principal and condemning those who oppose him. They do not believe in the correctness of acting by the others' views, as if the others belonged to an entirely different community. They exert and outdo themselves in refuting each other. They say, "Their books and our books differ, as do their scholars and ours and their schools and ours." All this they have done despite the fact that there is one Prophet, one Qur'an, one religion and one God. It is obligatory on all to submit to common terms between them. They must not follow anyone other than the Prophet. They must not appoint alongside him someone whose [ambiguous] words carry as much authority as his explicit ones. They must not take others as lords besides God. If they come to agreement on this, and if they all submit to the one who calls them to God and His Messenger, referring to the Sunnah and the narrations of the Companions for guidance, disagreement will be reduced, even if it does not entirely disappear from the world. This is why you will find that the people who have the least disagreement among themselves are the people of the Sunnah and *ḥadīth*. There is not, in the whole world, a faction more in harmony and with lesser disagreement in their midst than them because they base themselves on this principle [557]. The more a sect is removed from the *ḥadīth*, the greater and more severe is the disagreement in their midst. For every affair becomes confused and muddled for the one who rejects the

truth; it becomes ambiguous for him so he does not know where to turn, as the Most Majestic One said, *But they deny the Truth when it comes to them, so they are in a confused state.* [Q., Qāf, 50:5].

## ʿUmar Commanded Shurayḥ to Accord Precedence to the Qurʾan and Then the Sunnah

52. As for your statement, "ʿUmar wrote to Shurayḥ that he was to judge with the Book of God, and, if something was not to be found in it, then with what was in the Sunnah of His Messenger. If it is not found in that, then he was to judge according to what the righteous people decided." This is the clearest proof against you regarding the nullity of imitation. For ʿUmar commanded that Shurayḥ accord precedence to the Book of God over whatever else was besides it, and if he were not to find an answer in the Book and were to find it in the Sunnah, then he should not turn to anything other than that. And if he were not to find it in the Sunnah, then he should decide in the same manner as the Companions.

In the name of God, we ask the imitators if they do this, or anything resembling it. When a new situation presents itself before them, are any of them moved to try and discover a ruling thereupon from the Book of God and then to enforce it? If they do not find such a ruling in the Book of God, do they search for it in the Sunnah? If they do not find it in the Sunnah do they base their verdicts on those of the Companions? God and His angels bear witness over them, as they do over themselves, that they take their verdicts on such matters from the opinions of the ones they imitate. Even if a contrary opinion from the Book, the Sunnah, or the Companions is clear before them, they do not turn toward it, nor do they take anything from these sources except what agrees with the opinion of the one they imitate. The letter of ʿUmar, therefore, nullifies their statement and tears it down more than anything else. It demonstrates the perfect approach and the august guidance of the predecessors.

## The Way of Later Generations in Deriving Legal Rulings

When it came to the later generations, their practice was contrary to this, and they said, "If a new problem is presented before a *muftī* or a ruler, he must first see whether there is any disagreement in this area or not. If there is no disagreement, he does not need to look into the Book or the Sunnah. Rather, he issues a verdict and judgment based on consensus.* But if there is disagreement in it, then he exercises independent reasoning to find the view closest to the available evidence, and he issues a verdict and a ruling based on it." This is contrary to what is proved by the *ḥadīth* of Muʿādh, the letter of ʿUmar, and the statements of the Companions.

[The truth is that] what is proved by the Qurʾan, the Sunnah, and the Companions is preferable, as it is within our capacity, and it is what we have been commanded to follow. It is easier for the *mujtahid*s to know what the Qurʾan and Sunnah indicate than to know those rulings over which people in the far corners of the earth have reached agreement. The latter, if not absolutely impossible, is certainly the hardest and most burdensome of obligations (even though there are a few [major areas of agreement] that must be known of as a matter of religious necessity). How can God and His Messenger direct us to do something that is not within our reach? How can they direct us to abandon referring to His Book and the Sunnah of His Messenger, both of which He guided us to and made easy for us, so that we could reach and grasp the knowledge contained therein?

Further, people could well have disagreed without the scholar knowing this. The absence of knowledge about dispute does not indicate its [the dispute's] actual absence. So, how can he prefer this absence of knowledge about the occurrence of disagreement to the knowledge [attained through the Qurʾan and the Sunnah]? How, then, can it be permissible for him to abandon the truth which is known, and opt for [ruling on the basis of the supposed agreement of previous scholars], an affair about which he does not know, and about which the most that can be said is that it is likely. In the best case, there will still be as much doubt about the occurrence of this agreement as there is about those matters of which he does have knowledge. Or [there might even be] more.

On this basis, how can it be correct for one to say, "It is a necessary condition of consensus that the age of the people living during it should have ended? So long as their age has not passed, everyone is free to disagree with them." So it is not possible for the one who adopts this path to rely on consensus as a proof, until he knows that that age has passed, and there was no opposition in it to the views of the scholars of the time. In seeking guidance, has God directed the community to the Qurʾan and the Sunnah of His Messenger,

* A verdict is a *fatwa* issued by a *muftī*. It is a non-binding legal opinion by a scholar, while a judgment is a legally binding order issued by a *qāḍī*.

or has He directed them to gain knowledge of consensus that is impossible for them to attain and about which the people of the community can never know? Has He abandoned directing them to rely on the proof in their midst [the Qur'an], which remains till the end of time and by which it is possible for them to gain guidance and to discern truth? This is truly impossible.

When this trend started, the practice of abandonment of texts by relying on supposed consensus came into being. Then, claims in support of this began to surface. Now, when someone among the imitators who does not know of the disagreement [in a particular area of law] is argued against on the basis of the Qur'an and the Sunnah, he says, "This is against consensus." This is precisely what was rejected by the Imāms of Islam. They denounced the one who did this, and said, "Anyone making such a claim [of the existence of consensus] is a liar."

Imām Aḥmad, may God be pleased with him, said, in the narration of his son, 'Abdallāh, "Whoever [559] claims consensus has lied. It might well be that people actually did disagree. This [mistaken claim about the existence of consensus] is the claim of Bishr al-Marīrsī* and al-Aṣamm†. Rather, let [a person] say, 'We do not know of people disagreeing over this,' or, 'It has not reached us [that they did so].'"

He also said, in the narration of Marwazī‡, "How can it be permissible for a person to say, 'The scholars agreed'? When you hear them saying this, denounce them [as liars]. Had they said, 'I do not know of any disagreement,' that would have been acceptable."

He also said, in the narration of Abī Ṭālib§, "This [claim of consensus] is a lie. How can he have knowledge of the fact that all of mankind agreed on this? Rather he should say, 'I do not know of any disagreement herein.' This is better than saying that there is consensus among people."

He also said, in the narration of Abī al-Ḥārith**, "No one may claim consensus. It might be that people did indeed disagree."

---

* Abū 'Abd al-Raḥmān Bishr b. Ghiyāth b. Abī Karīmah al-Marīsī, one of the leading scholars of the Mu'tazilīs, who gained notoriety among the traditionalists for his espousal of heretical positions. He is reported to have debated al-Shāfi'ī.

† Abū Bakr 'Abd al-Raḥmān b. Kaysān al-Asamm (d. c. 225/840), a linguist and exegete, who was denounced for his association with various heretical sects.

‡ Muḥammad b. Naṣr b. al-Ḥajjāj al-Marwazī (d. 294/906), a leading jurist and traditionist.

§ Abū Ṭālib Aḥmad b. Ḥamīd al-Mishkānī (d. 244/858), a student of Aḥmad b. Ḥanbal.

** Abū al-Ḥārith Surayj b. Yūnus b. Ibrāhīm (d. 235/849), a contemporary of Aḥmad b. Ḥanbal.

## The Scholars of Islam Accord Precedence to the Book and the Sunnah

The scholars of Islam never ceased to accord precedence to the Book over the Sunnah and to the Sunnah over consensus, placing consensus in the third category [of sources from which law is derived]. Al-Shāfiʿī, may God be pleased with him, said, "Proof lies in the Book of God, the Sunnah [560] of His Messenger and the agreement of the scholars." In writing on his differences with Mālik, he said, "Knowledge is of different categories. In the first category is the Book and the confirmed Sunnah; then, consensus about that which is not found in the Book or the Sunnah; third, the statement of a Companion to which no other Companion is known to have objected; fourth, disagreement among the Companions; fifth, analogy." So he accorded precedence to examining the Qurʾan and Sunnah over consensus. Consensus is only to be resorted to when what the Qurʾan and Sunnah have to say on a matter is unknown. This indeed is the truth.

## The Way of the Knowledgeable Ones and the Scholars

Abū Ḥātim al-Rāzī* said, "Knowledge, for us, is what comes from God in the form of a Book that speaks and abrogates but is not itself abrogated [i.e., the Qurʾan], and those authentic reports about the Prophet about which there is no dispute. And whatever comes from the greatest of the Companions about that which they agreed on. If they disagreed, one may not venture outside the bounds of their disagreement. If this too is not clear and cannot be understood, then what comes from the Successors is adopted. If it is not found with the Successors, then with the righteous scholars from among those who followed here," such as Ayyūb al-Sakhtiyānī,† Ḥammād b. Zayd,‡ Ḥammād b. Salamah,§ Sufyān, Mālik,

*Abū Ḥātim Muḥammad b. Idrīs b. al-Mundhir al-Ḥanẓalī al-Rāzī (d. 77/697), a leading traditionist.

†Abū Bakr Ayyūb b. Abī Tamīmah Kaysān al-Sakhtiyānī (d. 131/748), a renowned traditionist.

‡Abū Ismāʿīl Ḥammād b. Zayd b. Dirham (d. 179/795), a Basran *ḥadīth* scholar.

§Abū Salamah Ḥammād b. Salamah b. Dīnār, a renowned Basran traditionist.

Awzāʿī,* and Ḥasan b. Ṣāliḥ.† If [the answer is] not to be found with their likes, then [it may be sought] among the likes of ʿAbd al-Raḥmān b. Mahdī,‡ ʿAbdallāh b. al-Mubārak,§ ʿAbdallāh b. Idrīs**, Yaḥyā b. Ādam,†† Ibn ʿUyaynah, Wakīʿ b. al-Jarrāḥ, and those after them, Muḥammad b. Idrīs al-Shāfiʿī, Yazīd b. Harūn,‡‡ al-Ḥumaydī,§§ Aḥmad b. Ḥanbal, Isḥāq b. Ibrahīm al-Ḥanẓalī,*** and Abū ʿUbayd al-Qāsim b. Sallām.†††

This is the way of the people of knowledge and the scholars of the religion. They regarded following the statements of the Companions (instead of the Qurʾan and the Sunnah) to be like purification with earth: it is only resorted to in the absence of water. These later imitators turned toward purification with earth, even while they had access to water, which was easier to use.

## The Way of the Later Imitators

After this came a group who were the enemies of knowledge and of its folk, who said, "If a matter comes before [561] a person who issues religious verdicts, whether he be a *muftī* or a judge, it is not permissible for him to look for an answer to it in the Book or the Sunnah of His Messenger nor to the statements of the Companions. Rather, he must only look to the statement of the one he imitates, his principal and the one whom he has made an authority over the Qurʾan and the Sunnah."

So he is to render judgments and verdicts according to whatever part [of the Qurʾan, the Sunnah, and the statements of the Companions] corresponds

---

*Abū ʿAmr ʿAbd al-Raḥmān b. ʿAmr al-Awzāʿī (d. 157/774), renowned jurist and founder of the school of law named after him.

†Abū ʿAbdallāh al-Ḥasan b. Ṣāliḥ b. Ṣāliḥ b. Muslim b. Ḥayy al-Hamadānī (d. 169/785), an early Kufan traditionist.

‡Abū Saʿīd ʿAbd al-Raḥmān b. Mahdī (d. 198/813), a Basran traditionist.

§Abū ʿAbd al-Raḥmān ʿAbdallāh b. al-Mubārak al-Ḥanẓalī (d. 181/797).

**ʿAbdallāh b. Idrīs al-Kūfī (d. 192/807), an early scholar and companion of Mālik.

††Abū Zakariyyā Yaḥyā b. Ādam b. Sulaymān al-Amawī (or al-Umawī), a renowned Kufan scholar. Some authorities report that he died in 203/818, while others report a much later date.

‡‡Abū Khālid Yazīd b. Hārūn (d. 206/821), an early scholar and Qurʾan commentator.

§§Abū Bakr ʿAbdallāh b. al-Zubayr al-Ḥumaydī (d. 219/834), an important traditionist.

***i.e. Ibn Rāḥawayh, whose details have been provided above.

†††Abū ʿUbayd al-Qāsim b. Sallām al-Khurāsānī (d. 224/838, in Mecca), a leading traditionist scholar.

to the views of the one he imitates. It is impermissible for him, [in their view,] to issue a verdict or judgment according to that part thereof that opposes the views of the one he imitates. If he does so, he is subject to dismissal from his post of delivering verdicts and judgments.

A verdict is then sought against him [by the imitators, in the following form]: "What do the noble scholars say about the one who is associated with a specific school which he imitates to the exclusion of all others, who then renders a verdict or a judgment opposing his school? Is it permissible for him to do this or not? Does this not establish his villainy?" The [scholars of the] imitators then lower their heads and say, "It is not permissible for him to do this, and it does establish his villainy." This they would do, even if the opinion the scholar inclined to was the opinion of Abū Bakr, ʿUmar, Ibn Masʿūd, ʿUbayy b. Kaʿb, Muʿādh b. Jabal, or their likes. The response of the one who has appointed himself to issue verdicts on behalf of God and His Messenger is that it is not permissible for him to oppose the statement of his principal for the statements of one who is more knowledgeable than him about God and His Messenger. This holds even though the Qurʾan and Sunnah are in support of the statement of the other scholar. This is one of the gravest crimes against the religion committed by the imitators.

If only they had confined themselves to their limit and rank and conveyed abstract theoretical knowledge about whatever they found to be suspect in the statement of their principals. If only they had acknowledged that they did not have any knowledge about whether these statements of their principals were right or wrong, they might have had an argument to present before God to justify their actions. But this is the limit of their knowledge. Such is their animosity toward the people of knowledge and those who uphold proofs based on knowledge. Success is with God.

## Did the Companions Imitate ʿUmar?

53. As for your statement, "ʿUmar forbade the sale of slave women who had borne children to their masters, and the Companions followed him in that, and he enforced the triple divorce as an irrevocable divorce, and they followed him in that as well," there are several answers.

First, they did not follow him in imitation of him. Rather, their independent reasoning in these matters led them to the same conclusions as his reasoning had led him to. Not a single one of them said, "I act thus because I imitate ʿUmar."

Second, not all of them followed him. Thus, Ibn Masʿūd opposed him regarding the sale of slave women who had borne children to their masters. Ibn ʿAbbās opposed him in the enforcement of the triple divorce [as an irrevocable one].[127] [562] So when the Companions and others disagreed, the ruler's [i.e., ʿUmar's] was the proof [which had to prevail].

Third, even if ʿUmar was followed, and even if it is supposed that he was imitated by the Companions, there is still no proof for the permissibility of imitating someone quite beneath him in everything that other person says, nor for abandoning the opinions of those who are more knowledgeable than him. To infer to the contrary is among the most pernicious of inferences, [a position so weak it is akin to] dangling from a spider's nest. You should imitate ʿUmar and abandon imitation of everyone else, although you are content that ʿUmar should not be imitated while Abū Ḥanīfah, al-Shāfiʿī, and Mālik should be imitated. You cannot argue on the basis of something you yourselves go against. How is it possible for a man to rely on an argument that he himself does not accept?

## An Explanation of ʿUmar's Statement: "Had I Done So, It Would Have Become a Practice"

54. As for your statement, "ʿAmr b. al ʿĀṣ said to ʿUmar, when he had a wet dream, 'Wear another garment.' But ʿUmar declined, saying, 'If I were to do so, it would become a Sunnah.'" So where is the proof in this that ʿUmar allowed imitation of himself and that he allowed turning away from the Qurʾan and the Sunnah of the Messenger? The extent of his dislike of this is that he did not wear another garment, lest he be followed by those who saw him. He did this to ensure that they would not follow him and in order that they would not be able to say, "If this was not the Sunnah of the Messenger of God, may the peace and blessings of God be on him, ʿUmar would not have done it." So this is what ʿUmar feared, for people tend to follow their scholars, whether the scholars like it or not. This, then, is the reality, even though it is necessary to explain this issue further.

## Acting upon That Which Is Clear and Leaving the Ambiguous to the One Who Has Knowledge of It

55. As for your statement, "'Ubayy said, 'Whatever seems doubtful to you, refer it to the one who knows more about it.'" [563] This is the truth. This is what is obligatory on everyone, other than the Messenger. For there is no doubt that all those after him will be confused about some matter that appears before them. Everyone in this position must refer this matter to the one who has more knowledge. If it then becomes clear to them, they become knowledgeable like him. If not, then, having referred it to the one who possessed greater erudition, they incur no liability for that which they do not know. This is what is obligatory on us in relation to the Book of our Lord, the Sunnah of His Messenger, and the statements of his Companions. God, the Exalted, has created over every knowledgeable one another who is yet more so. So, whoever finds some of the truth eluding him and refers it to the one who has more knowledge than him has done what is proper. Does this constitute turning away from the Qur'an, the Sunnah, and the reports of the Companions and choosing a specific individual to be an arbiter over all this? [How could this set a precedent allowing] abandonment of the texts because of their contradiction to his views, weighing the Qur'an and the Sunnah against them, accepting everything he delivers as a verdict and rejecting that which opposes it?

This report [of 'Ubayy] is the most convincing proof of the illegitimacy of imitation. The first part of it says, "Whatever is clear to you, act on it; and whatever is not clear, refer it to the one who knows about it." So we ask you, by God, if the Sunnah is clear to you, will you abandon the statement of the one you imitate in favor of it? Will you act on it and issue verdicts and judgments based on it or will you leave it and abandon it in favor of his opinion, with the excuse that he is more knowledgeable about it than we are? For that is the legacy of 'Ubayy, along with all the other Companions. They were firm on this legacy, which nullifies imitation absolutely. God grants success.

Then we say, "Did you refer those matters about which you were confused, to the ones who had knowledge about them from among the Companions of the Messenger of God, as they were the most knowledgeable of the community and the most exalted in rank? Or did you leave their opinions and turn away from them? Even if the ones whom you imitate are among those who are to be referred to in these matters, the Companions are more deserving of this than others."

## The Verdicts of the Companions, While the Prophet Was Alive, Were Narrations from Him

56. As for your statement, "The Companions used to issue verdicts while the Prophet was alive in their midst, so the people who sought verdicts from them were imitating them." The answer to this is that their verdicts consisted of relating rulings from God and His Messenger. So they were only acting as transmitters of the Sunnah. Their verdicts were not in imitation of others and were not followed, even if they were opposed by the texts of the Qur'an and the Sunnah. So they did not imitate in issuing verdicts nor did they do so without basing the latter on the texts. The ones seeking verdicts only relied on the ones being asked to deliver them for what the latter reported concerning their Prophet. [564] Therefore, the ones being asked would say, "He acted thus," or "He forbade this." Such were their verdicts, a proof for the ones seeking them, just as they were a proof for the Companions themselves. There was no difference between the Companions and the ones seeking verdicts, except in relation to the proximity between them and the Messenger, or the absence thereof. God, His Messenger, and all the people of knowledge know that the Companions and the ones who sought verdicts from them did not act, except on the basis of what they knew from their Messenger and what they had observed from him, or heard from him, some through an intermediary and some without.

There was no one among them who would adopt the opinions of one individual among the community and deem permissible whatever this individual had said was so and deem forbidden whatever this individual had declared so. Nor would they allow whatever this individual had allowed. The Prophet had admonished those among them who issued verdicts based on something other than the Sunnah. Just as he admonished* Abī al-Sanābil[128] and the one who issued a verdict that the virgin adulterer

*Abū l-Sanābil b. Ba'kak b. al-Ḥajjāj b. al-Ḥārith b. Quṣayy al-Qurashī, a poet and a Companion of the Prophet.

should be stoned to death,[129] and the one who issued a verdict that a wounded area must be washed, even though it led to the death of the man who washed his wound. He also admonished the one who delivered a verdict without knowledge and the one who issues verdicts whose authenticity he does not know about. The Prophet said that the sin in such cases was on the one who dispensed the verdict. Therefore, the verdicts of the Companions in the life of the Prophet were of two kinds: first, some of the verdicts of the Companions would reach the Prophet, and he would approve of them. These would become proofs by virtue of the Prophet's approval, not merely by the acts of the Companions who issued them. The second kind were the verdicts they issued in which they were only relating the affairs of their Prophet. So in this, they were narrators, neither imitating nor being imitated.

## The Real Meaning of God Obligating Some People to Accept Warnings from a Party that Gains Understanding in the Religion

57. As for your statement, "The Words of God, the Most High, *Nor should the Believers all go forth together,* [565] *if a party from every expedition remained behind, they could devote themselves to gain understanding in religion, and warn the people when they return to them* [Q., al-Tawbah, 9:122]—it is obligatory to accept their warnings and this is imitation of them."

There are several answers to this. First, God, the Most High, commands them to accept the warnings received from the revelation sent to the Prophet during the absence of the people in *jihād*. So where is the proof in this for the people of imitation in preferring the opinions of men over revelation?

Second, the verse is a clear proof against them. For the Most Perfect One divided their obedience to Him and their upholding of His Command into two categories. The first is going out for *jihād*, and the second, learning the religion. He linked the establishment of the religion with these two groups: the rulers and the scholars. So those who do battle fight on behalf of those who remain behind, whereas those who stay behind safeguard religious knowledge for those who have gone out to fight. When they return from their expedition, they are made aware of all the knowledge that escaped them, by someone who heard the same from the Messenger of God, may the peace and blessings of God be on him. People hold one of these two views regarding this verse.

According to the first of these, the meaning is, "Why does not a party from each group go forth to gain understanding into the religion and to warn those [gathered to fight at] the base camp?," so the meaning would be [going forth] for the acquisition of religious knowledge. This is the opinion of al-Shāfiʿī and a group among the commentators. They relied on this to prove the acceptability of a narration reported by one person, because it is not necessary that a "party" consist of the number of people required to reach the level of continuously recurrent testimony [*tawātur*].

According to the second view, the meaning of the verse is, "Why does not a party go forth to fight to allow those left behind to gain religious knowledge and to warn the party gone forth when they return to them and to inform them of the revelation that was sent down after they had left?" This, the opinion of the majority, is the correct one. This is because "party" [the word *nafīr* in the verse] is to go out for *jihād*, as said by the Prophet, "When you are called for *jihād*, then go forth."[130] Also, the term "Believers" could be common to those who stayed with the Prophet and those who were away. However, it is, without a doubt, those who stayed with him who are intended, they being the best of the Believers. So how can the word "Believers" not include them? According to the first group of interpreters, the term "Believers" applies only to those who are absent. So the meaning according to them is, "It is not for the Believers to go out altogether to the Prophet. Why does not a party of each go to him?" This is against the clear meaning of the word "Believers." It is also a departure from the way the root *n-f-r* is used in the Qur'an and Sunnah. Either way, there is nothing in the verse that would require acceptance of the condemned category of imitation as valid. Rather, it is a proof of its corruption and nullity. [566]

This is because warning is only achieved with proof. So the one on whom the proof is not established has not been warned. Likewise, the one who actually warns is the one who has established the evidence. Whoever does not present a proof is not a warner. If you name this kind of activity "imitation," then know that the real problem here is not with nomenclature. We do not deny the validity of this kind of imitation so you can name it whatever you like. What we denounce is appointing one specific individual and considering his opinions the arbiter of the Qur'an and Sunnah, so that whatever in them agrees with his views is accepted and whatever does not is rejected. You do all this while you accept the opinions of this individual without proof. You also reject the views of his peers or the one more knowledgeable than him, even while the proofs favor him. This is what we reject. Moreover, every scholar on the face of the earth declares his rejection and condemnation of this and of those who do it.

## Zubayr Adopted the View of Abū Bakr Regarding the Inheritance of the Grandfather

58. As for your statement that Zubayr was asked about the inheritance of the grandfather when he exists alongside the brothers of the deceased, and he said, "As for the one about whom the Messenger of God said, 'If I were to take a friend among the people of the earth, I would take him as one' (and by that he meant Abū Bakr), 'then he regarded the grandfather as being like the father.'" So is there anything in this that proves the validity of imitation in any way? The clear, irrefutable proofs which indicate that the opinion of the truthful one [i.e., Abū Bakr] about the inheritance of the grandfather is the most correct out of all the opinions on this matter, have already been mentioned. Ibn al-Zubayr did not put forth this view of his in imitation. Rather, he attributed this view to Abū Bakr to illustrate the majesty of the one who held this view and to clarify that he is the one to whom no other can be compared. Ibn al-Zubayr did not mention Abū Bakr in order that his opinion would be adopted without a proof, nor so that proofs from the Qur'an and Sunnah would be abandoned in favor of his view. Ibn al-Zubayr and the other Companions were among the most God-fearing of people. God's established Proof and His clear Statements were too dear to them to even countenance abandoning them for the opinions of mere men or the opinions of one man, whoever he may be. The statement of Ibn al-Zubayr, "The truthful one—i.e., Abū Bakr—regarded the grandfather as being like the father," therefore includes the ruling and the proof together.

## Accepting the Testimony of a Witness Does Not Imply That He Is Imitated

59. As for your statement, "God has commanded that we accept the testimony of the witness and this is imitation of him." This proof for the validity of imitation, had it existed without any other, would have been sufficient to establish its abhorrence. Do we base our acceptance of the testimony of a witness on anything other than a clear textual proof

from the Book of our Lord, the Sunnah of our Messenger and the consensus of the community, that his statement is to be accepted? It is God, the Most Glorious, who made the testimony of a witness an acceptable proof by which a judge can decide cases, just as he does so on the basis of confessions, which have also been made an acceptable means of proof in sacred law.

Now, the statement of the one who confesses to a crime is, likewise, a proof in the sacred law. Acceptance of that can also be referred to as imitation of him. So, just as you claim that accepting the testimony of a witness is imitation of him, you may call this acceptance of a confession whatever you desire. The fact is that God, the Exalted, has commanded us to judge on the basis of these confessions and testimonies. He validated these as proofs by which legal rulings are established [567]. Therefore, the one who judges on the basis of testimony and confession is enforcing the command of God and of His Messenger. If we were not to imitate the witness, no legal rulings could ever be enforced. The Prophet himself delivered judgments on the basis of witnesses and confessions,[131] but all this constitutes ruling according to the actual command that God had revealed. It does not fall under [the rubric of] ruling in accordance with imitation. It is a burial of the truth and a complete surrender of the intellect to argue on the basis of all this to prove the validity of the type of imitation which involves turning away from the Book, the Sunnah, and the views of the Companions, and to prefer the opinions of other people over all of these. To accord a less knowledgeable man precedence over a more knowledgeable one and to discard altogether the opinions of everyone who opposes him is the same thing.

In sum, when we accept the statement of a witness to an act, we do not accept it just because of the fact that he was a witness. Rather, we do so because God, the Most High, commanded us to accept his testimony. As for you, people of imitation, when you accept the statement of the one you imitate, do you accept it just because of the fact that he said it or is it because God commanded you to accept his statements and reject everything other than that?

## Accepting the Veracity of Someone Who Traces Ancestry Is Not Imitation

60. As for your statement, "The sacred law mandates accepting the statement of the one who traces ancestry and of those who estimate quantities of saleable goods, one who is called on to apportion commodities,

> the expert who appraises the cluster of ripening fruit, and the two judges who decide what qualifies as an equivalent atonement to be offered for hunting while in a state of ritual sanctity. And all this is manifest imitation." Do you mean by this that this is imitation of some scholars in accepting their views or in that which they relate? If you espouse the former position, this is erroneous. If you mean the latter, then there is no comfort to be had from this argument for the imitation whose falsity has been established through the evidence. Accepting the statements of these people falls in the category of accepting the narration of a reporter and witness. It is not from the category of accepting verdicts in the religion without establishing evidence for their veracity. Rather, this is allowed only because of a reasonable belief about the truthfulness of the one who makes this statement, while allowing for the possibility that he may have erred [568]. So how is the acceptance of news, testimony, and confessions comparable to imitation in issuing verdicts? The one who relates anything about these affairs informs others about matters that become perceptible to the senses by way of knowledge. He himself came to know of all this with his manifest senses and faculties of discernment. God, the Exalted, commanded that the statement of the one who informs us about all this is to be accepted if it is apparently true and honest. Accepting the statement of a person who conveys a report from the Messenger of God, about his actions or speech, may the peace and blessings of God be on him, is similar to this, as is accepting such a statement from the one who narrates it from the one who narrates it from the Prophet and so forth. This is the truth. Nobody disagrees on it.

Regarding the imitation of someone else's views in their entirety, all that we know thereof is that these are his opinions and deductions. Therefore, imitating him here is no different from imitating him when he relates what he saw, heard or knew. How does this obligate or even permit us to issue verdicts based on his opinion, to judge with it, to deem this our means of submission to God, and to say, "This is the truth and whatever opposes it is erroneous?" And to add, "We shall reject the texts of the Qur'an, the Sunnah, the narrations of the Companions, and the opinions of all the people of knowledge who opposed him!"

Also included in this category is the imitation by the blind man of someone who indicates the direction of Mecca so he can pray facing it, as well as [imitating him regarding] the arrival of the time of prayer. Ibn Umm

Maktūm would not make the call to prayer until he imitated someone who told him of the arrival of daybreak. It would be said to him repeatedly, "Daybreak has come." Similar to this is the imitation of the muezzin by the people regarding the commencement of the appointed time of prayer. Similar, too, is imitation by the one in an underground cove of the one who informs him of the times of prayers and the breaking and starting time of the fast and so forth. Also in this category lies the imitation related to [all the examples presented by the imitators, such as] the acceptance of translation, the authenticity of letters and introductions, and the pointing out of someone's flaws or merits. All of this is from the category of those reports in which God has commanded that the one transmitting the report be accepted if he is upright and truthful. People have unanimously agreed to accept a person's statement about the giving of a gift and the entry of one spouse unto the other [i.e., the occurrence of sexual intercourse in marriage]. Similarly, they agree over accepting the testimony of a woman (whether she is Muslim or a non-Muslim protected woman [*dhimmī*]), about the timing of the ending of her menstrual bleeding and the [resultant] permissibility of having intercourse with her or marrying her off in reliance on these statements.

None of this proves the validity of imitation in the issuance of verdicts or judgments. If this is imitation of her statement, then God has legislated for us that we accept this and imitate her in it. He would not have legislated for us that we take religious orders from Him through someone other than His Messenger, let alone that we abandon the Sunnah for the opinion of one man among the people of knowledge and prefer his views over those of all other scholars.

## Buying of Food Without Inquiry Regarding Its Lawfulness

61. As for your statement, "There is a consensus on the permissibility of purchasing different types of meat, [569] edibles, garments, and their likes without enquiring as to their permissibility and thus imitating their owners." The answer to all such arguments is that this is not imitation regarding a command of God and His Messenger without evidence. Rather, it is being satisfied with the declaration of the slaughterer or the seller. This is following and being guided by the command of God and His Messenger. Even if the slaughterers and sellers are Jews, Christians, or evil-doers, we would rely on their declarations in

these matters. We do not ask about the exact means by which these items were rendered permissible. As ʿĀʾishah said, "O Messenger of God, people come to us with varieties of meat, and we do not know whether the name of God has been recited on them or not," so he said, "You can pronounce the name of God over them and consume them."[132] So would imitation of the unbelievers and evil-doers in all matters of religion also be permissible for you as you claim to imitate them in matters dealing with slaughtering and foodstuffs?

Leave aside these lifeless arguments, and enter with us in a spirit of acceptance of proofs that distinguish between righteousness and falsehood. We shall enter a binding pact with you, that we accept the overarching authority of the Book of God and the Sunnah of His Messenger and that we shall make them the judge and abandon the opinions of mere men in favor of them. We shall follow the truth wherever it is and shall agree not to be biased in favor of anyone [as an authority], other than the Messenger whose every statement we accept, rejecting every opinion which goes against his. If not, then you may testify that we are the first to denounce this approach of imitation and we turn away from it, and call to its opposite. God is the Helper.

## Are All People Obliged to Perform *Ijtihād*?

62. As for your statement, "If all people had been obligated to perform *ijtihād* and to be scholars, the well-being of humanity would have come to an end, commerce and trade would have to be suspended. Such a thing is impossible in the religion and in divine decree."

There are several answers to this. It is among the mercies and kindnesses of God, the Most Perfect, upon us that He has not obligated us with performing imitation. If He had done so, our affair of existence would have come to an end, and our welfare would have been undermined. This is because we would not know who among the *muftī*s and religious scholars should be imitated. Their number is thought to be over two hundred—and actually, no one knows their real number, except God—for Muslims have populated the earth in the East, West, North, and South and Islam, by the Grace of God, spread as far as the distance of the night. If we were obligated with imitation, we would have become involved in things that were most futile and discordant. [And if we were obligated with imitation of every scholar], we would have been compelled to hold a thing both permissible and forbidden, and obligatory and prohibited, all at the same time [because of their differences]. If we were obligated with imitation of the most knowledgeable scholars, [570] it would remain far easier to gain knowledge of the rulings of the Qur'an and Sunnah than to gain knowledge of the identity of this scholar in whom all the qualifications for being imitated are met. Knowledge of this is, in fact, difficult to gain, even for the learned scholar, let alone the imitator who is like a blind person. If we were only obligated with imitation of some scholars and were left to choose this depending on our wishes and choices, the religion of God would have to follow our wills, choices, and desires. This is absolutely unthinkable. There is no doubt that all these differences are to be referred to the one whose obedience God Himself commanded and from whom we were commanded to acquire the religion. And that is Muḥammad, the son of ʿAbdallāh, the son of ʿAbd al-Muṭṭalib, the Messenger of God, the one who fulfilled the trust of revelation and the one whom He chose as a proof over all of creation. God did not create such a rank for anyone other than him.

Second, reasoning and refined deduction lead to the betterment of affairs, not to their corruption, while neglecting these and imitating someone who is sometimes right and sometimes wrong leads to the ruin and corruption of man's interests, as has been witnessed.

Third, we are all commanded to affirm the truthfulness of whatsoever is related from the Messenger and to obey his commands. But this cannot happen, except after knowing his commands and narrations. God did not obligate anything on the community, except that which would save its religion and its worldly affairs, thereby improving its present life along with the life to come. In neglecting this obligation of being guided by Him lies the abandonment of the community's welfare and the corruption of its affairs. The world is not rendered worse, except by ignorance, and is not built, except upon knowledge. When knowledge is prevalent in a city or a community, its residents are less prone to evil. Whenever it is absent, evil and corruption creep in. Whoever does not realize this is one of those whom God has not granted true insight. Imām Aḥmad said, "If it were not for knowledge, people would be like beasts." He also said, "People are in greater need of knowledge than of food and drink. For these are only needed twice or thrice a day, whereas knowledge is needed at all times."

Fourth, what is obligatory on man is to know the legal rulings that specifically concern him. There is no obligation on him to know that which is not needed. Acquiring this knowledge does not involve abandoning his welfare nor the suspension of his worldly life. The Companions were engaged in their daily lives, seeking sustenance through agriculture, livestock, and travelling around the earth for purposes of trade and concluding contracts in markets. Despite this they were the most knowledgeable of scholars, who cannot be equaled. [571]

Fifth, the useful knowledge that the Messenger came with was free of legal hypothetical what-ifs, guesswork, fictitious legal conundrums, puzzles, and riddles. And this religion, by the Grace of God, is the easiest thing for one to acquire, commit to memory, and comprehend. [This religion is] the Book of God which He has made easy to understand, as He says, *And We have indeed made the Qur'an easy to understand and remember, then is there anyone who will receive admonition?* [Q., al-Qamar, 54:17].

Al-Bukhārī said, in his *Ṣaḥīḥ,* that Maṭr al-Warrāq* said, "Is there anyone who seeks knowledge? Anyone who does will be helped." He did not say about such a person that "his interests will be ruined and his worldly life suspended." The Sunnah of the Messenger is, by the Grace of God, firm and safe. The principles underlying religious rulings are based on nearly five hundred *aḥādīth,* while its underlying foundation and details are based on around four thousand *aḥādīth.* What is extremely hard and difficult are the mental hypothetical what-ifs, the legal sophisms, captious questions, issues, sub-issues, and principles for which God did not reveal any authority or sanction. The success of the imitators' method is measured by excess, increase, and multiplication [in such hypotheticals]. As for the religion, its success is measured by its profound simplicity. God is the Helper.

## The Number of Reports on Which the Principles and Details of Rulings Are Based

63. As for your statement, "People have agreed on the validity of the groom imitating [i.e., being led by] the one who guides him to his bride on the night of their wedding; of the blind man, regarding the direction of Mecca for the prayer and its time; of the muezzins [for learning of the times of prayer]; of the prayer leaders, in matters of ritual purity and the recitation of the Opening Chapter†; and imitation

*Abū Rajā' Maṭr b. Ṭahmān al-Warrāq al-Khurāsānī (d. 229/843), a Successor.

†According to some schools of law, an *imām*'s recitation of the Opening Chapter of the Qur'ān in ritual prayer suffices for those praying behind him.

of the wife regarding the end of her period and intercourse and marriage with her."

The answer to this has preceded. Your inference in this is incorrect. This is not the imitation [572] that was condemned by the earliest and later generations at all. We do not accept the statements of these people because they inform us of them but because God and His Messenger commanded that their statements be accepted and they established them as proofs on the basis of which legal judgments could be issued. So the information [conveyed by these categories of people] carries the same weight as testimony and confession. How does any of this render it permissible to imitate in religious commands, turning away from the Qur'an and the Sunnah by appointing one specific person to act as an arbiter over the Book of God and the Sunnah of His Messenger?

## The Case of ʿUqbah b. al-Ḥārith Is Not a Proof for the Imitators

64. As for your statement, "The Prophet commanded ʿUqbah b. al-Ḥārith to imitate the woman who claimed she had breast-fed him and his wife [by separating from his wife]."

How wondrous, by God—for you yourselves do not imitate her in this matter! Even if she were one of the Wives of the Prophet [you would not imitate her in this], nor would you accept and act according to this *ḥadīth*. In fact, you reject it in favor of your principal whom you imitate. Is there anything in this that proves that imitation in the religion of God is permissible? Does this *ḥadīth* prove anything other than the validity of accepting the claim of a person about a physical, sensory matter about which she forwards a claim? Or, is it not like accepting the testimony of a witness? Was ʿUqbah's separation from his wife carried out in imitation of this woman or out of obedience to the Messenger of God when he commanded that ʿUqbah separate from her? It is the blessing of imitation that you yourselves do not command that the husband in a similar situation [i.e., one who finds that he and his wife were breast-fed by the same woman] separate from her. Rather, you say to such a man, "She is your wife, with whom it is lawful for you to have intercourse." As for us, the evidence compels us to command the one who is faced with a similar situation as the Prophet commanded ʿUqbah b. al-Ḥārith. Nor do we abandon the *ḥadīth* in imitation of a particular individual.*

## Refutation of the View That the Scholars Allowed Imitation

65. As for your statement, "The scholars have clearly stated the permissibility of imitation." For Sufyān said, "When you see a man performing an action that is wrong, according to you, do not stop him." And Muḥammad b. Ḥasan said, "It is permissible for a scholar to imitate one who is more knowledgeable than he is, not one who is of the same rank as him." Al-Shāfiʿī also said on more than one occasion, "I have said this imitating ʿUmar," or, "I have said this in imitation of ʿUthmān," or, "I have said this in imitation of ʿAṭāʾ," there are several answers to this.

First, if you are claiming that all the scholars issued clear statements regarding the permissibility of imitation [573], this is a false claim. We have mentioned a sufficient number of statements from the Companions, the Successors, and the scholars of Islam relating to their prohibition of imitation and their condemnation of it and of those who advocate it.

## How Did the Scholars Regard the Imitator?

They would call the imitator a freeloader, one who follows other people in his religion. As Ibn Masʿūd said, "the freeloader is one who follows others in his religion." They used to call such a person a blind man, having no insight. They also referred to the imitator as the one who followed every bawler having something to say and who thereby inclines to everyone who hollers. They said the imitator was the one who was not illuminated by the light of knowledge nor supported by any firm foundation, as was said by ʿAlī b. Abī Ṭālib about them. Al-Shāfiʿī labeled the imitator as the one who collects wood at night, and he prohibited imitation of him and of everyone else. So may God grant him a goodly reward for his services to Islam. He counseled sincerity to God, His Messenger, and the Muslims and called to the Book of God and the Sunnah of His Messenger. He commanded that these sources be followed instead of his own views. Al-Shāfiʿī also

*The reference here is to the Ḥanafīs, who do not require such a couple to separate.

commanded that we present his opinions before these sources, accepting from his opinions whatever conforms to them and rejecting whatever is opposed by them. We ask the imitators, "By God, have you preserved his legacy in this matter and obeyed him, or have you revolted, rebelled, and gone against what he said?" Besides, even if you claim that a particular scholar did allow imitation, this would only be the scholar's own view.

Second, those about whom you claim that they allowed imitation of the ones who were more knowledgeable than them were actually the ones who ran farthest in dread of imitation. They were among the most adamant followers of proofs and among the strongest critics of those who were more knowledgeable than themselves. You acknowledge that Abū Ḥanīfah was more knowledgeable than Muḥammad b. Ḥasan and Abū Yūsuf, whereas their disagreements with him [i.e., Abū Ḥanīfah] are well known. It has also been authentically reported from Abū Yūsuf that he said, "It is not permissible for anyone to say what we have said, unless he knows our reasons for saying so."

Third, you relentlessly deny that those whom you imitate among the scholars were themselves imitating others. Thus do you rise and fall with the statement of al-Shāfiʿī, "I have said this imitating ʿUmar," and "I have said this in imitation of ʿUthmān," and "I have said this in imitation of ʿAṭāʾ." However, when it came to deciding whether or not his dicta could be reconciled with his [fame for carrying out] *ijtihād*, you became extremely confused [574]. Thus, you claimed that he did not imitate Zayd in matters of inheritance law, but that he exercised *ijtihād* and that his conclusions [happened to] match those of Zayd, even in the inheritance case known as "al-Akdariyyah."* Thus, you claimed that it was his *ijtihād* [that happened to be carried out] in exactly the same way [as that of Zayd]. So how then can you ascribe being an imitator to him now? But this contradiction on your part has only come about as a mercy of imitation. If you had followed knowledge and evidence wherever they came from, being guided by the proofs, you would not have been involved in this contradiction and would have given everyone his due merit.

Fourth, this argument of yours is among the strongest proofs against you. Al-Shāfiʿī clearly said that he imitated ʿUmar, ʿUthmān, and ʿAṭāʾ, despite the fact that he was among the scholars who exercised *ijtihād*.

---

*A case in which the propositus is survived by her husband, her mother, full sister, and paternal grandfather.

Whereas you, despite your acknowledgement that you are mere imitators, do not allow imitation of a single one among the Companions. Rather, if al-Shāfiʿī has said one thing and ʿUmar, ʿUthmān, and Ibn Masʿūd—let alone Saʿīd b. al Muṣayyib, ʿAṭāʾ, and al-Ḥasan*—have said another, you leave imitation of all of them and imitate al-Shāfiʿī. This is manifest contradiction. So you have disagreed with his approach, even while thinking that you were imitating him. If you imitate al-Shāfiʿī, then imitate the one he imitated. If you were to say, "We do imitate them in those matters wherein Shāfiʿī imitated them," it would have to be said, "This is not the same as you imitating them, rather you are continuing to imitate him." Otherwise, whenever an opinion contradicting his had been related from them, you would not have accepted a single one of his opinions.

Fifth, those scholars whom you mention did not imitate in the same way as you do. They certainly did not allow it. Rather, the most that can be established about them is imitation in those trivial matters concerning which they could not find a clear text from God and His Messenger, and they were unable to find anything other than the opinions of someone more knowledgeable, so they imitated the latter. This is the practice of the people of knowledge, and it is obligatory. For imitation is permissible for the one who is compelled to do it. As for the one who turns away from the Book, the Sunnah, the opinions of the Companions, and knowledge of the truth with its proofs, while he had access to all this, in favor of imitation, he is like the one who has recourse to carrion while he has the ability to opt for that which has been ritually slaughtered. The basic principle is that the opinion of another may not be accepted without proof, except in cases of necessity. You have made this case of necessity your basic capital.

## [4:5] The Difference between the Rank of the Scholars and the Imitator

66. As for your statement, "al-Shāfiʿī, may God be pleased with him, said, 'The opinions of the Companions are better for us than our own opinions.' Likewise we, too, affirm that the view of al-Shāfiʿī is better for us than our own opinions," there are several answers.

* Abū Saʿīd al-Ḥasan b. Abī al-Ḥasan al-Baṣrī (d. 110/728), one of the most renowned Successors and a leading authority in traditionalist circles.

First, you are the foremost opponents of his view. You do not regard the opinions of the Companions as being better for you than the opinions of the scholars themselves. Rather, you say, "The opinions of the scholars are better for us than those of the Companions." So if one verdict comes from Abū Bakr, ʿUmar, ʿUthmān, ʿAlī, and the greatest of the Companions, and another from al-Shāfiʿī, Abū Ḥanīfah, and Mālik, you abandon that which comes from the Companions and adopt the verdict of the scholars. Would the Companions' opinions not have been better for you than those of the scholars, if you were sincere in desiring your own good?

## Excellence of the Companions and Their Knowledge

Second, this principle, even if it is accepted, does not obligate the imitation of anyone other than the Companions. This is because of how they were chosen by God in terms of knowledge, understanding, merit, and insight into the religion of God and His Messenger. They witnessed the revelation, and they acquired the religion from the Prophet, with no intermediary. It was revealed in their language while it was still unsullied, pure, and free of corruption. They could return to the Messenger of God to ask him to explain all that was difficult in the Qurʾan and the Sunnah, until it was clarified to them. So who had this privilege after them? Who is there who even shared this rank with them so that that he should be imitated just as they are, let alone that imitation of him should be made obligatory while forbidding it when it comes to them, as some of the extreme partisans among the imitators have done. By God, between the Companions and those whom you imitate there is as much difference of knowledge as of rank.

Al-Shāfiʿī said, in the *Old Epistle* [*Risālah al-qadīmah*], after mentioning the Companions and their greatness and merits, "They are better than us in every area of knowledge, legal reasoning, God-consciousness, intellect, and every matter which was rectified after them. Their opinions are more praiseworthy and preferable to us than our own." Al-Shāfiʿī also said, "God Himself praised the Companions in the Qurʾan, the Torah, and the Bible, and the Prophet has already praised them in a manner that does not apply to anyone after them."

In the two *Ṣaḥīḥ* collections of traditions [those of al-Bukhārī and Muslim] it is reported from the narration of ʿAbdallāh b. Masʿūd, from the

Prophet, that he said, [6] "The best of people are my generation, then those who come after them, then those who come after them. Then people will come who will hasten to testify even before taking oaths and who will hasten to take oaths even before they are called to testify." And in the two *Ṣaḥīḥs*, from the *ḥadīth* of Abū Saʿīd* it is reported that the Prophet said, "Do not curse my Companions. For even if one of you were to spend as much as the mountain of ʿUhud in charity, you would not come near any of them in reward by as much as a handful, or even half a handful."[133] Ibn Masʿūd said, "God looked into the hearts of His servants, and he found that the heart of Muḥammad was the best of hearts among His servants. Then He looked to the hearts of men and found the hearts of the Companions the best of hearts among His servants, so He chose them for his companionship. He chose them as helpers of His religion and deputies of His Prophet. So whatever the Believers regard as good is good in the sight of God, and whatever they regard as reprehensible is reprehensible in the sight of God."[134] [7] The Messenger of God commanded us to follow the Sunnah of the rightly guided Caliphs, and, in particular, to follow the two Caliphs [Abū Bakr and ʿUmar]. Abū Saʿīd said, "Abū Bakr was the most knowledgeable among us about the Messenger of God."[135] The Messenger bore witness to Ibn Masʿūd's knowledge.[136] He also prayed for Ibn ʿAbbās, that he be granted insight into the religion and taught the art of interpretation of the Qurʾan. He embraced him on one occasion and said, "O God, grant him wisdom."[137] And in his dream, he handed ʿUmar a bowl of milk from which ʿUmar drank [8] until he was sated and the milk emerged from beneath his fingernails, and he interpreted this as a sign of ʿUmar's great knowledge.[138] He also said that the people would be rightly guided if they followed Abū Bakr and ʿUmar.[139] Likewise, he said that if there were a Prophet after him, it would be ʿUmar.[140] He added that God had established truth through [ʿUmar's] speech and his heart.[141] He also said, "I am happy for you with that with which [10] Ibn Umm ʿAbd is happy for you,"[142] by which he meant ʿAbdallāh b. Masʿūd. Their virtues, rank, and those ways in which God favored them in terms of knowledge and excellence are too numerous to be mentioned. So, can imitation of these be similar to that of the ones who came after them, who are not comparable to the latter, even in the least?

---

*Abū Saʿīd Saʿd b. Mālik b. Sinān al-Khuḍrī (d. 74/693), a close Companion of the Prophet.

## [11] The Statements of the Companions Are Binding Proof

Third, the Muslims are agreed that the opinion of those whom you imitate is not a legal proof. But, at the same time, most scholars are agreed—in fact, those whom you imitate have said explicitly—that the opinions of the Companions are legal proofs that must be followed, and to abandon their opinions is forbidden, as will appear in the words of the scholars themselves. The most eloquent of them in this matter is al-Shāfiʿī. We shall clarify that there is no disagreement in his school over the view that the opinion of a Companion is a legal proof. We shall mention his statements in his later work on this matter, if God wills. We shall also show that the one who narrates two opinions from him about this issue does so by narrating the second as an extension of what he actually said. The second opinion is not an explicit statement of his. Now, if the opinion of a Companion is a proof then accepting his opinion is a specific obligation, while the best that can be said about accepting the opinion of someone else is that it is allowed. So analogy of one of these people [the Companions, who issue a statement] with another [i.e., scholars who are not Companions] is the worst and most futile of analogies.

## The Natural Disposition to Imitate Teachers That God Has Instilled in His Creation Does Not Necessitate the Permissibility of Imitation in the Religion

67. As for your statement, "God has instilled in mankind a natural disposition toward imitation of teachers by students in all crafts, sciences, and so forth." The answer to this is that this truth cannot be denied. But how does this obligate the acceptability of imitation in the religion of God? How does it obligate accepting the opinion of a principal without a proof? Also, how does it obligate according precedence to his view over those who are more knowledgeable than him and abandoning proofs for the sake of conformity to his views and leaving the opinions of all the people of knowledge from among the earlier and later generations in favor of this person's opinions? Did God create a disposition to do this in the nature of anyone in the universe? Then it is to be said, "Rather, God created in His servants a natural disposition toward seeking proofs and sound evidence for the opinion of every person who makes a claim."

God implanted in the dispositions of men that they do not accept the opinion of the one who does not establish evidence for the validity of what he says. It is for this reason that God, the Exalted, established decisive proofs, clear-cut arguments, lucid evidence, and luminous signs of the truthfulness of His Messengers, so that the proof would be established and so that all arguments for disbelief would be rendered void. This He did, even though the Messengers were the most truthful of God's creation, the most knowledgeable, righteous, and perfect. Still, they advanced clear signs and decisive proofs, despite the testimony of their nations that they were the most truthful ones. So how can we accept the opinions of others without proof that obligates accepting them? God, the Exalted, only obligated accepting the Messengers' claims after the evidence for what they said had been established and after the appearance of clear signs which necessarily showed the truthfulness of their claim. So God created the nature of mankind in such a way that it yields before evidence and accepts the one who provides it. This is something shared by all people, the believer and the disbeliever, the righteous and the wicked—that is, yielding to evidence and exalting the one who provides it. [12] If they go against this out of stubbornness and transgression, it is because their own desires would be nullified [by yielding in this way]. How apt are the words of the one who said:

*Enkindle the truth in the heart of the hearer*
*And leave him be, for the light of truth traverses and glows by itself.*
*With softness will it cling to it and forget its resistance*
*As the free man forgets what it was to be chained.*

So the innate disposition God instilled in mankind and His own law are among the strongest proofs against the imitators.

## Differences in Capacities Do Not Necessitate Imitation in Every Ruling

68. As for your statement, "God, the Exalted, distinguished between the mental abilities of people just as He did between their physical abilities. And by His divine wisdom and justice, it is not fitting that everyone be obligated to know the truth with its evidence in every issue," and so forth.

We do not deny this. Nor do we claim that God obligated everyone with the duty of knowing the truth with its evidence in every religious issue, whether it be minor or major. All we deny is what was rejected by the scholars and those who preceded them among the Companions, as well as those who followed them, and what only occurred in Islam after the passage of the meritorious generations in the fourth century, which had been condemned by the Messenger of God.

What we deny is selecting one individual and assigning the same rank to his verdicts as to the texts from the Lawgiver. Rather, to prefer them over these and to accord precedence to his view over the views of all the scholars of the community who came after the Messenger of God. We oppose being content with imitation of him rather than gaining rulings from the Book of God, the Sunnah of His Messenger and the statements of the Companions, and we oppose adding to this the claim that, "This scholar did not say anything except that which was in the Book of God and the Sunnah of His Messenger." Not only does issuing such a claim involve testimony about which the one testifying has no knowledge, it is also an ascription of something to God without any knowledge. We oppose the practice of saying of the scholar who disagreed with him, even if he was more knowledgeable, that "He was not correct in his interpretation of the Qur'an and Sunnah, and my principal is more correct." Or saying, "Both of them were right in their interpretation of the Book and Sunnah," even while their opinions are contradictory. Thus, the one who says this holds the evidences of the Book and the Sunnah to be contradictory and conflicting, holding that God and His Messenger command a thing and its opposite at the same time. He also maintains that His religion is subject to the opinions of men and that, in the meantime, there is no specific ruling for him to act on. So he either follows this approach, or he declares incorrect the one who disagrees with his principal. He has no choice but to follow one of these two courses—this is among the blessings of imitation on him.

Once you know this, then know also that we said and maintain, "God, the Exalted, obligated His servants [13] to remain conscious of Him, as much as they are able. The essence of remaining conscious of Him is to know what is to be avoided and then to refrain from it. So what is obligatory on every individual is to exert himself in knowing what he has to be conscious of in every matter that concerns him (from the commands and prohibitions of God). Then he must abide by the commands of God and His Prophet. If he could not learn some part of it, he would be similar to everyone other than the Messenger (for everyone other than him had defects in his knowledge). But, this does not remove such a person from the rank of scholars. God does not obligate him with anything except knowing the truth and following it to the extent that he is able." Abū ʿUmar said, "There is no one after the Messenger except that some of the Messenger's affairs were concealed from him." So, in terms of knowing the truth, God, the Most Perfect, has obligated everyone with that which he is able to perform, and which his strength allows him to achieve. Further, He has excused him regarding that which was concealed from him in which he therefore errs or imitates another. This is all dictated by His wisdom, justice, and mercy. The opposite would be the case if He allowed His creation to imitate whomever they wanted among the scholars, and if He allowed everyone to appoint a specific person as an arbiter of the revelation, evading the obligation of acquiring rulings from the light of revelation. This would go against His wisdom, mercy, and kindness. It would result in the abandonment of His religion, His Book and the Sunnah of His Messenger, as has happened among some people. God grants success.

## Major Difference between the Imitator and the Follower in Prayer

69. As for your statement, "In your imitation you are like the one who follows an *imām* in prayer, the one who traces footsteps, or the caravan that follows a guide." The response to the above is to say that, by God, this is exactly what we have been crooning about. However, the real issue is the identity of the *imām*, the guide, and the one who is to be followed. God obligated His creation to be guided by him [i.e., the Prophet], to follow him and to walk behind him. He, the Most Perfect, swore by His honor that, if His creation tried to come to Him by every path or to open every door leading to Him, it would not be opened except if they entered behind the Prophet. He, by God, is the Imām of creation, their guide and true leader. God did not create this stature of leadership for anyone after him, except for the one who calls to him, guiding people to him and ordering them to follow, obey and walk behind him, without appointing for themselves a principal, Imām, or guide other than him.

Rather, the scholars are, in relation to the people, like the leaders of prayers and those praying behind them. Everyone prays in obedience to God and in fulfillment of His command, so they cooperate and assist each other in the congregation, just as is the case with the guide and the caravan. Each one of them performs the pilgrimage [14] in obedience to God and in fulfillment of His command. It is not the case that the worshipper prays because the *imām* does. Rather, he prays whether or not the *imām* prays, unlike the imitator, who adopts the view of his principal because it is his view, not because it is the view of the Messenger. If the matter was as you said, then the imitator would follow the opinion of the Messenger at all times and would therefore not be an imitator. So their reliance on the proof of the *imām* of prayer and the guide of a caravan bound for pilgrimage is one of the most convincing arguments against them.

70. The one being led in prayer knows that this prayer that he is offering is that which God, the Exalted, has obligated on His servants and that he and his *imām* are equal in being commanded with this obligation. He also knows that this House of God, the Sacred Mosque, is the one whose pilgrimage God obligated on those who are able to perform it and that the obligation to do this applies equally to him and the caravan guide, so he does not perform the pilgrimage in imitation of the guide, nor does he pray in imitation of the imām.

The Prophet, may the peace and blessings of God be on him, hired someone to show him the way to Medina, when he undertook the migration which God had made obligatory on him.[143] He prayed behind ʿAbd al-Raḥmān b. ʿAwf,* as a follower.[144] And [it is acceptable in religious law that] the more knowledgeable one prays behind one who is like him or even lower than him [in rank]. Indeed, it is valid that he prays behind one who is not even a scholar. In none of this, therefore, is there any imitation.

71. The follower in prayer does exactly what the *imām* does, and likewise the caravan rider with the guide. Had they not done this, they would not be true followers. The one who follows the scholars must be the one who acts as they did. He must do the same in terms of knowing evidence, preferring proofs and ruling by them wherever they are and whomsoever they are with. The one who does this is the one who

---

*Abū Muḥammad ʿAbd al-Raḥmān b. ʿAwf (d. 32/653), a prominent Companion of the Prophet.

really follows them. But if he turns away from the principle on which the scholars' authority is established and adopts a path other than theirs, claiming that he is their follower, then these are merely his own delusions, and it will be said to him, *Say, "Bring forth your argument, if you are telling the truth!"* [Q., al-Naḥl, 16:64].

## [15] The Companions Would Convey the Commands of God and His Messenger to the People

72. As for your statement, "The Companions of the Messenger of God conquered countries while people were newly embracing Islam, and the people would seek verdicts from the Companions. But they would not respond to anyone by saying, 'You must seek the truth in this verdict with evidence.'" The answer to this is that they did not issue verdicts to them based on their own opinions. Rather, they conveyed to them whatever was said by their Prophet, as well as his actions and commands. So the verdicts that they issued themselves constituted both the ruling and the proof. They would say to the ones who asked them for verdicts, "This is the trust of our Prophet to us, and this is our trust to you." What they would convey to them would therefore be both the proof and the ruling. For the speech of the Messenger of God is both the ruling and the proof thereof. Likewise, the Qur'an. People at that time were eager to know what their Prophet said, did, and commanded, and this the Companions conveyed to them.

How is this comparable to a time in which those who only seem to resemble real men search for what was said by this or that individual? The later in time a person is, the more the contemporary scholars adopt his views and the more they abandon (or almost abandon) the views of those who preceded him. This continues until you find that the followers of the Imāms are the ones who most often ignore their opinions. The people of each age deliver judgments and verdicts based on the views of those lower than the Imāms—and lower still—and those closest to them. As time progresses, the abandonment of earlier opinions increases, as does the practice of turning away from them. This continues until the earlier scholar's own books almost disappear. The more distant in time he is, the more likely this is to be so. But where is the proof that the Companions of the Messenger of God said to the Successors, "Let each one of you appoint for himself a man whom he chooses in order to imitate him in his religion; you ought not to turn to anyone other than him or to gain rulings from the

Book and the Sunnah. Rather, you ought to acquire these rulings by imitating mere men. So, if you learn something from God and His Messenger, while something else comes to you from the one you appointed as your principal, do you adopt the view of the one you imitate and leave whatever comes to you from God and His Messenger"? By God, if the veil were lifted from your eyes and the truth were to become manifest to you, you would see your actions in relation to those of the Companions just as a poet has described:

*They desçended on Mecca amongst the tribes of Hāshim,*
*While I found myself in the open desert, the furtherest of places,*

And as another has versified:

*She went to the East. I, to the West*
*But what distance between those navigating East and West! [16]*

And as another said:

*You are marrying Pleiades to Canopus!*
*By God, can the twain e'er be wed?*
*She, in her stride, is Syrian-inclined*
*While Canopus' stride is all Sabaean.*

## Imitation Is Not Among the Necessities of Sacred Law

73. As for your statement, "Imitation is necessitated by sacred law and divine decree. Even those who reject it are forced to accept it as has preceded in the discussion on rulings." The answer to this is that the imitation that is rejected and condemned, even if it is among the matters that are necessitated by divine decree, is not among the obligations of sacred law. Rather, the law requires that it be viewed as void and corrupt, as is known by the reasons we have mentioned and many others besides them. Instead, what is a religious necessity is to be guided on the basis of proof. These issues that you mention as religious necessities are not imitation. Rather, they come under [the rubric of] following evidence and obeying the commands of the Lawgiver. If you refuse to accept this and persist in calling it imitation,

then from this perspective, imitation is correct, and it is part of the law. But this does not compel us to hold that this discordant imitation that emerged later is part of the religion or that is it one of its necessities. Rather, its nullity is a religious imperative.

74. The opposite of every religious obligation stands nullified necessarily. If imitation, about which there is disagreement, is among the obligations imposed by law, then the nullity of seeking proofs and following evidence is established [because imitation would be obligatory and *ijtihād*, its opposite, would therefore be forbidden]. So, accepting one of these two propositions necessitates the rejection of the other; the veracity of one, dictates the nullity of the other. We intend to mention this as evidence and say, "If imitation is part of the religion, then it cannot be permissible to abandon it in favor of *ijtihād* and the seeking of inferences, because that would necessitate its invalidity."

If it is said, "Both of them are religious obligations, but one of them is more complete than the other, so it is permissible to leave that which is less perfect for that which is more so." It is to be said in response, "As the doors of *ijtihād* are shut according to you, and, as you closed off the paths leading to it, the only thing that remains as an obligation is imitation. So, leaving it for something the doors to which are closed and the path thereto blocked, is, for you, a sin [17] and the one who traverses this path is a sinner." The effacement of the path of knowledge, nullification of the clear Signs and proofs of God, and the claim that the world can be empty of one who stands forth with God's proofs, implied in this view, are sufficient to render it void and worthy of being discarded. The Prophet guaranteed that a group of his community would not desist from the truth and would not be harmed by those who seek to disgrace them, nor by those who oppose them until the Last Hour is established. These are the people of knowledge and insight into that which God sent His Prophet with. They are the people of insight and clarity, as opposed to the blind one who testifies that he is not among the people of knowledge and vision and hence must imitate.

What is necessary by law is to follow evidence, to be guided by it, and to accord precedence to the clear divine texts over the opinions of men. Likewise, to regard the Book and Sunnah as arbiters in everything over which the scholars have differed. As regards being wary of the texts, leaving them for the opinions of men and preferring them over the texts, denouncing the one who considers the Book of God, the Sunnah of His Messenger, and the opinions of the Companions the arbiter (and judges the opinions of scholars by them and does not take an ally other than God and His Messenger), the invalidity of this is among the requirements of sacred law. Religion cannot be complete without denouncing and invalidating such a position. Following evidence is something entirely different from this imitation. God grants success.

## Narration Is Different from Imitation

75. As for your statement, "Every narrated proof which you rely on to establish the invalidity of imitation, you yourselves are imitators of those who bore that narration and transmitted it. So the scholar has no option but to imitate the one who narrates, the judge must imitate the witness, the layperson, a scholar," and so forth.

The answer to this has already been given many times. What you refer to as imitation here is, in fact, obedience to the command of God and His Messenger, and if this were imitation, every scholar in this world after the Companions would be an imitator. Rather, the Companions who adopted the opinions of their contemporaries would also be imitators. Such a comparison will not issue forth, except from a quarrelsome man or one who seeks to confuse the truth with falsehood and to conceal the truth with the cloak of falsehood. The imitator, because of his ignorance, takes a sound form of imitation and relies on it for proving the validity of its unsound forms, because of a common factor present in both. But he ignores the distinguishing factor between them. This is therefore, a type of invalid analogy, the reprehensibility of which is agreed upon, which is, in fact, related to this type of invalid imitation. Both are equal in their invalidity.

So if God declares the report of a truthful person a proof and likewise the testimony of the just person, [18] the one who follows this is not termed an imitator. If he is to be called that for following the evidence, then hasten to accept this kind of imitation, for are we crooning about anything other than this? God is the Helper.

## A Reply to Those Who Assert That Imitation Is Safer Than Seeking Evidence

76. As for your statement, "You do not allow imitation out of fear that the imitator will fall into error if the one whom he imitates is incorrect in his opinion. You then obligate him to look into the evidence and to

> weigh it in search of the truth. But there can be no doubt that he will be closer to the mark by imitating someone who is more knowledgeable than him than if he were to perform *ijtihād* for himself. Just as the one who wants to buy an article about which he has no knowledge, if he were to follow an expert, one who is informed, trustworthy, and sincere in giving advice, he would be more correct and more likely to attain what he desires than if he were to struggle for the truth by himself."

There are several responses to this.

First, we declare imitation to be prohibited out of obedience to God and His Messenger. It is God and His Messenger who have prohibited it. God also condemned those who perform it in His Book, as He commanded that He and His Messenger be made arbiters and that everything about which the community of Muslims disagrees be referred to Him and His Messenger. He informed us that He alone possesses dominion and forbade the practice of regarding anyone other than Him and His Messenger as an authority. He commanded that His Book be held on to, and He forbade that others should be taken as allies and lords beside Him, with what they declare lawful being considered so and what they declare unlawful being considered so. He designated those who do not know what He revealed to His Messenger as falling under the category of cattle, and He commanded obedience to those in authority, if this entails obedience to His Prophet, in that those in authority follow him and inform others about his affairs. He swore by His Own Most Glorious Self that we do not believe unless we make the Prophet alone the arbiter in everything that we disagree over and until we refer to the authority of no one but him. Then, we must not find in ourselves any opposition to his decision (as is the case of the imitators when an order of the Prophet appears against the opinion of the one they imitate). Instead, we must submit to his judgment completely, just as the imitators submit to the opinions of those they imitate. Rather, our submission must be more complete than theirs. God is the Helper!

God condemned those who seek an authority other than the Prophet. This was the established rule while the Prophet was alive and remains so, in just the same way, after his death. If he were alive in our midst and we were to refer to someone other than him as an authority, we would be among those who deserve condemnation and punishment. Similarly, his Sunnah, the true religion, and the guidance that he came with cannot perish. Even if his noble person is lost to the community, his Sunnah, message, and guidance are not. Knowledge and guidance are secure in their place, and whoever searches for them, finds them. God, the Exalted, guaranteed safekeeping of the religion [19] that He revealed to His Messenger. It will forever remain safe with the protection of God, so that the proof of God on His creation is established generation upon generation. Since their [the community's] Prophet was the last of the Prophets, and there is none after him, God's safeguarding of this religion and His revelation does not stand in need of another Messenger after him. So what God, the Exalted, obligated the Companions and what He ordered them to do, to spread the knowledge and guidance of the Qur'an and the Sunnah alone and of nothing other than these two, is exactly what has been made obligatory on those who come after them. This order is decisive, and it has not been abrogated, nor can abrogation ever approach it until God finishes and rolls up the world.

God condemns the one who turns away when he is called toward that which God has revealed to His Messenger. Such a person has been warned that he will be afflicted with a malediction because of his turning away from this. This affliction will affect his heart, religion, and worldly existence. God also warns the one who turns away from His command and follows another that he will be afflicted with a severe torment or a painful punishment. The affliction will affect his heart, and the painful torment will affect his body and spirit. Each is a corollary of the other. For the one who is afflicted in his heart because he turned away from what was revealed to the Messenger and opposed him by turning toward another must be thus afflicted. God, the Exalted, informs us that, when He decrees a matter through the words of His Prophet, it is not permissible for any believer to choose something other than what His Messenger chose. Indeed, there is no choice left for a believer after God's Messenger has delivered judgment. So we ask those who perform imitation, "Is it possible that in many cases the judgment of God and His Messenger was not known to those you imitate?" If they say, "Yes, it is not possible that this was not known to them," they have placed them in a rank greater than that of Abū Bakr, 'Umar, 'Uthmān, ʿAlī, and all of the Companions.

## Issues That Remained Concealed to the Major Companions

Some part of what God and His Messenger decided remained concealed from each one of the Companions.

## Issues That Eluded Abū Bakr

Consider the truthful one [i.e., Abū Bakr], may God be pleased with him, who was the most knowledgeable of the community, yet knowledge of the inheritance share of the grandmother eluded him until Muḥammad b. Maslamah* and Mughīrah b. Shuʿbah† informed him about it.[145] He was also unaware of the ruling that there is no blood money for the martyr [20], until ʿUmar informed him of this and then he adopted his view.[146]

## [21] Issues That Eluded ʿUmar

ʿUmar was not aware of the ruling regarding purification with dried earth [*tayammum*] for the one who was in a state of ritual impurity, so he said that such a person is not to pray, even if his impure state lasts for a month, unless he is able to bathe himself.[147] He was also unaware of the compensation to be awarded for the loss of fingers [in a criminal assault], so he ruled regarding the amputated thumb and the finger that comes next to it that 25 camels were due as compensation for these, until he was informed that the book of the children of ʿAmr b. Ḥazm‡ contained a ruling from the Prophet, in which he ruled that ten camels were the correct compensation in such cases. So he abandoned his view and went back on it.[148] He was also unaware of the manner in which consent has to be sought before entering someone's house, until he was informed about this by Abū Mūsā and Abū Saʿīd [22] al-Khuḍrī.[149] He was also unaware of the inheritance share of the widow from the blood money of her deceased husband, until Ḍaḥḥāk b. Sufyān al-Kilābī§ wrote to him—and he was a bedouin of the inner desert—that the Prophet, may the peace and blessings of God be upon him, commanded him to grant a share of inheritance to the widow of Ashyam al-Ḍibābī from the latter's blood money. He was similarly unaware of the ruling regarding a woman who delivered a child prematurely, until he asked about this and found the

---

*Abū ʿAbd al-Raḥmān Muḥammad b. Maslamah al-Anṣārī (d. 45/666), a Companion of the Prophet.

†Abū ʿAbdallāh Mughīrah b. Shuʿbah al-Thaqafī (d. 50/670), a Companion of the Prophet.

‡ʿAmr b. Ḥazm b. Zayd al-Khazrajī (d. 53/672), a Companion of the Prophet.

§Ḍaḥḥāk b. Sufyān b. ʿAwf al-Kilābī, a Companion from whom Ḥasan al-Baṣrī and others narrate but whose biographical details are sketchy.

answer with Mughīrah b. Shuʿbah.[150] He was also unaware of the ruling on Zoroastrians, in particular, whether or not they were required to pay the minority tax [*jizyah*], until ʿAbd al-Raḥmān b. ʿAwf informed him that the Messenger of God, may the peace and blessings of God be upon him, took the *jizyah* from the Zoroastrians of the region of Hajar.[151] He was also unaware of the ruling that the requirement of a farewell circumambulation around the Holy House in Mecca* was waived for a woman in her menstrual period, and he would send them back until they were pure and would then command them to perform the circumambulation [23], until it reached him that the Prophet, may the peace an blessings of God be upon him, had acted contrary to this, so he went back on his own view.[152] He was also unaware of the equal payment to be given for all fingers lost as a result of criminal assault, and he would distinguish between them, until the Sunnah regarding equality in compensation reached him, and so he adopted it. The issue of the *tamattuʿ* pilgrimage† also eluded him, and he would not allow it, until he came to know [24] that the Prophet commanded it, so he abandoned his view and acted according to the former.[153] He was also unaware of the permissibility of calling people by the names of the Prophets, and he ruled against the validity of this, until he was informed by Abū Ṭalḥah‡ that the Prophet, may the peace and blessings of God be upon him, had given him the teknonymic [*kunyah*] Abū Muḥammad so he abandoned his own view and did not stubbornly insist on his own view of prohibition.[154] He was ignorant of the correct ruling in this area, even though Abū Mūsā,§ Muḥammad b. Maslamah,** and Abū Ayyūb†† were among the most famous Companions. But still he did not know, so he issued orders regarding it, going so far as to prohibit it. He was also unaware of the correct interpretation of the words of the Most High, *Truly you will die, and*

*The farewell circumambulation around the Kaʿbah marks the end of the major pilgrimage.

†A pilgrimage in which the minor (*ʿumrah*) and major (*ḥajj*) pilgrimages are performed during one journey, with a break in between them.

‡Abū Ṭalḥah Zayd b. Sahl (d. 20/641), a close Companion of the Prophet.

§Mūsā is the Arabic form of "Moses."

**Muḥammad b. Maslamah al-Anṣārī (d. 43/663), a Companion of the Prophet.

††Abū Ayyūb Khālid b. Zayd al-Anṣārī (d. 50/670), a Companion of the Prophet. Ayyūb is the Arabic form of "Job."

*truly they (too) will die.* [Q., al-Zumar, 39:30] and His Words, *Muḥammad is no more than an Apostle, many were the Apostles that passed away before him. If he died or were slain, will you then turn back on your heels?* [Q., Āl-ʿImrān, 3:144], so that he said, "By God, it is as if I had not heard these words until this moment."[155]

[25] Likewise, the correct ruling regarding giving a dowry that involved an excess over the dowries given to the wives and daughters of the Prophet, may the peace and blessings of God be upon him, was concealed from him, until he was reminded by a woman of the words of the Most High, *Even if you had given the latter a whole treasure for dower, take not the least bit of it back.* [Q., al-Nisāʾ, 4:20] and he said, "Everyone has more insight than ʿUmar, yes, even the women."[156]

This is similar to the issue of the inheritance share of the grandfather and the one who dies without any heirs, in which the truth also eluded him. It also eluded him in certain areas of the law relating to interest; thus he expressed his wish that the Messenger of God, may the peace and blessings of God be on him, had issued them an authoritative directive in this.[157] It also escaped him on the day of [the treaty of] Ḥudaybiyyah [in 6/628] that the promise of God to His Messenger and the Companions regarding entry into Mecca was general and not specific to that particular year, until the Prophet, may the peace and blessings of God be on him, clarified this to him.[158] He was also unaware of the permissibility of using perfume for the one in a state of ritual sanctity and also regarding such an individual applying perfume after having completed the ritual of sacrifice and before the farewell circumambulation, even though this action is approved of in the Sunnah.[159] He was also unaware of the correct view regarding the permissibility of going to an area in which there was [26] a plague and the impermissibility of fleeing from such a place, until he was informed that the Messenger of God, may the peace and blessings of God be upon him, had said, "When you hear of the plague appearing in an area, do not enter it. And if it occurs while you are in an area, do not leave that area, and do not flee from it."[160]

This is the condition of the one who was definitely the most knowledgeable of the community after the truthful one. He was the one about whom Ibn Masʿūd said, "If the knowledge of ʿUmar was placed in one scale and the knowledge of all the people of earth was placed in the other, ʿUmar's knowledge would outweigh it." Aʿmash said, "I mentioned this to Ibrāhīm al-Nakhaʿī, so he said, 'By God, I estimate that ʿUmar walked off with nine-tenths of all knowledge.'"

## [27] Issues That Eluded ʿUthmān, Abī Mūsā, Ibn ʿAbbās, and Ibn Masʿūd

ʿUthmān was unaware of the minimum period of pregnancy, until Ibn ʿAbbās mentioned it by referring to the words of the Most High, *The carrying of the (child) to his weaning is (a period of) thirty months* [Q., al-Aḥqāf, 46:15], and His words, *The mothers shall give suck to their offspring for two whole years* [Q., al-Baqarah, 2:233], so he adopted this view.[161]

Abū Mūsā al-Ashʿarī was unaware that the inheritance share of the daughter of the son alongside the daughter of the deceased, was one-sixth, until it was mentioned to him that the Messenger of God, may the peace and blessings of God be on him, awarded her this much as her share of inheritance.[162] Ibn ʿAbbās was unaware of the impermissibility of eating the meat of domesticated donkeys, until it was recounted to him that the Messenger of God, may the peace and blessings of God be on him, had forbidden it on the day of [the battle of] Khaybar [in 7/628].[163] Ibn Masʿūd was unaware of the ruling regarding the dowry of a widow whose marriage was not consummated and who had not received a dowry, so he vacillated about it [28] for a month and issued a verdict based on his own reasoning, after which an explicit ruling on this from the Prophet reached him.

## That Which Eluded Others Was Even Greater than That Which Eluded the Companions

This is a vast area, and if we were to allow ourselves to be led into it, it would become a long narrative, so we suffice by asking the party of imitation, "Is it possible for some affair of the Messenger of God, may the peace and blessings of God be on him, to be unknown to those you imitate?" If they say, "The one we imitate was not unaware of any such matter, even though the Companions themselves were unaware of some of them, despite their proximity to the Prophet," they have truly indulged in extremism like the one who declares all scholars to be incapable of error. But if he acknowledges that it is possible for some of them to be unaware of this—and that this is, in fact, what occurred—and that they are of various ranks based on how much or how little they knew or did not know, then we say, "We ask you, by God, the One who is watching over every tongue and heart, if God and His Messenger have delivered a judgment about something that was unknown to the one you imitate, do you still have a choice between acceptance and rejection of their judgments, or is your choice nullified by your obligation to act exactly according to their commands. Is it not now impermissible for you to act according to the opinion of anyone else?" Prepare an answer to this question, and the truth alongside it. For the question is inevitable. And an answer, necessary. This is the main issue that keeps us from performing imitation. Can you bring forth even a single proof that would answer this charge and allow you an option regarding the imitation which you have happily chosen for yourself?

## Fallacy of the Imitator's Claim

Second, your statement that the imitator falls closer to the mark by imitating someone who is his peer or is more knowledgeable than him than by performing his own *ijtihād* is a false, baseless statement. This is because, if he imitates someone who himself was opposed by those who were more knowledgeable than him or those who were of his rank, then the imitator does not know whether he is correct or not by imitating his principal. Rather he is, [29] as al-Shāfiʿī said, a person who collects wood at night, who could return either with precious wood or with a snake that could bite him. If he exerts himself in *ijtihād* and in searching for the truth, then he is in one of two possible states. Either he is correct in it and so receives two rewards, or he is in error and so receives one reward only.[164] Thus, he gets rewarded no matter what. This is contrary to the case of the fanatic partisan imitator, because, even if he is correct, he does not get the reward, and, if he is wrong, he is not safe from earning a penalty. How can the veracity of the one who is blind be compared to the veracity of the one who exhausts himself in his search for the truth?

Third, he would be closer to the truth only if he knew that the truth lay with the one whom he imitates and not with anyone else. And if he truly knows this, then he is not an imitator of him but is, rather, someone who follows him based on evidence. If he truly does not know this, then how can you arrive at the conclusion that he is closer to the truth than the one who exhausts and devotes himself to searching for the truth?

Fourth, the one who is closer to the truth in cases of disagreement among the scholars is necessarily the one who follows the command of God and refers the dispute to the Qurʾan and Sunnah. As for the one who refers it to his principal without considering anybody else, how is he closer to the truth?

Fifth, the example which you yourself have offered argues strongly against you. For the one who seeks to buy an item or to traverse a path over which the people are divided into two or three groups, each commanding the opposite of what all the others command, such a person does not prefer imitating one group alone out of all of them. Rather, he goes back and forth, seeking the most correct opinion out of all of them. If he does prefer the opinion of just one, even while the rest are no less knowledgeable, sincere, and pious, or when the rest are in fact better than the one he has chosen, this person would be counted among those who had erred. He would be blameworthy and would not be praised for his conduct, even if he were to arrive at the truth. Indeed, God has created a natural disposition in people of intellect that, when faced with a situation such as this, they pause and seek to establish the superiority of one among the many discordant views through some external reference until the truth is apparent to them. He did not create their natures so as to converge and accept the view of one individual and abandon the views of all others.

77. It is said to the party of imitators, "Do you allow the imitation of every scholar among the earliest generations and the later ones, or only of some of them and not others?" If you allow imitation of all of them, [30] then your doing so for the one whose school you belong to and of someone other than him are comparable. So how do the opinions of this one scholar become the school for you, by which you issue verdicts and judgments, while you have allowed imitation of him, just as you have allowed imitation of another? How did this individual become the principal of your school and not the other? How did you make it permissible to leave the statements of one and to accept those of another while both were scholars whose imitation was allowed? If the opinions of one of these scholars was part of the religion, how can it be allowed for you to reject the religion? And if his opinions were not part of the religion, how did you allow imitation of him? To this you can have no answer.

## Two Narrations from One of the Scholars Are Like Two Opinions from the Imāms

78. If two opinions or narrations are transmitted from those whom you imitate, you deem it permissible to act on both. You justify this by saying, "He was a *mujtahid* who had two opinions, so we are free to choose either one." And both opinions together constitute the legal school [*madhhab*] for you. So why not treat the opinion of a rival *mujtahid* [whom you

oppose] like the alternative opinion of the first *mujtahid* and make both of them your *madhhab*? It may be that the opinions of the *mujtahids* who are more knowledgeable, whom you oppose, are preferable to the alternative opinion of the first *mujtahid* and also closer to the Book and the Sunnah.

79. O you, party of imitation, if some of your scholars from your own school, whom you imitate, issue an opinion that contradicts the opinion of the principal of the school, or if they derive a new opinion based on this, you regard this as acceptable and issue judgments and verdicts according to this new opinion [that comes from your own school]. Yet if an Imām who was a contemporary of your principal or even superior to him in rank has an opinion that contradicts that of your principal, you do not incline toward it nor is it of any great significance for you. Even though it is well known that just one of the scholars among those who were contemporaries of your principal is more exalted than all the subsequent scholars of your school from beginning to end. So how evil is your division and taxonomy of scholars that it would make the view of the lesser scholar a salient view in the school. By God, this is extraordinary. The verdict or judgment of one who supposedly decides in accordance with one of the scholars of the *madhhab* is more worthy of acceptance than the verdict of one who bases his verdicts on the opinions of the rightly guided Caliphs, as well as the opinions of Ibn Masʿūd, Ibn ʿAbbās, ʿUbayy b. Kaʿb, Abū l-Dardāʾ*, and Muʿādh b. Jabal. These [positions you find yourselves in] are among the blessings of imitation upon you.

80. You seek refuge from this strategy by saying, "Imitation of some scholars is allowed and imitation of] others is not." Now, every group among you says that it is allowed [31] or obligatory to imitate its own principals but no one else among the scholars of the religion who were like him or were more knowledgeable. The least that would occur as a result of this is contradiction between your opinion and that of the other party [which claims the same for its own principal], with these opinions clashing against each other. Then it will be said to you, "How does your principal come to be more deserving of being imitated than that of the rival party? Through which Book and through which Sunnah [do you resolve this contradiction]? Was it not

---

*Abū l-Dardāʾ (d. 32/653), a close Companion of the Prophet.

because of this that the affair of the community divided up into pieces between itself with *each sect rejoicing in that which is with itself* [Q., al-Muʾminūn, 23:53]?"

Every faction calls toward imitation of its principal, removing itself further from the others and preventing people from going toward them. This leads to division within the community and to the religion of God becoming subservient to the desires and whims of people and so becoming vulnerable to confusion and discord. All this is a proof that imitation is not from God, because of the tremendous disagreement that is inherent in it. The disagreements among them [the *muqallids*] and the fact that their opinions go against each other are sufficient to show the evil of this school of thought. [This disagreement, by itself, would have been sufficient to establish the corruption of this school] even if there was nothing worse in it than their upholding imitation of their principal while forbidding that of one of the major Companions, as has clearly been stated in their books.

## Imitators Obligate Imitation of Their Scholars and Forbid Imitation of Others

81. The imitators pass, explicitly, a void judgment against God regarding His divine decree and His law, one which opposes what His Messenger informed us of. They maintain that the world is void of those who would establish God's proof on it. They say, "There are no scholars left on the earth since the by-gone era." Another group among them says, "It is not permissible for anyone to choose an opinion of a scholar after Abū Ḥanīfah, Abū Yūsuf, Zufar b. al-Hudhayl,* Muḥammad b. al-Ḥasan, and al-Ḥasan b. Ziyād al Luʾluʾī,† this being the opinion of many among the Ḥanafīs. Bakr b. ʿAlā l-Qushayrī al-Mālikī‡ said, "It is not allowed for anyone to choose an opinion of a scholar after the first two centuries of Islam," and yet others say, "It is not allowed for anyone to choose after al-Awzāʿī and Sufyān al-Thawrī, Wakīʿ b. al-Jarrāḥ, and

*Zufar b. al-Hudhayl (d. 157/774), considered the third most important student of Abū Ḥanīfah.

† Ḥasan b. Ziyād al-Luʾluʾī (d. 204/820), an important Ḥanafī scholar.

‡ Bakr b. Muḥammad b. al-ʿAlā b. Muḥammad al-Qushayrī al-Mālikī (d. 344/955), a leading Mālikī scholar, who settled in Egypt.

> ʿAbdallāh b. al-Mubārak." Yet another group says, "It is not permissible for anyone to choose after al-Shāfiʿī." The imitators among his followers differed about the status of those who attributed themselves to him and also about the identities of the ones who possessed sufficient authority in the school for later verdicts and judgments in the school being rendered according to their views. So they divided these scholars who were affiliated to particular principals into three ranks: those whose views are authoritative, such as Ibn Surayj,* al-Qaffāl,† [32] and Abū Ḥāmid al-Isfarāʾīnī‡; those whose views were to be considered but were not authoritative, such as Abū l-Maʿālī§; and those who were neither, such as Abū Ḥāmid [al-Ghazālī],** among others.

They also disagreed and adopted several divergent views about the time at which the gates of *ijtihād* were closed, but for none of these views did God reveal any authority. According to them, it is acceptable for there to be a time when the earth is devoid of those who stand on the path of God with evidence and for it to be empty of those who speak on the basis of knowledge. They regard it as impermissible for anyone after that time to look to the Book of God or the Sunnah for the purpose of acquiring rulings from them. Nor do they deem it permissible for one to judge and render verdicts based directly on what is in the Qurʾan and Sunnah, unless this corresponds to the opinion of the principal and the one he imitates. If the latter's opinion happens to match [with what is in the Qurʾan and Sunnah], then a judgment can be delivered and a verdict passed according to [the sources]. If not, then the Qurʾan and Sunnah must not be accepted and therefore must be rejected.

These statements have, as can be seen, reached the limit of corruption, nullity, contradiction, and [the sin of] speaking about God without knowledge, rejecting His proofs, and turning away from His Book and the Sunnah of His Messenger and deriving rulings from them.

---

*Aḥmad b. ʿUmar b. Surayj (d. 306/918), the leading Shāfiʿī scholar of his generation.

†Abū Bakr Muḥammad b. ʿAlī b. Ismāʿīl al-Shāshī, known as al-Qaffāl (d. 365/976), a renowned Shāfiʿī scholar.

‡Abū Ḥāmid al-Isfarāʾīnī (d. 406/1015), the leading Shāfiʿī scholar of his generation.

§Abū l-Maʿālī al-Juwaynī (d. 478/1085), a renowned Shāfiʿī jurist and *kalām* scholar.

**Abū Ḥāmid al-Ghazālī (d. 555/1111), a renowned Shāfiʿī jurist and author of numerous theological and devotional treatises.

And God refuses to accept this. Rather, He is not satisfied until He manifests His light and ratifies His Messenger's statement, "This earth will never be devoid of someone who establishes God's authority," and that there will always be a group from his community who will remain firm on the truth with which he was sent and that someone will, at the turn of every century, be raised for this community to renew the religion for it.[165]

It is sufficient to establish the corruption of these statements [33] to say to the ones who utter them, "When it is not permissible for someone to choose [an opinion] after the passing of the scholars whom you have mentioned, how did you happen to choose imitation of them as opposed to others?" How have you prohibited a person from choosing the opinion his *ijtihād* compelled him to accept as the one that conforms to the Qur'an and Sunnah? While, at the same time, you deem it permissible for yourselves to choose the statement of your principal, obliging the community to imitate him, and prohibiting imitation of others, preferring imitation of him instead.

What has allowed you this choice, which does not carry any evidence from the Book, the Sunnah, consensus, analogy, and the statements of the Companions? And what authority has prohibited you from making a choice that is sanctioned by evidences from the Book, Sunnah, and the statements of Companions?

It will be said to you, "If it is not permissible according to you and others to choose [an opinion of a scholar] after the first two centuries of Islam, how is it permissible for you to choose the opinions of Mālik rather than the opinions of those who were superior to him from among the Companions and their followers or those who are like him, from among the scholars of different regions or those who came after him, while you yourself were not born until 60 years had passed since the passing of the first two centuries."

The corollary of this statement is that Ashhab*, Ibn Mājishūn,† Muṭarrif b. ʿAbdallāh,‡ Aṣbagh b. al-Faraj,§ Saḥnūn b. Saʿīd, Aḥmad b.

---

* Miskīn b. ʿAbd al-ʿAzīz Ashhab (d. 204/820), a renowned Egyptian Mālikī jurist.

† ʿAbd al-Malik b. ʿAbd al-ʿAzīz b. Mājishūn (d. 214/829), a renowned Medinese Mālikī jurist. He and his brother Muṭarrif are referred to as the "two brothers" in the Mālikī tradition.

‡ Muṭarrif b. ʿAbdallāh. b. Muṭarrif (d. 220/835), a renowned Medinese Mālikī jurist.

§ Aṣbagh b. al-Faraj b. Saʿīd (d. 225/840), a prominent Egyptian Mālikī scholar and student of Ibn al-Qāsim.

al-Muʿadhal,* and those scholars who are of their rank had a choice in the matter until the end of the twelfth month in the year two hundred. Then, when the new moon appeared for the first month in the year two hundred and one, and the sun set that evening, that which has been a completely permissible option for them became impermissible, without any reprieve.

It will be said to others, is it not among the woes and wonders of this world that you allow the scholars whom you have mentioned to choose an opinion as you allow them to use analogy and *ijtihād* and to issue opinions regarding the religion of God based on one's own views? Then you do not permit a choice and *ijtihād* for the scholars of Islam and the ones who were more knowledgeable about the Book of God, the Sunnah of His Messenger, and the statements of his Companions and their verdicts, such as Aḥmad b. Ḥanbal, al-Shāfiʿī, Isḥāq b. Rāhawayh, Muḥammad b. Ismāʿīl al-Bukhārī, Dāʾūd b. ʿAlī,† and their contemporaries. You do this, despite the extensive knowledge of these scholars regarding the Sunnah, their awareness of the authentic and ambiguous forms of it, their zeal to learn the opinions of the Companions and the Successors, and the subtlety and refinement of the inferences they drew from evidence. Whoever among them advocated analogy, his analogy [34] is closer to the truth, further away from its corrupt forms and closest in meaning and spirit to the texts. You advance the view that they should not be imitated, despite their exalted piety and the fact that God has bestowed the love of the Believers and the respect of the Muslim scholars and masses upon them.

If every sect from the imitators argues for the primacy of its principal for any possible reason such as his belonging to an earlier time, his asceticism and piety, his meeting with venerable and ordinary scholars whom those after him could not meet, or the large number of his followers who are not rivalled by anyone else, another group is able to argue for the primacy of their principal with these same arguments—or similar ones—or those even better.

It is also possible for someone else to say to them, "The implementation of your statement—provided you disdain contradiction—obligates you to leave the statements of your principal for the statement of the eldest Companions, the Successors, and those who were more knowledgeable, who possessed greater piety, asceticism, and a larger following and who were

---

*Abū l-Faḍl Aḥmad b. al-Muʿadhal b. Ghaylān b. al-Ḥakam al-Fahdī, a Basran jurist and *kalām* scholar and a disciple of Ibn Mājishūn.

† Dāʾūd b. ʿAlī al-Ẓāhirī (d. 270/883), founder of the Ẓāhirī school of law.

more respected. Is there any comparison between the rank and number of the followers of Ibn ʿAbbās, Ibn Masʿūd, Zayd b. Thābit, and Muʿādh b. Jabal, let alone the followers of ʿUmar and ʿAlī and the followers of later scholars?"

## Merit of the Companions and Those Who Followed Them

Here, [consider] Abū Hurayrah. Al-Bukhārī said, "Eight thousand men learned from him, including other Companions and the Successors." Here you have Zayd b. Thābit. ʿAbdallāh b. ʿAbbās is just one of his many associates. Where, in the followers of the later scholars, is there to be found anyone like ʿAtāʾ, Ṭāwūs,* Mujāhid, ʿIkramah,† ʿUbaydallāh b. ʿAbdallāh b. ʿUtbah,‡ and Jābir b. Zayd§? Where, among their followers, are the likes of the two Saʿīds,** al-Shaʿbī, Masrūq, ʿAlqamah,†† al-Aswad,‡‡ and Shurayḥ to be found? Where, among them, are to be found those of the rank of al-Nāfiʿ, Sālim,§§ al-Qāsim,*** ʿUrwah,††† Khārijah b. Zayd,‡‡‡ Sulaymān b. Yasār,§§§ and Abū Bakr b. ʿAbd al-Raḥmān****?

---

* Ṭāwūs b. Kaysān (d. 106/724), a renowned Successor.

† ʿIkramah b. ʿAbdallāh al-Barbarī (d. 105/723), a freed slave of Ibn ʿAbbās and a leading scholar.

‡ ʿUbāydallāh b. ʿAbdallāh b. ʿUtbah (d. 98/717), a prominent Medinese legal authority.

§ Jābir b. Zayd al-Azadī (d. 93/711), a Successor from Basra, who is considered one of the leading students of Ibn ʿAbbās.

** The two Saʿīds: Saʿīd b. Jubayr (d. 45/655), a renowned Successor, who was executed by Ḥajjāj b. Yūsuf, and Saʿīd b. al Muṣayyib.

†† ʿAlqamah b. Qays al-Nakhaʿī (d. 62/682), a renowned Successor.

‡‡ Al-Aswad b. Yazīd (d. 75/694), a renowned scholar, who accepted Islam in the lifetime of the Prophet but did not meet him and hence is not counted among the Companions.

§§ Sālim b. ʿAbdallāh b. ʿUmar (d. 106/724), a renowned Successor and grandson of the second caliph.

*** Al-Qāsim b. Muḥammad b. Abū Bakr (d. 108/726), one of the renowned seven jurists of Medina from the generation of the Successors and a nephew of the Prophet's wife ʿĀʾishah.

††† ʿUrwah b. al-Zubayr (d. 93/711), one of the renowned seven jurists of Medina from the generation of the Successors and a nephew of the Prophet's wife ʿĀʾishah.

‡‡‡ Khārijah b. Zayd b. Thābit al-Anṣārī (d. 100/719).

§§§ Sulaymān b. Yasār (d. 109/727), a client of Maymūnah, wife of the Prophet.

**** Abū Bakr b. ʿAbd al-Raḥmān (d. 94/712), one of the renowned seven jurists of Medina, from the generation of the Successors.

Are your scholars somehow more fortunate with their followers than these Companions were with theirs? The Companions and their followers were great, as was the age in which they lived, but it is almost as if it was this very fact, alongside their exaltedness and pre-eminence, that prohibited the later generations from following them!

In accordance with the spirit of the age in which they lived, the later generations said, "The Companions were far greater than us; we are not their patrons," just as they explicitly demonstrated and testified against themselves that their capacity to acquire knowledge from the Qur'an and Sunnah was lesser than that of the Companions. They said, "We are not capable of doing that, not because of the limitations of the Qur'an and Sunnah, but because of our own shortcomings and limitations. Consequently, we are content to follow someone who is more knowledgeable about them than we are." So it will be said to them, "Why do you denounce the one who follows them, rules according to them, seeks judgments from them, and presents the statements of the scholars before their statements, accepting whatever conforms to them, rejecting whatever opposes them?"

You should just accept that you have not reached this verdant grove of knowledge, so why [35] do you denounce the one who has reached it and tasted its sweetness? How have you restricted the vast blessings of God, which cannot be imagined or conceived by all the intellects of the universe? Thus, even if the followers [of the Qur'an, the Sunnah, and the opinions of the Companions] are present in your age, growing up alongside you, and even if there exists a close affinity between them and you, they could still attain this understanding, for God bestows His blessings upon whomever He wants from among His creation. God, the Exalted, denounced the one who refused to acknowledge the prophecy [of Muhammad, may the peace and blessings of God be on him] arguing that God had turned it away from the nobles and leaders of society and bestowed it on the one who did not have these characteristics, with His statement, *Is it they who would portion out the Mercy of your Lord? It is We Who portion out between them their livelihood in the life of this world: and We raise some of them above others in ranks, so that some may command work from others. But the Mercy of your Lord is better than the (wealth) which they amass.* [Q., al-Zukhruf, 43:32].

And the Prophet, may the peace and blessings of God be on him, said, "The example of my community is like the rainfall: it is not known whether the first or the last part is better."[166] God, the Exalted, has informed us about the ones who will be successful in the Hereafter that they will be

*A large number of people from those of old, and a few from those of later times.* [Q., al-Wāqiʿah, 56:13–14]. And the Exalted One informs us that, *It is He Who has sent among the unlettered people an Apostle from among themselves, to recite to them His signs, to sanctify them, and to instruct them in scripture and wisdom, although they were, before this, in manifest error*; then He said, *As well as (to confer all these benefits upon) others of them, who have not already joined them: And He is exalted in Might, Wise.* And then He also said, *Such is the Bounty of God, which He bestows on whom He wills: and God is the Lord of the highest bounty.* [Q., al-Jumʿah, 62:2–4].

# *Glossary*

***akdariyyah*** A case in inheritance law in which the propositus is survived by her husband, her mother, full sister, and paternal grandfather.

***ahl al-ḥadīth*** The people of *ḥadīth*, scholars who favored reliance on scripture in legal and theological matters.

***ahl al-rā'y*** Scholars who favored the use of personal reasoning or opinion (*ray'*) in legal and theological matters.

***ahl al-ẓāhir*** Textualist and literalist scholars.

***dhawq*** Experience, taste, intuition.

***fatwā* (pl. *fatāwā*)** Legal verdict issued by a *muftī*.

***faqīh*** Legal scholar.

***furū'*** Substantive law.

***fiqh*** Positive law.

***ḥadīth* (pl. *aḥādīth*)** Narrative or report of the deeds and sayings of the Prophet.

***ḥajj*** Major pilgrimage.

***ḥalālah*** A marriage conducted in order to allow a divorced couple to return to each other.

***ḥikmah*** Rationale, wisdom.

***ḥīlah* (pl. *ḥiyal*)** Legal fiction.

***iftā'*** The discipline of issuing verdicts (by a *muftī*).

***iḥrām*** State of ritual consecration at the time of the major or minor pilgrimage.

***ijmā'*** Consensus.

***ijtihād*** Independent legal reasoning; a jurist's effort to deduce the law from its sources.

***ikhtilāf*** Disagreement, difference of opinion.

***imām*** Scholar, ruler, prayer leader.

***iqāmah*** The second call to prayer.

***istiḥsān*** Juristic preference.

***istijmār*** Cleaning oneself with dry material.

***istinjā'*** Washing oneself after defecation.

***i'tikāf*** Worship carried out in seclusion in a mosque.
***ittibā'*** Following another person or his practice, based on evidence.
***ittifāq*** Agreement.
***jihād*** Fighting in God's cause.
***jizyah*** Tax paid by a minority community living in the Islamic state.
***kashf*** Mystical unveiling.
***kalālah*** A case in inheritance law in which the propositus leaves behind no ascendants or descendants.
***kalām*** Speculative theology.
***khabar* (pl. *akhbār*)** News, report; also, a synonym for *ḥadīth*.
***kunyah*** A personal name derived from the name of one's child.
***madhhab* (pl. *madhāhib*)** A juristic/theological school.
***maqṣad* (pl. *maqāṣid*)** Goal, objective.
***marfū'*** A *ḥadīth* report that is raised to the Prophet (lit., elevated).
***mashhūr*** Well-known, widespread.
***maṣlaḥāh*** Considerations of public interest.
***mawqūf* (lit., halted)** A report from a Companion only, which, barring exceptions, is not treated as a *marfū'* tradition.
***mu'āmalāt*** Civil transactions and affairs.
***mudabbar*** A slave with a contractual agreement to be freed after his/her master's death.
***mudhāmmatān*** A dark green color.
***muftī*** A jurist who issues *fatāwā*.
***muḥaqqib*** One who follows other people in religion without proof or evidence.
**Muḥarram** The first month of the Islamic calendar.
***muḥkam*** Perspicuous, said of a word or text conveying a firm and unequivocal meaning.
***muḥrim*** A person in the state of ritual consecration (*iḥrām*).
***mujmal*** Ambiguous, referring to a category of unclear words.
***mujtahid*** Legist competent to derive law based on his *ijtihād*.
***mukātib*** A slave who was contracted to be freed upon payment of an agreed sum.
***mukhtaṣar*** Compendium.
***muqallid*** One who performs *taqlīd*.
***mursal*** A discontinued or disconnected *ḥadīth*, especially at the level of a Companion.
***muṣarrāh*** Purchase of an animal with milk in its udders.
***musnad*** A *ḥadīth* with a continuous chain of transmitters.
***nafīr*** A party or expedition going forth for *jihād* (cf. 9:122).
***naṣab*** Patronymic.
***naṣṣ* (pl. *nuṣūṣ*)** A text; a clear injunction; an explicit textual ruling.
***qiblah*** Direction of prayer, towards the Sacred Mosque in Mecca.
***qiṣāṣ*** Lex talionis (law of retaliation).
***qiyās*** Analogical reasoning, rationality.

***qullah*** A volume measurement of water.

**Qur'an** The literal word of God as revealed to the Prophet Muhammad in Arabic and transmitted through continuous testimony.

***radd*** Amount left over after one's property has been divided among the Qur'ānic sharers.

***rak'āh*** Unit of prayer.

***ray'*** Personal reasoning or opinion.

***sadd al-dharā'i'*** Blocking the means to evil.

***ṣaḥīḥ*** Valid, authentic.

***salaf*** The pious forefathers, referring to the Companions, their successors, and the generation following them.

***salām*** Salutation offered at the end of the prayer.

***sharī'ah*** The sacred law as contained in scripture.

**Sunnah** An established practice or course of conduct, specifically that of the Prophet.

***tābi'ī* (pl. *tābi'īn*)** One from the generation following that of the Companions.

***tajdīd*** Renewal.

***takbīr*** The prefatory formula ("God is Great") recited during ritual prayer.

***takhrīj*** The process whereby legal opinions are derived, based on extant legal opinions of a scholar or school.

***ṭalāq*** Divorce.

***talbiyah*** The prefatory formula recited on arrival at the Sacred Precincts of the Holy Mosque at Mecca, during the *ḥajj*.

***talfīq*** Combining the rulings of two or more schools regarding a particular action.

***tamattu'*** A case in which the minor and major pilgrimages are performed together in one journey, separated by an interval.

***taqlīd*** Imitation; following the views and opinions of others.

***ṭarīqah* (pl. *ṭuruq*)** A Sufi sect.

***tawātur*** Continuous recurrence.

***tayammum*** Purification or dry ablution with clean earth, in the absence of water.

***'ulamā'* (sing. *'alim*)** Religious scholars.

***ummah*** The faith community of Islam.

***umm al-walad*** A slave woman who has borne children to her master.

***'umrah*** Minor pilgrimage.

***uṣūl*** Basic principles.

***uṣūl al-fiqh*** Jurisprudence. The principles by which law is derived from scripture.

***walījah*** Friend, protector.

***wuḍū'*** Ablution with water.

***zakāt* (lit., purity)** Legal alms.

***zinā*** Unlawful sexual intercourse.

# *Notes*

## INTRODUCTION

1. Ḥabīb Aḥmad Kīrānwī, *al-Dīn al-qayyim*, in Zafar ʿUthmānī, *Iʿlāʾ al-sunan* (Beirut: Dār al-Fikr, 2001), 19:9106.
2. A recent and welcome change to this trend is Caterina Bori, *A Scholar in the Shadow: Essays in the Legal and Theological Thought of Ibn Qayyim al-Ǧawziyyah* (Rome: Istituto per l'Oriente C. A. Nallino, 2010). See also Birgit Krawietz, "Ibn Qayyim Al-Jawzīyah: His Life and Works," *Mamlūk Studies Review* 10, no. 2 (2006): 19–64; Livnat Holtzman, "Ibn Qayyim Al-Jawziyyah," in *Essays in Arabic Literary Biography*, edited by Joseph E. Lowry and Devin J. Stewart (Wiesbaden: Harrassowitz, 2009), 202–223.
3. See Yossef Rapoport and Shahab Ahmed, *Ibn Taymiyya and His Times*. Karachi: Oxford University Press, 2010.
4. See Abdul-Hakim al-Matroudi, "The Hanbalī School of Law in the Light of Contemporary Western Studies," *Journal of Qurʾanic Studies* 8, no. 2 (2006): 260–203 (an Arabic article in an English/Arabic journal).
5. By far the most comprehensive biographical work on Ibn al-Qayyim remains Bakr Abū Zayd, *Ibn Qayyim al-Jawziyyah: Ḥayātuh, āthāruh, mawāriduh* (Riyadh: Dār al-ʿĀṣimah, 1992). A representative sample of biographical notices on Ibn al-Qayyim can be found in al-Ziriklī, *al-Aʿlām* (Beirut: Dār al-ʿIlm li-l-Malāyīn, 2002), 6:56; Ibn Ḥajar, *al-Durar al-kāminah fī aʿyān al-miʾah al-thāminah* (Hyderabad: Majlis Dāʾirah al-Maʿārif al-ʿUthmāniyyah, 1972), 5:137; al-Shawkāni, *al-Badr al-ṭāliʿ bi-maḥāsin man baʿd al-qarn al-sābiʿ* (Cairo: Maṭbaʿah al-Saʿādah, 1348/1930), 2:143; Ibn Mufliḥ, *al-Maqṣad al-arshad fī dhikr aṣḥāb al-Imām Aḥmad* (Riyadh: Maktabah al-Rushd, 1990), 2:384; al-Suyūṭī, *Bughyah al-wuʿāh fī ṭabaqāt al-lughawiyyīn wa-l-nuḥāh* (Beirut: al-Maktabah al-ʿAṣriyyah, 1964), 1:63; al-Dhahabī, *al-Muʿjam al-mukhtaṣṣ bi-l-muḥaddithīn* (al-Ṭāʾif: Maktabah al-Ṣiddīq, 1408/1988), 269; al-Dāʾūdī, *Ṭabaqāt al-mufassirīn* (Beirut: Dār al-Kutub

al-ʿIlmiyyah, 1983), 2:93–97; Ibn al-Taghrībirdī, *al-Manhal al-ṣāfī wa-l-mustawfā baʿd al-wāfī* (Cairo: Maṭbaʿah Dār al-Kutub wa-l-Wathāʾiq al-Qawmiyyah, 2002), 9:240–242; Ibn Kathīr, *al-Bidāyah wa-l-nihāyah* (Beirut: Dār Ibn Kathīr, 2010), 15:353–354 al-Ṣafadī, *Kitāb al-Wāfī bi-l-wafayāt* (Beirut: Dār ʾIhyāʾ al-Turāth al-ʿArabī, 2000), 2:195–197; Ibn Rajab, *Dhayl ʿalā ṭabaqāt al-Ḥanābilah* (Mecca: Maktabah al-ʿUbaykān, 2005), 5:170–179; Ibn ʿImād, *Shadharāt al-dhahab fī akhbār man dhahab* (Beirut: Dār Ibn Kathīr, 1992), 8:287–291.

6. Zafar ʿUthmānī, *Iʿlāʾ al-sunan* (Beirut: Dār al-Kutub al-ʿIlmiyyah, 1997). On the Deobandī movement, see Barbara Daly Metcalf, *Islamic Revival in British India: Deoband, 1860–1900*, (Princeton: Princeton University Press), 1982. Henceforth, all references to the *Iʿlaʾ al-sunan* are to this edition.
7. al-Shawkānī, *al-Qawl al-mufīd fī adillah al-ijtihād wa-l-taqlīd*, ed. ʿAbd al-Raḥmān ʿAbd al-Khāliq (Kuwait: Dār al-Qalam, 1976), 56–57; al-Ṣanʿānī, *Irshād al-nuqqād ilā taysīr al-ijtihād*, ed. Ṣalaḥ al-Dīn Maqbūl Aḥmad (Kuwait: Dār al-Salafiyyah, 1405/1985); Shāh Walī Allāh, *ʿIqd al-jīd fī aḥkām al-ijtihād wa-l-taqlīd* (Cairo: al-Maṭbaʿah al-Salafīyyah, 1965); Rashīd Riḍā, *al-Manār* (16 Shaʿbān 1319/28 November 1901). In another issue of *al-Manār* (16 Rajab 1321/8 October 1903), Riḍā published an abridged version of Ibn al-Qayyim's essay on *taqlīd*.
8. See Muhammad Naasir Al-Albaani (al-Albānī), *The Prophet's Prayer, Sallallaahu ʿalaihi Wasallam, Described from the Beginning to the End as Though You See It*, trans. Usama Hasan (Ipswich, Suffolk: Al-Haneef Publications, 1993), especially the introduction and appendices, for the author's criticism of *taqlīd*. For a contemporary Wahhābī critique of *taqlīd*, see Saʿd al-Shithrī, *al-Taqlīd wa-aḥkāmuh* (Riyadh: Dār al-Waṭan, 1995); Yūsuf Qaraḍāwī, *Kayfa nataʿāmal maʿ al-turāth wa-l-tamadhhub wa-l-ikhtilāf* (Beirut: Muʾassasah al-Risālah, 2005).
9. Taqī Usmānī, *The Legal Status of Following a Madhhab*, trans. Mohammad Amin Kholwadia and ed. Muhammad Dhakir Shaikh (Karachi: Zam Zam Publishers, 1998, 2nd ed. 2001); Muḥammad Saʿīd Ramaḍān al-Būṭī, *al-Lā madhhabiyyah akhṭar bidʿah tuhaddid al-sharīʿah al-Islāmiyyah* (Damascus: Dār al-Fārābī, 2005); see also al-Būṭī's *al-Salafiyyah: Marḥalah zamāniyyah mubārakah lā madhhab Islāmī* (Damascus: Dār al-Fikr, 1988); ʿAbd al-Fattāḥ al-Yāfiʿī, *al-Tamadhhub: Dirāsah taʾṣīliyyah muqāranah li-masāʾil wa-aḥkām al-tamadhhub* (Beirut: Muʾassasah al-Risālah Nāshirūn, 2006).
10. Muhammad Asad, *This Law of Ours* (Gibraltar: Dar al-Andalus, 1987); Abdal Hakim Murad (Timothy Winter), *Understanding the Four Madhhabs: The Facts about Ijtihād and Taqlīd* (Oneonta NY: Islamic Publications, 1998?); Ibn al-Naqīb, *Reliance of the Traveller: The Classic Manual of Islamic Sacred Law ʿUmdat al-Salik by Ahmad Ibn Naqib al-Misri (d. 769/1368) in Arabic with Facing English Text, Commentary, and Appendices*, ed. and trans. Nuh Ha Mim Keller (Evanston IL: Sunna Books, 1994).
11. ʿAbd Allāh ʿAzzām, *Join the Caravan* (London: Azzam Publications, 2001), 53.

12. Cheryl Bernard, *Civil Democratic Islam: Partners, Resources and Strategies* (Santa Monica: RAND Corporation, 2003), 64.
13. Roscoe Pound, "The Decadence of Equity," *Columbia Law Review* 5 (1905): 20–35; Max Rheinstein, ed. *Max Weber on Law in Economy and Society* (Cambridge MA: Harvard University Press, 1954); Scott Alan Kugle, "Framed, Blamed and Renamed: The Recasting of Islamic Jurisprudence in Colonial South Asia," *Modern Asian Studies* 35, no 2 (2001): 257–313.
14. W. M. Watt, *Islamic Political Thought* (Edinburgh: Edinburgh University Press, 1998), 73–74.
15. See Mohammad Fadel, "The Social Logic of Taqlīd and the Rise of the Mukhtaṣar," *Islamic Law and Society* 3 (1996), 193.
16. For an excellent discussion of the issue, see *Abḥāth hay'ah kibār al-'ulamā' bi-l-mamlikah al-'Arabiyyah al-Sa'ūdiyyah* (Riyadh: Ri'āsah 'Idārah al-Buḥūth al-'Ilmiyyah wa-l-'Iftā', 1421/2001), 3:115. See also Frank E. Vogel, *Islamic Law and Legal System: Studies of Saudi Arabia* (Leiden: Brill, 2000), chap 8.
17. Sherman Jackson, *Islamic Law and the State: The Constitutional Jurisprudence of Shihāb al-Dīn al-Qarāfī* (Leiden: Brill, 1996), 77.
18. Muḥammad Sa'īd Albānī, *'Umdāh al-taḥqīq fī l-taqlīd wa-l-talfīq* (Damascus: al-Maktab al-Islāmī, 1981), 110.
19. Albānī, *'Umdāh al-taḥqīq*, 100; Ibn Mullā Farrūkh, *al-Qawl al-sadīd fī ba'ḍ masa'il al-ijtihād wa-l-taqlīd*, ed. Jāsim Yāsīn and 'Adnān Sālim (Kuwait: Dār al-Da'wah, 1988), 79; Birgit Krawietz, "Cut and Paste in Legal Rules: Designing Islamic Norms with *Talfīq*," *Die Welt des Islams* 42 (2002) 3–40.
20. See Jackson, *Islamic Law and the State*, 99, where he cites Alan Watson, and p. xl, where he lays out his concept of legal scaffolding.
21. Ṣāliḥ b. Muḥammad Fulānī, *Īqāẓ himam ūlī l-abṣār li-l-īqtiḍā' bi-sayyid al-muhājirīn wa-l-anṣār* (Gujranwala: Dār Nashr al-Kutub al-Islāmiyyah, 1975), 39.
22. Ibn al-Qayyim, *I'lām al-muwaqqi'īn 'an Rabb al-'Ālamīn*, ed. Mashhūr b. Ḥasan Āl Salmān (Riyadh: Dār Ibn al-Jawzī, 1423/2002), 6:203.
23. See Ibn 'Ābidīn, *Radd al-muḥtār 'alā l-durr al-mukhtār* (Beirut: Dār al-Kutub al-'Ilmiyyah, 1415/1994), 1:140, where he quotes the Ḥanafī scholar Ibn al Humām's words to this effect.
24. Ibn 'Ābidīn, *Radd al-Muḥtār*, 1:176.
25. Ibn 'Ābidīn, *Radd al-Muḥtār*, 1:177. On the idea that *taqlīd* was related to concerns for the layman, see Fadel, *Social Logic*, 199–200.
26. Ibn al-Qayyim, *I'lām*, 6:206.
27. Jackson, *Islamic Law and the State*, 213.
28. Al-Qurṭūbī, *al-Jāmi' li-aḥkām al-Qur'ān*, ed. 'Abd al-Razzāq al-Mahdī (Beirut: Dār al-Kitāb al-'Arabī, 1423/2003), commentary on verse 2:188.
29. Ibn al-Najjār, *Sharḥ al-Kawkab al-munīr* (Riyadh: Maktabah al-'Ubaykān, 1997), 4:574; al-Nawawī, *Rawḍah al-ṭālibīn* (Beirut: Maktab al-Islāmī, 1991), 11:117; Ibn

Taymiyyah, *al-Fatāwā al-kubrā*, ed. Muḥammad ʿAbd al-Qādir ʿAṭāʾ and Muṣṭafā ʿAbd al-Qādir ʿAṭāʾ (Beirut: Dār al-Kutub al-ʿIlmiyyah, 1987), 5:556.

30. al-Shurunbulālī, *al-ʿIqd al-farīd li-bayān al-rājiḥ min al-khilāf fī jawāz al-taqlīd*, ed. Khālid Muḥammad al-ʿArūsī, *Majallah jāmiʿah umm al-qurā li-ʿulūm al-sharīʿah* 17, no. 32 (1425/2004), 674–768.
31. Albānī, *ʿUmdāh al-taḥqīq*, 97.
32. Ibn al-Qayyim, *Iʿlām*, 6:203–205.
33. Ibn ʿĀbidīn, *Radd al-muḥtār*, 1:168; Zafar ʿUthmānī, *Iʿlaʾ al-sunan* (Beirut: Dār al-Kutub al-ʿIlmiyyah, 1997), 14, sect. 2, p. 19.
34. Fadel, *Social Logic*, 203. See also Ibn al-Qayyim, *Iʿlām*, 6: 99–101, for a discussion of whether transmission could count as *fatwā* and whether a *muqallid* could be a *muftī*.
35. Shah Wali Allah (Shāh Walī Allāh), *The Conclusive Argument from God: Shah Wali Allah of Delhi's Hujjat Allah al-Bāligha*, trans. Marcia K. Hermansen (Islamabad: Islamic Research Institute, 2003), 472–473.
36. Jackson, *Islamic Law and the State*, 100.
37. Jackson, *Islamic Law and the State*, 209.
38. Muhammad Qasim Zaman, *Ashraf ʿAli Thanawi: Islam in Modern South Asia* (Oxford: Oneworld, 2008), 62–65.
39. Ahmad Atif Ahmad, *Structural Interrelations of Theory and Practice in Islamic Law: A Study of Six Works of Medieval Islamic Jurisprudence* (Leiden, Brill, 2006). See also the concluding discussion in Bernard G. Weiss (ed.), *Studies in Islamic Legal Theory* (Leiden: Brill, 2002).
40. Norman Calder, "Taḳlīd," *Encyclopaedia of Islam*, 2nd ed., P. Bearmanet al. (Leiden: Brill, 1998), 10:137.
41. Norman Calder, "Al Nawawī's Typology of *Muftīs* and its Significance for General Theory of Islamic Law," *Islamic Law and Society* 4 (1997): 139, 140, 150, 159, 161. Calder even translates al-Nawawī as requiring "manipulation" of arguments by the jurist, at 144.
42. Calder, *Al Nawawī's Typology of Muftīs*, 159.
43. Norman Calder, "The 'Uqūd Rasm al-Muftī' of Ibn 'Ābidīn," *Bulletin of the School of Oriental and African Studies* 63 (2000): 219.
44. See for example, Jackson, 128.
45. Wael Hallaq, "Was the Gate of Ijtihad Closed?," *International Journal of Middle East Studies* 16, no. 1 (1984): 3–41.
46. Calder, *The "Uqūd Rasm al-Muftī" of Ibn ʿĀbidīn*, 226. Compare with Ahmad Atif Ahmad, *Structural Interrelations*, 182–196 and passim.
47. Calder, *Al Nawawī's Typology of Muftīs*, refers to the interpretive tradition as intellectual play but also as an enactment of a religious duty (140). He claims that the complexity and delight to be enjoyed in the study of *fiqh* were things established in the juristic community, (141) and that *uṣūl* was something to be studied for its own sake (158).

48. Al-Karkhī, *al-Uṣūl allatī 'alayhā madār furū' al-Ḥanafiyyāh* (Cairo: al-Maṭba'ah al-Adabiyyah, n.d.), 84–85. In this view, the primary aim of *uṣūl* would, of course, be justification. See Wael Hallaq, *A History of Islamic Legal Theories: An Introduction to Sunni Uṣūl al-Fiqh* (Cambridge: Cambridge University Press, 1997), ix.
49. 'Uthmānī, *I'lā' al-sunan*, 14/2:5.
50. See Ibn al-Qayyim, *I'lām*, 6:100–101; Fullānī, *Īqāẓ*.
51. See al-Dhahābī, *Zaghl al-'Ilm*, ed. Muḥammad b. Nāṣir al-'Ajmī (n.p., Maktabāh al-Ṣaḥwah al-Islāmiyyah, 1404/1983–1984), 41.
52. Fadel, *Social Logic*, 226.
53. Jackson, *Islamic Law and the State*, xx.
54. Jackson, *Islamic Law and the State*, xxii. See also Adam Sabra, "Review of Islamic Law and the State: The Constitutional Jurisprudence of Shihab al-Din al-Qarafi," *The Journal of Law and Religion*, 15, no. 2 (2001): 413–416.
55. Jackson, *Islamic Law and the State*, 88.
56. Ibn Abī al-'Izz al-Ḥanafī, *al-Ittibā'*, ed. Muḥammad 'Atā Allah Ḥanīf and 'Asim b. 'Abdallāh al-Qaryūti (Lahore: al-Maktabah al-Salafiyyah, 1410/1989–1990), 76–77.
57. S. A. A. Mawdudi, *The Islamic Law and Constitution* (Lahore: Islamic Publications, 1980), 79–80.
58. Fadel, *Social Logic*, 208.
59. Concerning the use of the word "imitation" for *taqlīd*, see Joseph Schacht, *An Introduction to Islamic Law* (Oxford: Clarendon Press, 1964), 71. See also Haim Gerber, "Rigidity Versus Openness in Late Classical Islamic Law: The Case of the Seventeenth-Century Palestinian Muftī Khayr al-Dīn al-Ramlī," *Islamic Law and Society* 5, no. 2 (1998): 165–195, esp. 173. Sherman Jackson, on the other hand, argues that *muqallid* jurists often regarded themselves equal to the eponymous Imāms in their ability to derive law from scripture; see Jackson, *Islamic Law and the State*, 81.
60. Jackson, *Islamic Law and the State*, 81, and Adam Sabra, "Review of Islamic Law and the State: The Constitutional Jurisprudence of Shihab al-Din al-Qarafi," *The Journal of Law and Religion*, 15, no. 2 (2001): 413–416.
61. See Jackson, *Islamic Law and the State*, passim. Calder states that in the system of *taqlīd*, an *imām*, because of his interaction with scripture, is the mediator of authority to the *muqallid muftī*. See Calder, *Al Nawawī's Typology of Muftīs*, 152.
62. Wael Hallaq, *Authority, Continuity, and Change in Islamic Law* (Cambridge: Cambridge University Press, 2001). This trend is also apparent in standard legal *tafāsīr*, such as that of al-Qurṭūbī, texts that discuss inter-*madhhab ikhtilāf*, such as Ibn Qudamah's *Mughnī*, and polemical pro-*madhhab* works, such as the *I'lā' al-sunan*, all of which denounce the substantive positions of a variety of schools and scholars and the authoritative status of those positions.
63. Sherman Jackson, "Setting the Record Straight: Ibn al-Labbād's Refutation of al-Shāfi'ī," *Oxford Journal of Islamic Studies* 11, no. 2 (2000): 121–146.

64. William Graham, "Traditionalism in Islam: An Essay in Interpretation," *The Journal of Interdisciplinary History* 23, no. 3 (1993): 495–522.
65. Jackson, *Islamic Law and the State*, 81.
66. Ibn al-Qayyim, *I'lām*, 6:144–145. Similar comments by Abū Bakr al-Ṭarṭūshī (d. 566/1170) are cited in Jackson, *Islamic Law and the State*, 159.
67. Ibn al-Qayyim, *I'lām*, 6:49, 64, 200.
68. Calder, *The "Uqūd Rasm al-Muftī" of Ibn 'Ābidīn*.
69. Calder, *The "Uqūd Rasm al-Muftī" of Ibn 'Ābidīn*, 217.
70. See Ibn Baṭṭah, *al-Ibānah al-kubrā*, ed. Raḍā Mu'ṭī et al. (Riyadh: Dār al-Rāyah, n.d.), 1:419; Ibn Ḥazm, *al-Iḥkām fī uṣūl al-aḥkām* (Cairo: Dār al-Ḥadīth, 1404/1983–1984), 8:509; Khaṭīb al-Baghdādī, *al-Faqīh wa-l-mutafaqqih* (Riyadh: Dār Ibn al-Jawzī, 1417/1996–1997), 1:245, 2:56; al-Shawkānī, *al-Qawl al-mufīd fī adillah al-ijtihād wa-l-taqlīd* (Kuwait: Dār al-Qalam, 1396/1976), 1:80; al-Ṭabarī, *Jāmi' al-bayān fī ta'wīl al-Qur'ān*, ed. Aḥmad Muḥammad Shākir (n.p: Mu'assasah al-Risālah, n.d.), 22:390.
71. Abū Bakr al-Ṭarṭūshī, as cited in Jackson, *Islamic Law and the State*, 159.
72. Ibn al-Qayyim, *I'lām*, 2:22, 38–48.
73. See Scott Lucas, "Where Are the Legal "*Ḥadīth*"?: A Study of the "*muṣannaf*" of Ibn Abī Shayba," *Islamic Law and Society* 15, no. 3 (2008): 303, 310, and passim.
74. See also al-Ṣan'āni, *Irshād al-nuqqād ilā taysīr al-ijtihād*, ed. Salaḥ al-Dīn Maqbūl Aḥmad (Kuwait: Dār al-Salafiyyah, 1405/1984–1985), 100–112.
75. George Makdisi, "The Significance of the Sunni Schools of Law in Islamic Religious History," *International Journal of Middle East Studies* 10, no. 3 (1979): 1–8.
76. This criticism of *muqallid* scholars is repeated at several places in Ibn al-Qayyim's work; see his *I'lām*, 6:127–128.
77. Ibn 'Ābidīn, *Radd al-muḥtār*, 1:160.
78. Al-Ṣan'āni, *Irshād*, 17.
79. Nimrod Hurvitz, "Schools of Law and Historical Context: Re-examining the Formation of the Ḥanbalī Madhhab," *Islamic Law and Society*, 7, no. 3 (2000): 37–64. See also Michael Cooperson, "Ibn Ḥanbal and Bishr Al-Ḥāfī: A Case Study in Biographical Traditions," *Studia Islamica* 86 (1997): 71–101; Khaṭīb al-Baghdādī, *Ta'rīkh Baghdād aw Madīnah al-Salām* (Cairo: Maktabah al-Khānjī, 1931), 4:412.
80. Al-'Imrānī, *al-Bayān fī madhhab al-Imām al-Shāfi'ī*, ed. Qāsim Muḥammad al-Nūrī (Damascus: Dār al-Minhāj, 2000), 72 (editor's introduction).
81. Nawawī, *al-Majmū': Sharḥ al-muhadhdhab* (Beirut: Dār al-Fikr, 2000), 1:11–23.
82. Ibn Qudāmah, *al-Mughnī*, ed. 'Abdallāh 'Abd al-Muḥsin al-Turkī and 'Abd al-Fattāh Muḥammad al-Ḥulw (Cairo: Ḥajr 1986–1990), 1:5.
83. George Makdisi, "The Significance of the Sunni Schools of Law,", 6.
84. Ibn 'Aqīl, *al-Wāḍih fī uṣūl al-fiqh*, ed. 'Abdallāh b. 'Abd al-Muḥsin al-Turkī, (Beirut: Mu'assasah al-Risālah, 1999), 5:423–4.

85. Al-Ṣan'ānī, *Irshād*, 90.
86. See Ibn Mullā Farrūkh, *al-Qawl al-sadīd*, 117.
87. Ibn 'Ābidīn, *Radd al-muḥtār*, 1:143–145.
88. Ibn 'Ābidīn, *Radd al-muḥtār*, 1:149.
89. See Albaani, *The Prophet's Prayer Described*, app. 5.
90. 'Uthmānī, *I'lā' al-sunan*, 14:2:84.
91. Nimrod Hurvitz, *Schools of Law and Historical Context*, 38. See also George Makdisi, *Ibn 'Aqil: Religion and Culture in Classical Islam* (Edinburgh: Edinburgh University Press, 1997).
92. Al-Ṣan'ānī, *Irshād*, 146.
93. See Christopher Taylor, *In the Vicinity of the Righteous: Ziyāra and the Veneration of Muslim Saints in Late Medieval Egypt* (Leiden: Brill, 1998); Josef Meri, *The Cult of Saints Among Muslims and Jews in Medieval Syria* (Oxford: Oxford University Press, 2002).
94. Al-Fullānī, *Īqāẓ*, 49.
95. See, for instance, Oussama Arabī, "Early Muslim Legal Philosophy: Identity and Difference in Islamic Jurisprudence," December 1, 1999, G. E. von Grunebaum Center for Near Eastern Studies, Paper 1, http://escholarship.org/uc/item/7c8253bt, at 29.
96. See al-Fullānī,*Īqāẓ*, 24–25, 31–33, for numerous quotations by Ibn 'Abd al-Barr on this point.
97. Khaṭīb al-Baghdādī, *Ta'rīkh Baghdād*, (Beirut: Dār al-Kutub al-'Ilmiyyah, 1417), 13: 420.
98. See Scott Lucas, "The Legal Principles of Muḥammad b. Ismā'īl al-Bukhārī and Their Relationship to Classical Salafi Islam," *Islamic Law and Society* 13, no. 3 (2006): 289–324.
99. See Hallaq, "On the Origins of the Controversy about the Existence of *Mujtahids* and the Gate of Ijtihād," *Studia Islamica* 63 (1986), 129–141. See also 'Abdallāh b. 'Abd al-Muḥsin al-Turkī, *Uṣūl madhhab al-Imām Aḥmad* (Beirut: Mu'assasah al-Risālah, 1996), 705–718.
100. See Ibn al-Qayyim, *I'lam*, 5:567–580; al-Ṣan'ānī, *Irshād*, 84, also rejects this idea and calls it an erroneous conjecture (*khayāl bāṭil*).
101. Ibn al-Qayyim, *I'lam*, 4:234.
102. See John O. Voll "Renewal and Reform in Islamic History: *Tajdīd* and *Islāh*," in *Voices of Resurgent Islam*, ed. John Esposito (New York: Oxford University Press, 1983), 32–48. See also Ella Landau-Tasseron, "The 'Cyclical Reform': A Study of the Mujaddid Tradition," *Studia Islamica* 70 (1989): 79–117.
103. Ibn al-Qayyim, *I'lam*, 6:125.
104. Marshall Hodgson, *The Venture of Islam* (Chicago: University of Chicago Press, 1974), 3:160. See also *Tadwīn al-rājiḥ*, an essay contained in the *Abḥāth* (see bibliography).

105. Ibn ʿĀbidīn, *Radd al-muḥtār*, 1:151.
106. See Marie Bernard, "Ḥanafī *Uṣūl al-Fiqh* through a Manuscript of al-Ǧassās," *Journal of the American Oriental Society*, 105, no. 4 (1985): 623–635, at 624.
107. George Makdisi, "The Juridical Theology of Shāfiʿī: Origins and Significance of *Uṣūl al-Fiqh*," *Studia Islamica* 59 (1984): 5–47.
108. Makdisi, *Juridical Theology*, 12; Ibn Taymiyyah, *Kitāb al-Tisʿīniyyah*, ed. Muḥammad Ibrāhīm al-ʿAjlān, (Riyadh: Maktabah al-Maʿārif lil-Nashr wa-l-Tawzīʿ, 1999), 3:876–879; see also al-ʿImrānī, *al-Bayān*, 1: 69, where al-Ḥumaydī is cited as saying that we (i.e., the *ahl al-ḥadīth*) wanted to refute the *ahl al-rāʾy* and were unsuccessful until Shāfiʿī came to us.
109. Ibn al-Qayyim, *Iʿlām*, 6:125.
110. Hallaq, *Was the Gate of Ijtihād Closed?*, 12.
111. See Marie Bernard, *Ḥanafī Uṣūl al-Fiqh*, 625, 632, where the connection is made with other Muʿtazilī works, such as those of ʿAbd al-Jabbār.
112. See Ibn ʿĀbidīn, *Radd al-muḥtār*, 1: 140.
113. See al-Māwardī, *al-Ḥāwī al-kabīr fī fiqh madhhab al-Imām al-Shāfiʿī* (Beirut: Dār al-Kutub al-ʿIlmiyyah, 1994), 1:18–21.
114. Hallaq, *Was the Gate of Ijtihād Closed?*
115. Makdisi, *Juridical Theology*, 45, mentions several scholars who condemned al-Juwaynī for his criticism of al-Ashʿarī.
116. George Makdisi, "Ashʿarī and the Ashʿarites in Islamic Religious History. I," *Studia Islamica* 17 (1962): 37–80. Makdisi observes, significantly, that a full study of the influence of Ashʿarism on legal theory had been hindered by the habit of Muslim chroniclers to present disputes between theological schools as disputes between legal schools, such as Ḥanbalī against Shāfiʿī or more frequently, Ḥanafī against Shāfiʿī, when the term "Shāfiʿī" here actually referred to the Ashʿarīs. See Makdisi, *Juridical Theology*, 22, 42.
117. Al-Ṣanʿānī, *Irshād*, 9 (editor's introduction). The editor also cites al-Maqrīzī for his account of the trials suffered by those who would not adhere to a *madhhab*. For the *fatwā* on marriages between a Ḥanafī woman and a Shāfiʿī man, which was issued by al-Nasafī, see al-Ṣanʿānī, *Irshād*, 16–23 (editor's introduction). The issue is raised also by the *taqlīd* critic al-Albānī (Albaani), in his *The Prophet's Prayer Described*.
118. See Bernard Weiss, "Ibn Taymīyya on Leadership in the Ritual Prayer," in *Islamic Legal Interpretation: Muftīs and Their Fatwās*, ed. Muhammad Khalid Masud, Brinkley Messick, and David S. Powers (Karachi: Oxford University Press, 2005), 63–71, and Ibn Mullā Farrūkh, *al-Qawl al-sadīd*.
119. Ibn ʿAqīl, *al-Wādih*, 5:422.
120. See Ibn Mullā Farrūkh *al-Qawl al-sadīd*, which begins with the basic argument that God has not obligated anyone to be a follower of any school and then develops the argument to conclude that one may pray behind an *imām* from a different school.

121. Ibn Abī al-ʿIzz, *al-ʾIttibāʿ*, 25, 79–81.
122. Ibn al-Qayyim, *Iʿlām*, 4:234–5.
123. For more on this point, see Muḥammad al-ʿArūsī ʿAbd al-Qādir, *al-Masāʾil al-mushtarakah bayn uṣūl al—fiqh wa uṣūl ul-dīn* (Riyadh: Maktabah al-Rushd, 2009), 270–284, 288–295, 322–325.
124. Jackson, *Islamic Law and the State*, xxv.
125. al-Juwaynī, *al-Talkhīṣ fī uṣul al-fiqh*, (Beirut: Dār al-Bashāʾir al-Islāmiyyah, 1417/1996), 3:334; al-Ghazālī, *al-Mustaṣfā*, (Beirut: Dār al-Kutub al-ʿIlmiyyah, 1413/1993), 352. See also Ibn Mullā Farrūkh, *al-Qawl al-sadīd*, 53–57, where this view is attributed to the Muʿtazilīs, and later Ḥanafī scholars are shown trying to distance themselves from it. The issue is also discussed in Ibn ʿAqīl, *al-Wāḍiḥ*, 5: 379–390.
126. Qarāfī dicusses this issue at several places in his works. See, for instance, Qarāfī, *Nafāʾis al-uṣūl fī sharḥ al-maḥṣūl*, (Makkah: Maktabah Nizār Muṣṭafā al-Bāz, 1416/1995), 1:161.
127. This is the first issue discussed by al-Rāzī in his commentary on the verse 2:29: "He it is who created *for you* all that is on the earth"; see Fakhr al-Dīn al-Rāzī, *Tafsīr mafātīḥ al-ghayb* (Beirut: Dar al-Kutub al-ʿIlmiyyah, 2000), 2:142.
128. ʿAlī b. ʿAbd al-Kāfī al-Subkī and Tāj al-Dīn al-Subkī, *al-Ibhāj fī Sharḥ al-minhāj* (Beirut, Dār al-Kutub al-ʿIlmiyyah, 1995), 3:41, 62. For a discussion of the tension in the works of *kalām* theologians who also practiced jurisprudence, see Ahmad al-Raysūnī, *Imām al-Shātibī's Theory of the Higher Objectives of Islamic Law*, 197–221. Shāh Walī Allāh also briefly refers to this debate in his *Hujjat Allāh al-Bāligha*, 11. See also ʿAlī b. ʿAbbās b. ʿUthmān al-Ḥukmī, "Ḥaqīqah al-Khilāf fī l-Taʿlīl bi-l-Ḥikmah wa ʾAthruh fī l-Fiqh al-Islāmī,"*Majallah jāmiʿah ʾUmm al-Qurā*, 7, no. 9 (1414/1993–1994): 11–85.
129. See Ibn al-Najjār, *Sharḥ al-kawkab al-munīr*, 4:39.
130. For a discussion of the theological significance of this debate, see Shirāzī, *Sharḥ al-Lumaʿ*, (Beirut: Dār al-Gharb al-Islāmī, 1408/1988), 2:1043–1044.
131. Note that Jackson himself believes that al-Qarāfī's Ashʿarism had a negligible influence on his legal theory. See also al-ʿArūsī ʿAbd al-Qādir, *al-Masāʾil al-mushtarakah*, 322–323.
132. Al-Rāzī might be said to be one of the major influences on al-Qārafī's thought. Qārafī wrote two major commentaries (the *Tanqīḥ al-fuṣūl* and its commentary, *Sharḥ tanqīḥ al-fuṣūl*) on al-Rāzī's famous *uṣūl* work, *al-Maḥṣūl*; see Jackson, *Islamic Law and the State*, 7.
133. The construction of scholarly authority by developing a cult of piety has been explored briefly in Jonathan E. Brockopp, "Competing Theories of Authority in Early Mālikī Texts," in *Studies in Islamic Legal Theory*, ed. Bernard G. Weiss (Leiden: Brill, 2002), 3–22, in which he discusses the existence of a "great sheikh theory" in Mālikī law. The creation of a "super-human" founder- Imām paradigm has also been commented on by Scott Lucas, "Abū Bakr Ibn

al-Mundhir, Amputation, and the Art of *Ijtihād*," *International Journal of Middle Eastern Studies* 39 (2007): 351–368, at 363.

134. See al-Sha'rānī, *al-Mīzān al-kubrā* (Beirut: Dār al-Kutub al-'Ilmiyyah, 1997), 1:40–41.
135. Jackson asserts that, in the regime of *taqlīd*, claims of *ijmā'* actually came to conceal the biases of *muqallid* scholars.
136. Ibn al-Qayyim, *I'lām*, 6:181–181.
137. See Jackson's introduction to his *Islamic Law and the State*, and Fadel, *Social Logic*, 209–210. Fadel also says that it was possible, within the regime of *taqlīd*, to speak of correct or incorrect interpretations because of the conventions or "rules of recognition" of particular schools. He argues that this was not possible under a system of *ijtihād*. This is a confusing statement. If it is particular linguistic or legalistic conventions that determine the correctness or inaccuracy of a statement, there is no reason that such rules of language cannot also work in the system of *ijtihād*, provided there is agreement in the interpretive community over how this is to be done. If the point is that, in the regime of *ijtihād*, there are various interpretive communities following different rules, then this problem applies equally to divergent rules between schools in the regime of *taqlīd*.
138. Ibn al-Qayyim's view might also go back to an older Shāfi'ī and Ḥanbalī skepticism about the occurrence of *ijmā'*. See Jonathan Brown, *The Canonization of al-Bukhārī and Muslim: The Formation and Function of the Sunni Ḥadīth Canon* (Leiden: Brill, 2007), 144–145.
139. Jackson, *Islamic Law and the State*, 56.
140. Jackson, Islamic Law and the State, 64. On the importance of theological arguments in the debates on *maṣlaḥah*, see Felicitas Opwis, Maṣlaḥa and the Purpose of the Law: Islamic *Discourse on Legal Change from the 4th/10th to 8th/14th Century* (Leiden: Brill, 2010).
141. Jackson, *Islamic Law and the State*, 24.
142. Jackson, *Islamic Law and the State*, 177.
143. Al-Rāzī, *al-Maḥṣūl fī 'ilm uṣūl al-fiqh*, (Beirut: Mu'assasah al-Risālah, 1992), 5:176, 179.
144. See al-Ṣafadī, *Kitāb al-wāfī bi-l-wafayāt*, 2:195–197; Bori, *A Scholar in the Shadow*, 13–44. In the same volume, see Birgit Krawietz, "Transgressive Creativity in the Making: Ibn Qayyim al Ǧawziyyah's Reframing Within Ḥanbalī Legal Methodology," 47–66; Ahmad al-Raysūnī, *Imām al-Shātibī's Theory of the Higher Objectives and Intents of Islamic Law* (London: International Institute of Islamic Thought, 2005), 393.
145. Ibn al-Qayyim states clearly that there is no restriction on a *qāḍī* also delivering *fatwās*; *I'lām*, 6:139.
146. Ibn al-Qayyim, *I'lām*, 6:203–205.
147. Ibn al-Qayyim, *I'lām*, 6:167.

148. See, for instance, Ibn al-Qayyim, *I'lām*, 5:209–520, 584–605. In this section of the book, Ibn al-Qayyim lists the *fatāwā* of the Prophet in both theological and legal matters. A similar approach is adopted in *I'lām*, 4:58–336, where Ibn al-Qayyim discusses the ways in which certain groups maintain that there is often a conflict between the Qur'an and the Sunnah. His examples are drawn from theological and legal sects.
149. See for instance the comments of the prominent Mu'tazilī *qāḍī* 'Abd al-Jabbār, cited in Oussama Arabī, *Early Muslim Legal Philosophy*, 50. This work also explores the significance of al-Shāfi'ī's *Uṣūl* as a riposte to Mu'tazilī legal theory and theology.
150. See al-Shāfi'ī, *al-Risālah*, trans. Majid Khadduri (Cambridge: Islamic Texts Society, 1997), 288; Ibn al-Qayyim, *I'lām*, 1:92, 3:116. For a discussion of the theological significance of al-Shāfi'ī's insistence on the authority of solitary *ḥadīth*, see Umar F. Abd-Allah, "Theological Dimensions of Islamic Law," in *The Cambridge Companion to Classical Islamic Theology*, ed. Tim Winter (Cambridge: Cambridge University Press, 2008), 245.
151. Ibn al-Qayyim, *I'lām*, 4:47, 6:517.
152. Ibn al-Qayyim, *I'lām*, 1:369–383.
153. Ibn al-Qayyim, *I'lām*, 2: 359, 3: 168, 5:579.
154. Ibn al-Qayyim, *I'lām*, 4:337.
155. Ibn al-Qayyim goes further than most Muslim scholars in attempting to identify the rationale behind specific religious rulings. See the very long section in which he attempts to do this, Ibn al-Qayyim, *I'lām*, 3:281–425.
156. Ibn al-Qayyim, *I'lām*, 4:553–565. Ibn al-Qayyim offers 99 proofs for the validity of *sadd al-dharā'i'*, one proof for each of the 99 enumerated names of God, see Ibn al-Qayyim, *I'lām*, 5:66. On *sadd al-dharā'i'*, see Mohammad Hashim Kamali, *Principles of Islamic Jurisprudence*, (Cambridge: Islamic Texts Society, 2003), 397–409.
157. Ibn al-Qayyim, *I'lām*, 3:91–99, 116.
158. Ibn al-Qayyim, *I'lām*, 3:220–225, 4:134, 355.
159. See, for instance, Ibn al-Qayyim, *I'lām*, 5:5–65. For a Ḥanafī perspective on this issue, see Satoe Horii, "Reconsideration of Legal Devices (*hiyal*) in Islamic Jurisprudence: The Ḥanafīs and Their "Exits" (*makhārij*)," *Islamic Law and Society* 9, no. 3 (2002): 312–357. The author argues that the Ḥanafīs regarded *ḥiyal* as legal solutions drawn from an understanding of the spirit of the law (such as the principle of creating ease) as interpreted by their scholars. Horii also points to the existence of a traditionalist critique based on the kind of arguments advanced by Ibn al-Qayyim, *I'lām*, at 342. Makdisi also refers to several Ḥanafī scholars, such as al-Bazdawī, who came up with alternative views on this subject; see John Makdisi, "Legal Logic and Equity in Islamic Law," *American Journal of Comparative Law*, 33, no. 1 (1985); see also Brown, *Canonization*, 237.
160. Ibn al-Qayyim, *I'lām*, 6:74, 100.
161. Ibn al-Qayyim, *I'lām*, 6: 169–179.

162. See also Ibn al-Qayyim, *I'lām*, 4:191–192 for the author's views on how to determine which of several conflicting *aḥādīth* to follow.
163. Ibn al-Qayyim, *I'lām*, 6:180–181. See also Ibn 'Aqīl, *al-Wāḍiḥ*, 5: 379–390, for an entire chapter devoted to a refutation of those scholars who support the opinions of their schools by refusing to accept the idea that scriptural evidence can be used to favor one set of legal principles over others.
164. Ibn al-Qayyim, *I'lām*, 6:209.
165. Ibn al-Qayyim, *I'lām*, 6:169.
166. Ibn al-Qayyim, *I'lām*, 6:235.
167. Ibn al-Qayyim, *I'lām*, 6:68.
168. Ibn al-Qayyim, *I'lām*, 6:179–180.
169. Ibn al-Qayyim, *I'lām*, 6:200.
170. Ibn al-Qayyim, *I'lām*, 6:49, 64, 200–1.
171. Ibn al-Qayyim, *I'lām*, 6:201. Note that for Norman Calder, a *muftī* who presents proofs for his view is somehow blurring the boundaries between *muftī* and author, a view clearly rejected by Ibn al-Qayyim who calls on *muftī*s to mention proofs for their verdicts.
172. Ibn al-Qayyim, *I'lām*, 4:84–107.
173. Ibn al-Qayyim, *I'lām*, 4:239–273; see also Shāfi'ī *Risālah*, 109–123.
174. Ibn al-Qayyim, *I'lām*, 4:240.
175. Ibn al-Qayyim, *I'lām*, 4:239–249. Ibn al-Qayyim's examples of the issues in which the knowledge of the people of Medina would be preferred (e.g., weights and measures, the nature of the call to prayer, the number of units of prayer, the imposition of *zakāt* (alms taxes) on fruits, etc., relies on 'Abd al-Wahhāb al-Baghdādī's (d. 422/1031) discussion of such issues. Ibn al-Qayyim had praised the *qāḍī* for his *fiqh* and his staunch defense of the traditionalist stance on affirming the attributes of God. See Baghdādi, *al-Ma'ūnah*, ed. Hāmish 'Abd al-Ḥaqq (Riyadh: Maktabah al-Tijāriyyah), 1:89 (editor's notes).
176. Ibn al-Qayyim, *I'lām*, 4:267–268.
177. Ibn al-Qayyim, *I'lām*, 4:273.
178. Ibn al-Qayyim, *I'lām*, 3: 349.
179. Ibn al-Qayyim, *I'lām*, 4:388–389. For a discussion of this principle in relation to the Companions in particular, see Ibn al-Qayyim, *I'lām*, 4:394–408.
180. Ibn al-Qayyim, *I'lām*, 4:408.
181. Ibn al-Qayyim, *I'lām*, 4:394–408.
182. Ibn al-Qayyim, *I'lām*, 6:165–166.
183. Ibn al-Qayyim, *I'lām*, 5:242–247.
184. Ibn al-Qayyim, *I'lām*, 2:355.
185. Ibn al-Qayyim, *I'lām*, 5:243.
186. See the section on "The Reasons for Aḥmad's Numerous Narrations and Their Opposition to Each Other," in *Sharḥ al-zarkashī 'alā mukhtaṣar al-khiraqī*, ed. Ibn Jibrīn (Riyadh: Maktabah al-'Ubaykān, 1993), 19–21.

187. Ibn al-Qayyim, *I'lām*, 4:470.
188. Ibn al-Qayyim, *I'lām*, 4:316, 431, 441, 448, 473, 488, 505. Ibn al-Qayyim also brings up this issue when discussing the triple *talāq*; see *I'lām*, 4:377, 408–421, 424–425. The issue of the words used to signify divorce was also discussed extensively by al-Qārafī, whose views were similar to those of Ibn al-Qayyim but were strongly opposed by more loyal adherents to the Mālikī school in his time; see Jackson, *Islamic Law and the State*.
189. Ibn al-Qayyim, *I'lām*, 4:338–340.
190. Ibn al-Qayyim, *I'lām*, 4:340–342.
191. Ibn al-Qayyim, *I'lām*, 4:496, 505.
192. Ibn al-Qayyim, *I'lām*, 4:158, 166. See also Binyamin Abrahamov, "Ibn Taymiyya on the Agreement of Reason with Tradition," *The Muslim World*, 82, nos. 3–4 (1992): 256–273.
193. For an interesting discussion of this topic from a theological perspective, see Sherman A. Jackson, "The Alchemy of Domination? Some Ash'arite Responses to Mu'tazilite Ethics," *International Journal of Middle East Studies*, 31, no. 2 (1999): 185–201.
194. On the role of intuition in legal reasoning, especially in relation to the notion of *istiḥsān*, see John Makdisi, "Legal Logic and Equity in Islamic Law," 70, 73–75, 80–85.
195. A similar argument is found in Taqī Uthmānī, who argues that even if a Ḥanafī *muqallid* scholar finds a *ḥadīth* that supports a Shāfi'ī opinion, he should believe that Abū Ḥanīfa or Ḥanafī scholars must have had a stronger reason for not acting according to the *ḥadīth*. See Taqī Usmānī, *The Legal Status of Following a Madhhab*, 70.
196. See, for instance, Ibn 'Aqīl, *al-Wādiḥ*, 5: 379–390, and al-'Arūsī, *al-Masā'il al-mushtarakah*, 295–298, 322–324.
197. Ibn al-Qayyim, *I'lām*, 6:119, 128.
198. Ibn al-Qayyim, *I'lām*, 4:234, 337.
199. Ibn al-Qayyim, *I'lām*, 4: 337. For more on Ibn al-Qayyim's views on *qiyās* see *I'lām*, 2:251, 3:88–89. For different ways in which Ibn al-Qayyim uses the word *qiyās*, see *I'lām*, 2:359, 460–466. For Ibn Qayyim's general discussion on *qiyās*, see 2:329–383. On *qiyās* generally, see Kamali, *Principles of Islamic Jurisprudence*, 264–305. See also Wael Hallaq, "Non-Analogical Arguments in Sunni Juridical Qiyās," *Arabica*, 36, no. 3 (1989): 286–306, which discusses the various ways in which the term *qiyās* was used in Islamic legal thought. Note that al-Shāfi'ī too, in his *Risālah*, seems to accommodate all forms of *ijtihād* under the rubric of *qiyās*.
200. Ibn al-Qayyim, *I'lām*, 4:58–336.
201. Ibn al-Qayyim, *I'lām*, 4:85–93.
202. See, for example Shah Walī Allāh of Delhi's discussion of this debate in *Hujjat Allāh al-Bāligha*, 433–434. Virtually the same account can also be found in Walī

Allāh, *al-Inṣāf fī bayān sabab al-ikhtilāf* (Lahore: Auqāf Department, Government of the Punjab, 1971), 20.

203. Ibn Qayyim's teacher, Ibn Taymiyyah, had even accused some *ḥadīth* scholars of unfairly presenting their own proofs and concealing those of their opponents. Al-Bayhāqī and al-Ṭaḥāwī were mentioned in particular for evincing this trend.
204. See Shāh Walī Allāh, *Hujjat Allāh al-Bāligha*, 470.
205. See Ibn Mullā Farrūkh, *al-Qawl al-sadīd*, 45–46, where he condemns this view as pure partisanship.
206. Brown points out that such claims were actually made by scholars such as Khaṭīb al-Baghdādī in the context of the debate on the continuity of the *ḥadīth* tradition. See Brown, *Canonization*, 243, and Hallaq, "*Was the Gate of Ijtihād Closed?*," 24.
207. See Fullānī, *Īqāẓ*, 54, where this is reported as Mullā ʿAli Qārī's *mashhūr* narration of the Ḥanafī opinion on the issue.
208. Hallaq, *Authority, Continuity, and Change in Islamic Law*, 14–23. See also Hallaq, *Was the Gate of Ijtihād Closed?*," 29.
209. See Calder, *Al-Nawawī's Typology of Muftīs*, 137–164. Many of the categories of *muqallid* jurists cited by Nawawī would not even be called *muqallid* by Ibn al-Qayyim and his sympathizers. See also Ibn al-Ṣalāḥ, *Fatāwā wa-masāʾil Ibn al-Ṣalāḥ* (Beirut: Dār al-Maʿrifah, 1986), 21–39.
210. Ibn al-Qayyim, *Iʿlām*, 6: 125–128.
211. Hallaq, "*Was the Gate of Ijtihād Closed?*," 29–30; see also Abū Ẓahrah, *Muhāḍarāt fi taʾrīkh al-fiqh al-Islāmī*, (Cairo: Dār al Fikr al-ʿArabī, n.d.), 128.
212. Ibn al-Shāṭṭ, *Idrār al-shurūq ʿalā anwār al-furuq*, published with al-Qarāfī, *al-Furūq* (n.p.: Ālam al-Kutub, n.d.), 1:220.
213. Al-Shaʿrānī, *al-Mīzān al-kubrā*, 1:21.
214. See al-Ṣanʿānī, *Irshād*, 104. See also Abdul Hakim I. Al-Matroudi, *The Hanbalī School of Law and Ibn Taymiyyah: Conflict or Conciliation* (Routledge: New York, 2006).
215. For Ibn ʿAqīl's views on *ijtihād* and *taqlīd*, see *al-Wāḍiḥ*, 5:351–424.
216. Ibn al-Qayyim, *Iʿlām*, 6:166.
217. Al-Biri, *al-Ashbāh ʿan Sharḥ al-Hidāyah*, quoted in Ibn ʿĀbidīn, *Radd al-muḥtār*, 1:167. For a discussion of whether a *mujtahid* can adopt the opinion of someone more knowledgeable than himself, see Ibn Mullā Farrūkh, *al-Qawl al-sadīd*, 100, where he suggests that there is considerable disagreement on this issue among the Ḥanafī Imāms.
218. See also Ibn ʿĀbidīn, *Radd al-muḥtār*, 1:140, for a discussion of the opinions of Ibn al-Humām and Ibn Ḥajar on how a layman is to decide which scholarly opinion he is to follow.
219. Calder, *Al-Nawawī's Typology of Muftīs*.

220. Ibn al-Qayyim, *I'lām*, 6:125. Compare also the comments of Benjamin Jokisch, *Islamiches Recht in Theorie und Praxis: Analyse einiger kaufrechtlicher fatwās von Taqi'd-Dīn Ahmad b. Taymīyya* (Berlin 1996), 206, 253ff., wherein he argues that almost no scholar would claim to be an absolute independent *mujtahid* in the sense of consulting scripture and nothing more, cited in Krawietz, "Cut and Paste in Legal Rules: Designing Islamic Norms with *Talfīq*."
221. Ibn al-Qayyim, *I'lām*, 6:125. See also 'Uthmānī, *Ī'lā' al-sunan*, 14:2:16.
222. Ibn al-Qayyim, *I'lām*, 6:203.
223. Ibn 'Aqīl, *al-Wādiḥ*, 5: 244–256.
224. Ibn al-Qayyim, *I'lām*, 6:203–205.
225. The *rājiḥ* could also be referred to as the *ẓāhir*. See Mardāwī, *al-Inṣāf fī mā'rifah al-rājiḥ min al-khilāf 'alā madhhab al-imām al-mubajjal Aḥmad b. Ḥanbal*, ed. Muḥammad Ḥāmid al-Fīqī (Cairo: Maṭbū'ah al-Sunnah al-Muḥammadiyyah, 1955), 1:7.
226. Al-Ḥajjāwī, *Zād al-mustaqni' fī ikhtiṣār al-muqni'* (Riyadh: Madār al-Waṭan lil-Nashr, 2004).
227. Al-Ṣan'ānī, *Irshād*, 14–15 (editor's introduction).
228. Hallaq, "*Was the Gate of Ijtihād Closed?*," 74. See also Rudolph Peters, "Ijtihād and *Taqlīd* in 18th and 19th Century Islam," *Die Welt des Islams* 20 (1989): 132–145, at 137, where the author suggests that it is not even correct to refer to this kind of activity as *taqlīd*, because an affiliated scholar fully understands his Imām's argument.
229. Jackson, *Islamic Law and the State*, 87; Fadel, *Social Logic*, 205.
230. Al-Ṣan'āni, *Irshād*, 106–107.
231. Al-Ṣan'āni, *Irshād*, 156.
232. Jackson, *Islamic Law and the State*, 83–89. Ibn 'Aqīl argues that in making *tarjīḥ* a jurist must give preference to one scriptural interpretation over another, or to one *ḥadīth* over another and proceeds to identify the criteria on which he may do so. See *al-Wādiḥ*, 2: 302–309, 350–357.
233. See for instance, al-Laknawī, *Fawātiḥ al-raḥamūt* (Beirut: Dār al-Kutub al-'Ilmiyyah, 2002), 2:431, where various established Ḥanafī and non-Ḥanafī opinions in support of this proposition are cited and then refuted.
234. Hallaq, *Authority, Continuity and Change in Islamic Law*, 203–208.
235. Hallaq, "*Was the Gate of Ijtihād Closed?*," 30; al-Ṣan'ānī, *Irshād*, 65 (editor's notes).
236. See Jackson, *Islamic Law and the State*, 120.
237. Ibn al-Qayyim, *I'lām*, 2:56–59, 4: 232.
238. Ibn al-Qayyim, *I'lām*, 2:56.
239. Walī Allāh, *al-Inṣāf*, 18–19. See also al-Ṣan'ānī, *Irshād*, 14–15. Ibn al-Humām, too, was considered by some a *mujtahid*. See al-Albānī, '*Umdāt al-taḥqīq*, 109.
240. See for example 'Uthmānī, *I'lā' al-sunan*, 14:2:71.

241. See Ibn Jibrīn, *Sharḥ al-Zarkashī*, 9, 15 (editor's introduction).
242. See Scott Lucas, "Abū Bakr Ibn al-Mundhir, Amputation, and the Art of *Ijtihād*," 352, referring to al-Subkī's *Ṭabaqāt al Shāfiʿiyyah*. Ibn al-Mundhīr's personal opinions continued to be evaluated alongside those of the four established schools in *madhhab* works such as the *Mughnī* of Ibn Qudāmah, ibid., 353.
243. Brown, *Canonization*, 71–73.
244. See Joseph Schacht, *The Origins of Muhammadan Jurisprudence* (Oxford: Clarendon Press, 1950), 86.
245. See for instance, Calder, *Al-Nawawī's Typology of Muftīs*; Gerber, "Rigidity Versus Openness in Late Classical Islamic Law," 187, states that *istiḥsān* was a way of quietly introducing innovations that were socially desirable, sometimes under the guise of *qiyās khafī* (hidden analogy). On the inconsistency occasioned by this and by the use of custom, see Gerber, ibid., 186–192.
246. Calder, *The "Uqūd Rasm al-Muftī" of Ibn ʿĀbidīn*, 175.
247. Ibn ʿĀbidīn, *Radd al-muḥtār*, 1:167.
248. Ibn ʿĀbidīn, *Radd al-muḥtār*, 180–181.
249. Hallaq, *Authority, Continuity, and Change in Islamic Law*, 221–235.
250. See Abdal Hakim Murad (Timothy Winter), *Understanding the Four Madhhabs: The Facts about Ijtihād and Taqlīd* (New York, n.d.), 14. In the same work (p. 10) he states that the *ḥadīth* scholars were "all loyal adherents of one or another of the *madhhabs*," which they continued to improve and refine.
251. See Matroudi, *The Hanbalī School of Law and Ibn Taymiyyah*, 129–169.

## CHAPTER 1

1. Ibn ʿAbd al-Barr, *al-Jāmiʿ* (1861, 1864). Similar narrations exist in Sufyān al-Thawrī's *Tafsīr*, 124 (333); ʿAbd al-Razzāq, *Muṣannaf*, II. (272); al-Ṭabārī, *Tafsīr*, X. (815); Ibn Abī Ḥātim, *Tafsīr*, VI. (1784) (10058); al-Khaṭīb al-Baghdādī, *al-Faqīh wa-l-mutafaqqih*, II. (67); al-Bayhaqī, *Sunān*, X. (116), *al-Madkhal*, 258–259.
2. Al-Tirmidhī, al-Jāmiʿ, ʿAbwāb al-tafsīr," (Bāb Sūrah al-Tawbah), V. 278 (3095); al-Ṭabarī, *Tafsīr*, X. (81); al-Ṭabarānī, *al-Kabīr*, XVII. 92 (218–219); Ibn Abī Ḥātim, *al-Tafsīr*, VI. 1784 (10057); al-Wāḥidī, *al-Wāsiṭ*, II. (490) (491); al-Bayhaqī, *Sunān al-kubrā*, X. (116), *al-Madkhal* (261); Ibn Ḥazm, *al-Iḥkām*, VI. 132–133; al-Mizzī, *Tahdhīb al-kamāl* (1090).
3. Ibn ʿAbd al-Barr, *al-Jāmiʿ* (1863).
4. Al-Ṭabarānī, *al-Kabīr*, XVII. 14; al-Bazzār, *Musnad* (182); al-Bayhaqī, *al-Madkhal* (830); Abū Nuʿaym, *al-Ḥilyah*, II. 10; Ibn ʿAbd al-Barr, *al-Jāmiʿ* (1865). MH says its chain is very weak.
5. Ibn ʿAbd al-Barr, *al-Jāmiʿ* (1865).
6. Al-Bayhaqī, *al-Madkhal* (831), *Sunān al-kubrā*, XX. 211; Ibn ʿUdayy, *al-Kāmil*, VI. 2081.

7. Al-Bayhaqī, *al-Madkhal* (832), *Shu'b al-imān* (10311); al-Khaṭīb al-Baghdādī, *Faqīh wa-l-mutafaqqih*, II. 13.
8. Ibn 'Abd al-Barr, *al-Jāmi'* (1069, 1870).
9. Abū Dā'ūd, *al-Sunnah*, "Luzum al-sunnah" (4611); al-Bayhaqī, *al-Madkhal* (834). MH says its chain is authentic.
10. Ibn 'Abd al-Barr, *al-Jāmi'* (1872).
11. Ibid. (1873).
12. Ibn Abī Shaybah, *Muṣannaf*, VI. 188; Ibn 'Abd al-Barr, *al-Jāmi'* (1874–1876); al-Bayhaqī, *al-Madkhal* (378); Ibn Ḥazm *al-Iḥkām*, VI. 68, 147.
13. Ibn Ḥazm *al-Iḥkām*, VI. 97–98.
14. Ibn 'Abd al-Barr, *al-Jāmi'* (1881).
15. Al-Ṭabarānī, *al-Kabīr* (8764); Ibn Ḥazm *al- Iḥkām*, VI. 97, 147; Ibn 'Abd al-Barr, *al-Jāmi'* (1882).
16. Al-Bukharī, *Ṣaḥīḥ*, "Kitāb al-'Ilm," (100), "Kitāb al-I'tiṣām' (7307); Muslim, "Kitāb al-'Ilm," (2673).
17. Ibn 'Abd al-Barr, *al-Jāmi'* (1885).
18. Ibn 'Abd al-Barr, *al-Jāmi'* (1889); Ibn Abī Shaybah, *Muṣannaf*, VIII. 762; Aḥmad, *Musnad*, II. 321; al-Ṭaḥāwī, *al-Mushkal* (411); Ibn al-Jawzī, *Muqaddimāh al-mawḍū'āt*, I. 74.
19. Aḥmad, *Musnad*, II. 321, 365; Abū Dā'ūd, *Sunan*, "Kitāb al-'Ilm," (3657); Bayhaqī, *al-Madkhal* (186); Ibn Ḥazm *al- Iḥkām*, VI. 45; Ibn 'Abd al-Barr, *al-Jāmi'* (1626).
20. Al-Bukhārī, *Ṣaḥīḥ*, "al-Nikaḥ," (5143); Muslim (2563).
21. Ibn 'Abd al-Barr, *al-Jāmi'* (1900).
22. Ibn 'Udayy, *al-Kāmil*, VI. 2080; al-Bayhaqī, *al-Zuhd* (207).
23. Al-Bayhaqī, *al-Madkhal* (262).
24. Ibn Ḥazm *al- Iḥkām*, VI. 120–121.

## CHAPTER 2
## *Ḥadīth References*

The *aḥādīth* in the notes below are reproduced with the kind permission of the editor of the Arabic text, Shaykh Mashhūr Ḥasan (MH), who has provided exhaustive references for all the *aḥādīth* and narrations cited in the work. He then proceeds to give his own verdicts on the *aḥādīth* in the light of the comments of classical *ḥadīth* scholars. Although all the *ḥadīth* references that follow are the work of Shaykh Mashhūr Ḥasan, I have reproduced only some of the references to the more renowned collections. MH's own additional comments have been included only rarely.

The *ḥadīth* collections are referred to by their popular names and their titles are shortened. The name of the chapter in which the *ḥadīth* is found is in quotation marks. The volume number is in roman numerals. Page numbers follow volume numbers. The *ḥadīth* number is always indicated in brackets.

1. Ibn Mājah, *Sunan*, "al-Ṭahārah" (572); al-Dāraquṭnī, *Sunan*, I. 190–191; Abū Nuʿaym, *Ḥilyah*, III. 317–318; al-Bayhaqī, *Khilāfīyāt* (836); al-Khaṭīb al-Baghdādī, *al-Faqīh wa-l-mutafaqqih*, II. 68; Aḥmad, *Musnad*, I. 330; al-Bukhārī, *al-Taʾrīkh*, VIII. 288; Abū Dāʾūd, *Sunan* (337); ʿAbd al-Razzāq, *Muṣannaf* (867); al-Ṭabarānī, *al-Kabīr* (11472).
2. Al-Bukhārī, *Ṣaḥīḥ*, "al-Ḥudūd" (6827–6828).
3. Ibn Ḥazm, *al-Iḥkām*, VI. 127; ʿAbd al-Razzāq, *Muṣannaf*, X. 304 (19191); Ibn Abī Shayba, *Muṣannaf*, XI. 415–416.
4. Ibn Ḥazm, *al-Iḥkām*, VI. 67.
5. Aḥmad, *Musnad*, V. 246; Abū Dāʾūd, *Sunan*, "Ṣalāh," (507); Ibn Ḥazm, *al-Iḥkām*, VI. 70–71.
6. Al-Bayhaqī, *al-Madkhal* (152); al-Khatīb, *al-Kifāyah*, 48; Ibn ʿAbd al-Barr, *al-Jāmiʿ*, II. 925 (1760); Ibn Ḥazm, *al-Iḥkām*, VI. 82.
7. Aḥmad, *Musnad*, IV. 126–127; Abū Dāʾūd, *Sunan*, "Kitāb al-Sunnah," IV. 200–201 (4607); al-Tirmidhī, *al-Jāmiʿ*, "Abwāb al-ʿilm," V. 44 (2676); Ibn Majah, *Sunan*, "al-Muqaddimah," I. 15–17 (42) (43) (44).
8. Al-Nisāʾī, *al-Mujtabā*, "Kitāb Ādāb al-quḍāh," VIII. 231; al-Dārimī, *Sunan*, I. 60; Ibn Abī Shaybah, *Muṣannaf*, VII. 241; al-Khaṭīb al-Baghdādī, *al-Faqīh wa-l-mutafaqqih*, II. 99; Ibn ʿAbd al-Barr, *al-Jāmiʿ*, II. 846 (1595); Ibn Ḥazm, *al-Iḥkām*, VI. 29–30. MH says that its chain is authentic.
9. Abū Dāʾūd, *Sunan*, "Kitāb al-ʿItq" (3954); al-Bayhaqī, *Sunan*, X. 347.
10. Muslim, *Ṣaḥīḥ*, "Kitāb al-Ṭalāq" (1472).
11. Mālik, *al-Mawaṭṭa*," I. 50 (137); al-Bayhaqī, *Sunan al-kubrā*, I. 170.
12. Ibn Abī Shaybah, *Muṣannaf*, X. 489; al-Bukhārī, *al-Taʾrīkh al-kabīr*, II. 39–40; Ibn Ḥazm, *al-Iḥkām*, VI. 93.
13. Aḥmad, *Musnad*, IV. 4–5; al-Bukhārī, *Ṣaḥīḥ*, "Faḍāʾil al-Ṣaḥābah" (3658).
14. Al-Bukhārī, *Ṣaḥīḥ*, "Kitāb al-ʿIlm" (88) (2052) (2640) (2659) (2660) (5104).
15. Abū Dāʾūd al-Ṭayālisī, *Musnad* (1252); Abū Dāʾūd, *Sunan*, "al-Ṭahārah" (82); Aḥmad, *Musnad*, V. 66; al-Tirmidhī, *al-Jāmiʿ*, "al-Ṭahārah (64); Ibn Mājah, *Sunan*, "al-Ṭahārah" (373); al-Bayhaqī, *Sunan*, I. 191.
16. Al-Bukhārī, *Ṣaḥīḥ*, "Kitāb al-wuḍūʾ" (238); Muslim, *Ṣaḥīḥ*, "al-Ṭahārah" (281).
17. Al-Bukhārī, *Ṣaḥīḥ*, "Kitāb al-wuḍūʾ" (162); Muslim, *Ṣaḥīḥ*, "al-Ṭahārah" (278); al-Dāraquṭnī, *Sunan*, I. 132.
18. Al-Dāraquṭnī, *Sunan*, I. 132.
19. Mālik, *al-Mawaṭṭaʾ*, "Kitāb al-Ṭahārah" I. 22 (12); Ibn Abī Shaybah, *Muṣannaf*, I. 131; Aḥmad, *Musnad*, II. 237 (361) (393); al-Nisāʾī, *al-Mujtabā*, "Kitāb al-Ṭahārah," I. 176; al-Tirmidhī, *al-Jāmiʿ*, "Abwāb al-Ṭahārah," I. 100–101 (69); Abū Dāʾūd, *Sunan*, "al-Ṭahārah," I. 64 (83); Ibn Mājah, *Sunan*, "al-Ṭahārah," I. 136 (386), II. 1081 (3246); al-Dāraquṭnī, *Sunan*, I. 36.
20. Al-Bukhārī, *Ṣaḥīḥ*, "Kitāb al-wuḍūʾ" I. 274 (172); Muslim, *Ṣaḥīḥ*, "al-Ṭahārah," I. 234 (279) (280).
21. Al-Bukhārī, *al-Taʾrīkh al-kabīr*, III. 308–309; al-Dāraquṭnī, *Sunan*, I. 401; al-Bayhaqī, *Sunan*, II. 404; Ibn al-Jawzī, *al-Mawḍūʿāt*, II. 76. MH says that al-Bukhārī

said, "This tradition is false and is the essence of rejected traditions." Ibn Ḥibbān said, "It is fabricated, without a doubt. The Prophet, may the peace and blessings of God be upon him, did not say such a thing, but the people of Kufah preferred this tradition."

22. Al-Bayhaqī, *Sunan al-kubrā*, IV. 92.
23. Al-Ḥākim, *al-Mustadrak*, I. 359, 397; al-Bayhaqī, *Sunan*, IV. 89–90.
24. Al-Bukhārī, *Ṣaḥīḥ*, "Kitāb al-Buyū'" (2148); Muslim, *Ṣaḥīḥ*, "Kitāb al-Buyū'" (1158) (1524).
25. Al-Bayhaqī, *al-Ma'rifah* (3326), *Sunan al-kubrā*, V. 273; al-Dāraquṭnī, *Sunan*, III. 54–55; al-Ḥākim, *al-Mustadrak*, II. 22.
26. Muslim, *Ṣaḥīḥ* (1111); al-Bukhārī, *Ṣaḥīḥ* (1937).
27. Aḥmad, *Musnad*, II. 498, al-Dārimī, *Sunan*, II. 14; Abū Dā'ūd, *Sunan*, "al-Ṣawm" (2380); al-Tirmidhī, *al-Jāmi'*, "al-Ṣawm" (720); Ibn Mājah, *Sunan* (1676); al-Dāraquṭnī, *Sunan* (18412); al-Bayhaqī, *Sunan*, IV. 219.
28. Al-Bukhārī, *Ṣaḥīḥ*, "Taqṣīr al-ṣalāh" (1086–1087); Muslim, *Ṣaḥīḥ*, "al-Ḥajj" (1338) (414).
29. Al-Bukhārī, *Ṣaḥīḥ*, "al-Zakāt" (1448).
30. Abū Dā'ūd, *Sunan*, "al-Ḥudūd" (4408); al-Tirmidhī, *al-Jāmi'*, "al-Ḥudūd" (1474); al-Nisā'ī, *Sunan*, VIII. 91; Aḥmad, *Musnad*, IV. 181; al-Dārimī, *Sunan*, II. 231; al-Bayhaqī, *Sunan al-kubrā*, IX. 104.
31. Abū Dā'ūd, *Sunan*, "al-Buyū'" (3332); Aḥmad, *Musnad*, V. 92–93; al-Bayhaqī, *Sunan al-kubrā*, V. 335; al-Dāraquṭnī, *Sunan*, IV. 285–286.
32. Al-Bukhārī, *Ṣaḥīḥ*, "al-Zakāt" (1499) (2355) (6912) (6913); Muslim, *Ṣaḥīḥ*, "al-Ḥudūd" (1710).
33. Aḥmad, *Musnad*, II. 216; al-Dāraquṭnī, *Sunan*, III. 88; al-Bayhaqī, *Sunan*, VIII. 67.
34. 'Abd al-Razzāq, *Muṣannaf*, II. 96 (2632); Aḥmad, *Musnad*, VI. 15; Abū Dā'ūd, *Sunan*, "al-Ṣalāh" (937); al-Bayhaqī, *Sunan al-kubrā*, II. 22–23. MH says that in other versions it is the Prophet who says these words to Bilāl. See for instance, Aḥmad, *Musnad*, VI. 12; al-Bayhaqī, *Sunan*, II. 23, 56.
35. Muslim, *Ṣaḥīḥ*, "Kitāb al-Ṭahārah" (274).
36. Al-Bukhārī, *Ṣaḥīḥ*, "al-Adhān" (734); Muslim, *Ṣaḥīḥ* (414).
37. Al-Bukhārī, *Ṣaḥīḥ*, "al-Adhān" (757) (793) (6251); Muslim, *Ṣaḥīḥ*, "al-Ṣalāh" (397).
38. Aḥmad, *Musnad*, V. 424; al-Bukhārī, *Ṣaḥīḥ*, "Juz' Raf' al-yadayn fī l-ṣalāh," 5; Abū Dā'ūd, *Sunan* (730) (733) (734) (963) (966) (967); al-Tirmidhī, *al-Jāmi'*, "al-Ṣalāh" (304) (305); al-Nisā'ī, *Sunan*, "al-Sahw," III. 34; Ibn Mājah, *Sunan*, "al-'Iqāmah" (1061); al-Bayhaqī, *Sunan*, II. (62) (72) (73) (101) (116) (118) (123) (129).
39. Al-Bukhārī, *Ṣaḥīḥ*, "al-Jum'ah" (930) (931); Muslim, *Ṣaḥīḥ* (875).
40. Muslim, *Ṣaḥīḥ*, "al-Ṣalāh" (431).
41. Muslim, *Ṣaḥīḥ*, "al-Ṣalāh" (431).
42. Al-Bukhārī, *Ṣaḥīḥ*, "al-Adhān" (684) (1201) (1218) (2690) (7190); Muslim, *Ṣaḥīḥ*, "al-Ṣalāh" (421).

43. Al-Bukhārī, *Ṣaḥīḥ*, "al-Adhān" (664) (683) (687) (712) (713); Muslim, *Ṣaḥīḥ*, "al-Ṣalāh" (418).
44. Al-Bukhārī, *Ṣaḥīḥ*, "al-Adhān" (617) (620) (623) (1918) (2656) (7248); Muslim, *Ṣaḥīḥ*, "al-Ṣiyām" (1092).
45. Al-Bukhārī, *Ṣaḥīḥ*, "al-Adhān" (617) (620) (623) (1918) (2656) (7248); Muslim, *Ṣaḥīḥ*, "al-Ṣiyām" (1092).
46. Al-Bukhārī, *Ṣaḥīḥ*, "al-Wuḍūʾ (144) (394); Muslim, *Ṣaḥīḥ*, "al-Ṭahārah" (264).
47. Al-Bukhārī, *Ṣaḥīḥ*, "al-Iʿtikāf" (2032) (2042) (2043) (3144) (4320) (6697); Muslim, *Ṣaḥīḥ*, "al-Aymān" (1656).
48. Aḥmad, *Musnad*, III. 490; Abū Dāʾūd, *Sunan*, "al-Farāʾiḍ" (2906); al-Tirmidhī, *al-Jāmiʿ*, "al-Farāʾiḍ" (2115); Ibn Mājah, *Sunan*, "al-Farāʾiḍ" (2742); al-Dāraquṭnī, *Sunan*, IV. 89–90; al-Bayhaqī, *Sunan al-kubrā*, VI. 240, 259.
49. Abū Dāʾūd al-Ṭayālisī, *Musnad* (1443); Aḥmad, *Musnad*, V. 347; Abū Dāʾūd, *Sunan*, "al-Farāʾiḍ" (2903) (2904); al-Bayhaqī, *Sunan al-kubrā*, VI. 243.
50. Abū Dāʾūd, *Sunan*, "al-Diyyāt" (4564); al-Bayhaqī, *Sunan*, VI. 220.
51. Al-Bukhārī, *Ṣaḥīḥ*, "al-Tayammum" (337); Muslim, *Ṣaḥīḥ* (369).
52. Al-Bukhārī, *Ṣaḥīḥ*, "al-Wuḍūʾ (156).
53. Al-Bukhārī, *Ṣaḥīḥ*, "al-Ṣulh" (2699) (4251).
54. Aḥmad, *Musnad*, I. 97–98; al-Bayhaqī, *Sunan*, IX. 127.
55. Al-Bukhārī, *Ṣaḥīḥ* (2412) (4638) (6916) (6917) (7427); Muslim, *Ṣaḥīḥ* (2373). MH adds that this version does not say that he took retribution. In fact, retribution is not mentioned in any version of this tradition.
56. Muslim, *Ṣaḥīḥ*, "al-Aymān" (1657).
57. Aḥmad, *Musnad*, II. 216.
58. Al-Nisāʾī, *Sunan*, "al-Qasāmah," VIII. 55; Abū Dāʾūd, *Sunan*, "al-Diyyāt" (4567).
59. Al-Bukhārī, *Ṣaḥīḥ*, "al-Hibah" (2586).
60. Abū Dāʾūd, *Sunan*, "al-Ṭahārah" (385); al-Ḥākim, *al-Mustadrak*, I. 166; al-Bayhaqī, *Sunan al-kubrā*, II. 430.
61. Al-Bukhārī, *Ṣaḥīḥ*, "al-Maghāzī" (4261).
62. Abū Dāʾūd, *Sunan* (4388); al-Nisāʾī, *Sunan*, "Qatʿ al-sāriq," VIII. 87; al-Bayhaqī, *Sunan al-kubrā*, VIII. 262.
63. Aḥmad, II. 180; Abū Dāʾūd, *Sunan* (1708) (1710); al-Nisāʾī *Sunan*, V. 44; al-Tirmidhī, *al-Jāmiʿ* (1289).
64. Al-Bukhārī, *Ṣaḥīḥ*, "al-Ḥudūd" (6792); Muslim, *Ṣaḥīḥ*, "al-Ḥudūd" (1684).
65. Al-Bukhārī, *Ṣaḥīḥ*, "al-Ḥudūd" (6795); Muslim, *Ṣaḥīḥ*, "al-Ḥudūd" (1686).
66. Al-Bayhaqī, *Sunan al-kubrā*, VI. 200.
67. Ibn Mājah, *Sunan*, "al-Shufʿah" (2500) (2501); al-Bayhaqī, *Sunan*, VI. 108. MH says that its chain is very weak.
68. MH says that the narration that matches the above most closely is one with a different wording and is to be found in al-Bukhārī, *Taʾrīkh al-kabīr*," III. 182; al-Bayhaqī, *Sunan*, VIII. 36; Aḥmad, *Musnad*, I. 22; Ibn Mājah, *Sunan* (2662); al-Tirmidhī, *al-Jāmiʿ* (1400).

69. Muslim, *Ṣaḥīḥ*, "al-Ṣiyām" (1154).
70. Al-Bukhārī, *Ṣaḥīḥ*, "al-Buyū'" (2141); Muslim, "al-Aymān" (997).
71. Muslim, *Ṣaḥīḥ*, "al-Aymān" (1668).
72. 'Abd al-Razzāq, *Muṣannaf*, X. 305 (19194); Ibn Ḥazm, *al-Iḥkām*, VI. 128.
73. Al-Bayhaqī, *Sunan al-kubrā*, IX. 73; al-'Asqalānī, *Fatḥ al-bārī*, XII. 280.
74. Al-Bukhārī, *Ṣaḥīḥ* (2334); al-Bayhaqī, *Sunan al-kubrā*, IX. 134; Aḥmad, *Musnad*, I. 31.
75. Al-Bukhārī, *Ṣaḥīḥ*, "al-Maghāzī" (4022).
76. Muslim, *Ṣaḥīḥ*, "al-Imārah" (1823).
77. Ibn Qayyim discusses this issue elsewhere in his book. See also Ibn Ḥazm, *al-Iḥkām*, VI. 66.
78. Al-Bukhārī, *Ṣaḥīḥ*, "al-Aḥkām" (7221); al-Bayhaqī, *Sunan al-kubrā*, VIII. 335. MH says that its chain is authentic, according to the conditions of the two shaykhs [al-Bukhārī and Muslim].
79. Ibn Abī Shaybah, *Muṣannaf*, VI. 438; 'Abd al-Razzāq, *Muṣannaf*, VII. 289 (13214); al-Bayhaqī, *Sunan al-kubrā*, X. 248; Ibn Ḥazm, *al-Iḥkām*, VI. 16. MH says that its chain is authentic.
80. Muslim, *Ṣaḥīḥ* (534); Ibn Abī Shaybah, *Muṣannaf*, I. 277; 'Abd al-Razzāq, *Muṣannaf*, II. 152; Ibn Ḥazm, *al-Iḥkām*, VI. 62.
81. Al-Nisā'ī, *Sunan*, "al-Taṭbīq" II. 185; al-Bayhaqī, *Sunan al-kubrā*, II. 85.
82. 'Abd al-Razzāq, *Muṣannaf* (11366).
83. 'Abd al-Razzāq, *Muṣannaf* (11391); al-Bayhaqī, *Sunan*, VII. 351; Ibn Abī Shaybah, *Muṣannaf*, IV. 56.
84. Al-Bayhaqī, *Sunan*, VII. 156; 'Abd al-Razzāq, *Muṣannaf* (12798).
85. Al-Bayhaqī, *Sunan*, VII. 155; Ibn Abī Shaybah, *Muṣannaf*, III. 360; 'Abd al-Razzāq, *Muṣannaf* (12793).
86. 'Abd al-Razzāq, *Muṣannaf* (13169); Ibn Abī Shaybah, *Muṣannaf*, IV. 64; al-'Asqalānī, *Fatḥ al-bārī*, IX. 404.
87. Ibn Abī Shaybah, *Muṣannaf*, IV. 65.
88. Al-Bukhārī, *Ṣaḥīḥ*, "Kitāb Faḍā'il al-Qur'ān" (5000); Muslim, *Ṣaḥīḥ*, "Kitāb Faḍā'il al-ṣaḥābāh" (4262); Ibn Ḥazm, *al-Iḥkām*, VI. 62.
89. Al-Bukhārī, *Ṣaḥīḥ*, "Kitāb Faḍā'il al-Qur'ān" (5002); Muslim, *Ṣaḥīḥ*, "Kitāb Faḍā'il al-ṣaḥābāh" (2463); Ibn Ḥazm, *al-Iḥkām*, VI. 63.
90. Al-Bukhārī, *Ṣaḥīḥ*, "Kitāb Faḍā'il al-ṣaḥābāh" (3763); Muslim, *Ṣaḥīḥ*, "Kitāb Faḍā'il al-ṣaḥābāh" (2460).
91. Muslim, *Ṣaḥīḥ*, "Kitāb Faḍā'il al-ṣaḥābāh" (2461); Ibn Ḥazm, *al-Iḥkām*, VI. 63.
92. Al-Ḥākim, *al-Mustadrak*, III. 388; al-Bayhaqī, *Madkhal* (101); Ibn Ḥazm, *al-Iḥkām*, IV. 211.
93. Ibn Ḥazm, *al-Iḥkām*, IV. 214.
94. Aḥmad, *Musnad*, I. 337.
95. Aḥmad, *Musnad*, IV. 43; Abū Dā'ūd, *Sunan* (499); Ibn Mājah, *Sunan* (706).
96. Ibn Qayyim has already mentioned that this was the position of 'Umar and Abū Bakr.

97. MH says that this is the position of Ibn Masʿūd.
98. MH says that this is the position of ʿUmar.
99. MH says that this is the position of ʿAmmār. See Ibn Abī Shaybah, *Muṣannaf*, III. 306.
100. MH says that this is the position of ʿUthmān.
101. Al-Ṭaḥāwī, *Mushkal* (1864). This is the position of Anas.
102. MH says that Bazzār says, "We do not know of anyone adopting this position except Abū Ṭalḥah."
103. MH says that this is the position of Ibn ʿAbbās. See al-Bukhārī, *Ṣaḥīḥ*, "al-Tafsīr" (4909); Muslim, *Ṣaḥīḥ*, "al-Ṭalāq" (1485).
104. MH says that this is the position of Ibn Masʿūd. See al-Bukhārī, *Ṣaḥīḥ*, "al-Tafsīr" (4910).
105. MH says that this is the position of ʿUmar. See Mālik, *al-Mawaṭṭaʾ*, I. 329; Muslim, *Ṣaḥīḥ*, "al-Ḥajj" (1192).
106. MH says that this is the position of Ḥuṣayn b. ʿAlī and many others. See Ibn Abī Shaybah, *Muṣannaf*, III. 284.
107. MH says that this is the position of Ibn ʿAbbās.
108. Al-Bukhārī, *Ṣaḥīḥ* (2178); Muslim, *Ṣaḥīḥ* (1596).
109. MH says that this is the position of a group of Companions including ʿUmar and his son, Abū Hurayrah, Abū Bakr, and others. See Mālik, *al- Mawaṭṭaʾ*, I. 45, 46, 147; ʿAbd al Razzāq, *Muṣannaf*, I. 245 (940) (942) (947) (949) (950) (951); al-Bayhaqī, *Sunan al-kubrā*, I. 166, 264.
110. MH says that this is the position of ʿUthmān. See al-Bukhārī, *Ṣaḥīḥ*, "al-Ghusl" (292). The same position is attributed to ʿAlī, Zubayr, and others. See Aḥmad, *Musnad*, V. 115; Abū Dāʾūd, *Sunan* (214); Ibn Mājah, *Sunan* (609).
111. These include ʿUmar. See ʿAbd al-Razzāq, *Muṣannaf* (19112); Ibn Abī Shaybah, *Muṣannaf*, VII. 336. This is also the position of ʿĀʾishah. See ʿAbd al-Razzāq, *Muṣannaf* (19124); al-Dāraquṭnī, *Sunan*, IV. 85; al-Dārimī, *Sunan*, II. 366.
112. MH says that this is the position of ʿUmar. See Mālik, *al-Mawaṭṭaʾ*, II. 516; Ibn Abī Shaybah, *Muṣannaf*, VI. 377.
113. MH says that this is the position of ʿĀʾishah. See Muslim, *Ṣaḥīḥ* (1453) (1454); al-Bukhārī, *Ṣaḥīḥ* (4000) (5088).
114. MH says that this is the position of ʿUmar and his son. See ʿAbd al-Razzāq, *Muṣannaf* (13889).
115. MH says that this is the position of ʿUmar and Ibn Masʿūd. See al-Bukhārī, *Ṣaḥīḥ*, "al-Tayammum" (338); Muslim, *Ṣaḥīḥ*, "al-Ḥayḍ" (368) (110) (111) (112) (113).
116. MH says that this is the position of ʿAlī. See Ibn Abī Shaybah, *Muṣannaf*, I. 183, al-Ṭabārī, *Tafsīr*, V. 62.
117. MH says that this is the position of Ibn ʿAbbās, who maintained that this was the universal practice during the time of the Prophet and Abū Bakr and the first two years of ʿUmar's reign. See Muslim, *Ṣaḥīḥ*, "al-Ṭalāq" (1472).

118. MH says that this is the position of ʿUmar. See Muslim, *Ṣaḥīḥ*, "al-Ṭalāq" (1472); ʿAbd al-Razzāq, *Muṣannaf* (11340). This is also the position of Abū Hurayrah, Ibn ʿAbbās, and Ibn ʿUmar.
119. MH says that this is the position of ʿAlī. See Muslim, *Ṣaḥīḥ*, "al-Ḥajj" (1223).
120. MH says that this is the position of ʿUthmān. See Muslim, *Ṣaḥīḥ*, "al-Ḥajj" (1223).
121. MH says that this is the position of Ibn ʿAbbās. See al-Bukhārī, *Ṣaḥīḥ* (4227) (5529).
122. MH says that this is the position of Saʿd b. Abī Waqqās. See Mālik, *al-Mawaṭṭa'*, I. 142; ʿAbd al-Razzāq, *Muṣannaf* (414); al-Bayhaqī, *al-Sunān al-kubrā*, I. 131. This is also the position of Ibn ʿUmar and ʿĀ'ishah. See al-Bayhaqī, *al-Sunān al-kubrā*, I. 133.
123. MH says that this is the position of Ḥudhayfah b. al-Yamān. See ʿAbd al-Razzāq, *Muṣannaf* (429); Ibn Abī Shaybah, *Muṣannaf*, I. 190. It is also the position of Ibn Masʿūd. See Ibn Abī Shaybah, *Muṣannaf*, I. 190; ʿAbd al-Razzāq, *Muṣannaf* (430).
124. MH says that this is the position of Ibn Masʿūd. See al-ʿAsqalānī, *Fatḥ al-bārī*, IX. 404.
125. MH says that this is the position of ʿUmar.
126. MH says that this is the position of Ibn Masʿūd. See ʿAbd al-Razzāq, *Muṣannaf* (11640); al-Bayhaqī, *al-Sunān al-kubrā*, VII. 380.
127. Muslim, *Ṣaḥīḥ*, "al-Ṭalāq" (1472).
128. Al-Bukhārī, *Ṣaḥīḥ*, "al-Ṭalāq" (5319) (5320); Muslim, *Ṣaḥīḥ*, "al-Ṭalāq" (1484); Aḥmad, *Musnad*, IV. 304; al-Nisā'ī, *Sunan*, VI. 190–191; al-Tirmidhī, *al-Jāmiʿ* (1193).
129. Al-Bukhārī, *Ṣaḥīḥ* (2314); Muslim, *Ṣaḥīḥ* (1697).
130. Al-Bukhārī, *Ṣaḥīḥ* (1834) (2783) (2825) (3077); Muslim, *Ṣaḥīḥ* (1353).
131. Muslim, *Ṣaḥīḥ* (1692) (1694); al-Bukhārī, *Ṣaḥīḥ* (2314).
132. Al-Bukhārī, *Ṣaḥīḥ*, "al-Buyūʿ" (2075) (5507) (7398).
133. Al-Bukhārī, *Ṣaḥīḥ*, "Faḍā'il al-ṣaḥābah" (3673); Muslim, *Ṣaḥīḥ*, "Faḍā'il al-ṣaḥābah" (2541).
134. Abū Dā'ūd al-Ṭayālisī, *Musnad* (246); al-Bayhaqī, *al-Madkhal* (49); Aḥmad, *Musnad*, I. 379.
135. Al-Bukhārī, *Ṣaḥīḥ*, "al-Ṣalāh" (466) (3654) (3904).
136. Aḥmad, *Musnad*, I. 379; Abū Dā'ūd al-Ṭayālisī, *Musnad* (2456).
137. Al-Bukhārī, *Ṣaḥīḥ*, "Faḍā'il al-ṣaḥābah" (3756); al-Bukhārī, *Ṣaḥīḥ*, "al-ʿIlm" (75).
138. Al-Bukhārī, *Ṣaḥīḥ*, "al-ʿIlm" (82) (3681) (7006); Muslim, *Ṣaḥīḥ*, "Faḍā'il al-ṣaḥābah" (2391).
139. Muslim, *Ṣaḥīḥ*, "al-Masājid" (681).
140. Aḥmad, *Musnad*, IV. 154; al-Tirmidhī, *al-Jāmiʿ* (3695).
141. Aḥmad, *Musnad*, V. 165, 177; Abū Dā'ūd, *Sunan* (2962).
142. Al-Ḥākim, *al-Mustadrak*, III. 317–318; al-Bayhaqī, *al-Madkhal* (96).

143. Al-Bukhārī, *Ṣaḥīḥ*, "al-Ijārah" (2263).
144. Muslim, *Ṣaḥīḥ*, "al-Ṣalāh" (421).
145. Mālik, *al-Mawaṭṭa'*, II. 513; Abū Dā'ūd, *Sunan* (2894); al-Tirmidhī, *al-Jāmi'* (2101); Ibn Mājah, *Sunan* (2724).
146. Al-Bayhaqī, *al-Sunān al-kubrā*, VIII. 335.
147. Al-Bukhārī, *Ṣaḥīḥ*, "al-Tayammum" (338); Muslim, *Ṣaḥīḥ*, "al-Ḥayḍ" (368).
148. 'Abd al-Razzāq, *Muṣannaf* (17698); Ibn Abī Shaybah, *Muṣannaf*, VI. 306; Ibn Ḥazm, *al-Iḥkām*, VI. 86. MH points out the contrast between this narration and that in 'Abd al-Razzāq, *Muṣannaf* (17706).
149. Al-Bukhārī, *Ṣaḥīḥ*, "al-Buyū'" (2062) (7353); Muslim, *Ṣaḥīḥ*, "al-Ādāb" (2154).
150. Al-Bukhārī, *Ṣaḥīḥ*, "al-Diyyāt" (6905) (6906) (6907) (6908); Muslim, *Ṣaḥīḥ*, "al-Qisāmah" (1689).
151. Al-Bukhārī, *Ṣaḥīḥ*" (3156) (3157).
152. Al-'Asqalānī, *Fatḥ al-bārī*, III. 587; al-Bukhārī, *Ṣaḥīḥ* (1757) (4401); Muslim, *Ṣaḥīḥ* (1211).
153. Al-Bukhārī, *Ṣaḥīḥ*, "al-Ḥajj" (1559); Muslim, *Ṣaḥīḥ*, "al-Ḥajj" (1221).
154. Aḥmad, *Musnad*, IV. 216.
155. Al-Bukhārī, *Ṣaḥīḥ*, "Kitāb al-Janā'iz" (1242); Ibn 'Abd al-Barr, *al-Jāmi'* (2387).
156. 'Abd al-Razzāq, *Muṣannaf*, VI. 180.
157. Al-Bukhārī, *Ṣaḥīḥ*, "al-Ashribah" (5588); Muslim, *Ṣaḥīḥ*, "al-Tafsīr" (3032).
158. Al-Bukhārī, *Ṣaḥīḥ*, "al-Shurūṭ" (2731) (2732).
159. Al-Bukhārī, *Ṣaḥīḥ*, "al-Ḥajj" (1539); Muslim, *Ṣaḥīḥ*, "al-Ḥajj" (1189).
160. Al-Bukhārī, *Ṣaḥīḥ*, "Kitāb al-Ṭibb" (5728); Muslim, *Ṣaḥīḥ*, "Kitāb al-Salām" (2218).
161. Mālik, *al-Mawaṭṭa'*, II. 825; al-Bayhaqī, *al-Sunān al-kubrā*, VII. 442.
162. Al-Bukhārī, *Ṣaḥīḥ*, "al-Farā'iḍ" (6736).
163. Al-Bukhārī, *Ṣaḥīḥ*, "al-Maghāzī" (4227); Muslim, *Ṣaḥīḥ*, "al-Ṣayd wa-l-Dhabā'iḥ" (1939).
164. Al-Bukhārī, *Ṣaḥīḥ*, "Kitāb al-I'tiṣām" (7352); Muslim, *Ṣaḥīḥ*, "al-'Aqdiyah" (1716).
165. Abū Dā'ūd, *Sunan*, "al-Malāḥim" (4291); al-Ḥākim, *al-Mustadrak*, IV. 524.
166. Abū Dā'ūd al-Ṭayālisī, *Musnad* (647) (2023); Ibn Ḥibbān, *Sunan*, VII. 226; Aḥmad, *Musnad*, III. 130, 143; Tirmidhī, *al-Jāmi'* (2869).

# *Bibliography*

*Abḥāth hay'ah kibār al-'ulamā bi-l-Mamlikah al-'Arabiyyah al-Sa'ūdiyyah*. Riyadh: Ri'āsah Idārah al-Buḥūth al-'Ilmiyyah wa al-Iftā', 1421/2001.

Abd-Allah, Umar F. "Theological Dimensions of Islamic Law." In *The Cambridge Companion to Classical Islamic Theology*, ed. Tim Winter (Cambridge: Cambridge University Press, 2008), 237–257.

Abū Zayd, Bakr. *Ibn Qayyim al-Jawziyyah: Ḥayātuh, āthāruh, mawāriduh*. Riyadh: Dār al-'Āṣimah, 1992.

Arabi, Oussama. "Early Muslim Legal Philosophy: Identity and Difference in Islamic Jurisprudence." December 1, 1999. G. E. von Grunebaum Center for Near Eastern Studies, Paper 1. http://escholarship.org/uc/item/7c8253bt, at 29.

'Abd al-Qādir, Muḥammad al-'Arūsī. *Al-masā'il al-mushtarakah bayn uṣūl al-fiqh wa-uṣūl al-dīn*. Riyadh: Maktabah al-Rushd, 2009.

Abrahamov, Binyamin. "Ibn Taymiyya on the Agreement of Reason with Tradition." *The Muslim World* 82, no 3–4 (1992): 256–273.

Abū Ẓahrah, Muḥammad. *Muhāḍarāt fi ta'rīkh al-fiqh al-Islāmī*. Cairo: Dār al-Fikr al-'Arabī n.d.

Ahmad, Ahmad Atif. *Structural Interrelations of Theory and Practice in Islamic Law: A Study of Six Works of Medieval Islamic Jurisprudence*. Leiden: Brill, 2006.

Albānī, Muḥammad Sa'īd. *'Umdāh al-taḥqīq fī al-taqlīd wa-l-talfīq*. Damascus: al-Maktab al-Islāmī, 1981.

al-Albānī, Nāṣir al-Dīn. *The Prophet's Prayer, Sallallaahu 'alaihi Wasallam, Described from the Beginning to the End As Though You See It*. Translated by Usama Hasan. Ipswich, Suffolk: Al-Haneef Publications, 1993.

Al-Matroudi, Abdul Hakim I. *The Hanbalī School of Law and Ibn Taymiyyah: Conflict or Conciliation*. Routledge: New York, 2006.

Asad, Muhammad. *This Law of Ours*. Gibraltar: Dar al-Andalus, 1987.

'Azzām, 'Abd Allāh *Join the Caravan*. 2nd ed. London: Azzam Publications, 2001.

al-Baghdādi, 'Abd al-Wahhāb. *Al-ma'ūnah*. Edited by Hāmish 'Abd al Haqq. Riyadh: Maktabah al-Tijāriyyah.

Bernard, Cheryl. *Civil Democratic Islam: Partners, Resources and Strategies*. Santa Monica: RAND Corporation, 2003.

Bernard, Marie. "Ḥanafī *uṣūl al-fiqh* through a Manuscript of al-Ğassās." *Journal of the American Oriental Society* 105, no. 4 (1985): 623–635.

Bori, Caterina. *A Scholar in the Shadow: Essays in the Legal and Theological Thought of Ibn Qayyim al-Ğawziyyah*. Rome: Istituto per l'Oriente, 2010.

Brockopp, Jonathan E. "Competing Theories of Authority in Early Mālikī Texts." In *Studies in Islamic Legal Theory*, edited by Bernard G. Weiss (Leiden: Brill, 2002), 3–22.

Brown, Jonathan. *The Canonization of al Bukhārī and Muslim: The Formation and Function of the Sunni Hadīth Canon*. Leiden: Brill, 2007.

al-Būṭī, Muḥammad Sa'īd Ramaḍān. *Al-lā madhhabiyyah akhṭar bid'ah tuhaddid al-sharī'ah al-Islāmiyyah*. Damascus: Dār al-Fārābī, 2005.

———. *Al-salafiyyah: Marḥalah zamāniyyah mubārakah lā madhhab Islāmī*. Damascus: Dār al-Fikr, 1988.

Calder, Norman. "Al-Nawawī's Typology of *Muftīs* and its Significance for General Theory of Islamic Law." *Islamic Law and Society* 4 (1997): 137–164.

———. "Taḳlīd." In *Encyclopaedia of Islam*. 2nd ed. Edited by P. Bearman et al., 10: 137 (Leiden: Brill, 1998).

———. "The 'Uqūd Rasm al-Muftī' of Ibn 'Ābidīn." *Bulletin of the School of Oriental and African Studies* 63 (2000): 215–228.

Cooperson, Michael. "Ibn Ḥanbal and Bishr al-Ḥāfī: A Case Study in Biographical Traditions." *Studia Islamica* 86 (1997): 71–101.

al-Dā'ūdī. *Ṭabaqāt al-Mufassirīn*. Beirut: Dār al-Kutub al-'Ilmiyyah, 1983.

al-Dhahābī. *Zaghl al-'ilm*. Edited by Muḥammad b. Nāṣir al-'Ajmī. N.p.: Maktabāh al-Ṣaḥwah al-Islāmiyyah, 1404/1983–1984.

———. *Al-mu'jam al-mukhtaṣṣ bi-l-muḥaddithīn*. Al-Ṭā'if: Maktabah al-Ṣiddīq, 1408/1988.

Fadel, Mohammad. "The Social Logic of Taqlīd and the Rise of the Mukhtaṣar." *Islamic Law and Society* 3 (1996): 193–233.

al-Fullānī. *Īqāẓ himam ulī al-abṣār lil-īqtiḍā' bi-sayyid al-muhājirīn wa-l-anṣār*. Gujranwala: Dār Nashr al-Kutub al-Islāmiyyah, 1975.

Graham, William. "Traditionalism in Islam: An Essay in Interpretation." *The Journal of Interdisciplinary History* 23, no. 3 (1993): 495–522.

Gerber, Haim. "Rigidity Versus Openness in Late Classical Islamic Law: The Case of the Seventeenth-Century Palestinian Muftī Khayr al-Dīn al-Ramlī." *Islamic Law and Society* 5, no. 2 (1998): 165–195.

Ghazālī, al-Mustaṣfā, Edited by Muḥammad 'Abd al-Salam 'Abd al-Shāfī. (Beirut: Dār al-Kutub al-'Ilmiyyah, 1413/1993).

al-Ḥajjāwī, *Zād al-mustaqni' fī ikhtiṣār al-muqni'*. Riyadh: Madār al-Waṭan lil-Nashr, 2004.

Hallaq, Wael. *Authority, Continuity, and Change in Islamic Law*. Cambridge: Cambridge University Press, 2001.

———. *A History of Islamic Legal Theories: An Introduction to Sunni Uṣūl al-Fiqh*. Cambridge: Cambridge University Press, 1997.

———. "Non-Analogical Arguments in Sunni Juridical Qiyās." *Arabica* 36, no. 3 (1989), 286–306.

———. "On the Origins of the Controversy about the Existence of Mujtahids and the Gate of *Ijtihād*." *Studia Islamica* 63 (1986), 129–141.

———. "Was the Gate of Ijtihad Closed?" *International Journal of Middle East Studies* 16, no. 1 (1984): 3–41.

Holtzman, Livnat. "Ibn Qayyim Al-Jawziyyah," in *Essays in Arabic Literary Biography*, edited by Joseph E. Lowry and Devin J. Stewart (Wiesbaden: Harrassowitz, 2009), 202–223.

al-Ḥukmī, ʿAlī b. ʿAbbās b ʿUthmān. "Ḥaqīqah al-khilāf fī al-taʿlīl bi-l-ḥikmah wa-athruh fī al-fiqh al-Islāmī." *Majallah Jāmiʿah Umm al-Qurā* 7, no. 9 (1414/1993–1994), 11–85.

Hodgson, Marshall. *The Venture of Islam*. 3 vols. Chicago: University of Chicago Press, 1974.

Horii, Satoe. "Reconsideration of Legal Devices (*hiyal*) in Islamic Jurisprudence: The Hanafīs and Their "Exits" (*makhārij*)." *Islamic Law and Society* 9, no. 3 (2002): 312–357.

Hurvitz, Nimrod. "Schools of Law and Historical Context: Re-examining the Formation of the Ḥanbalī Madhhab." *Islamic Law and Society* 7, no. 1 (2000): 37–64.

Ibn Abī al-ʿIzz al-Ḥanafī. *Al-ittibāʿ*. Edited by Muḥammad ʿAtā Allah Ḥanīf and ʿAsim b. ʿAbdallāh al-Qaryūti. Lahore: al-Maktabah al-Salafiyyah, 1410/1989–1990.

Ibn ʿĀbidīn. *Radd al-muḥtār ʿalā l-durr al-mukhtār*. Beirut: Dār al-Kutub al-ʿIlmiyyah, 1415/1994.

Ibn ʿAqīl. *Al-wāḍih fī uṣūl al-fiqh*. Edited by ʿAbdallāh b. ʿAbd al-Muḥsin al-Turkī. Beirut: Muʾassasah al-Risālah, 1999.

Ibn Baṭṭa. *Al-ibānah al-kubrā*. Edited by Raḍā Muʿṭī et al. Riyadh: Dār al-Rāyah, n.d.

Ibn Ḥajar. *Al-durar al-kāminah fī aʿyān al miʾah al-thāminah*. Hyderabad: Majlis Dāʾirah al-Maʿārif al-ʿUthmāniyyah, 1972.

Ibn Ḥazm. *Al-iḥkām fī uṣūl al-aḥkām*. Cairo: Dār al-Ḥadīth, 1404/1983–1984.

Ibn ʿImād, *Shadharāt al-dhahab fī akhbār man dhahab*. Beirut: Dār Ibn Kathīr, 1992.

Ibn Jibrīn, ed. *Sharḥ al-Zarkashī ʿalā Mukhtaṣar al-Khiraqī*. Riyadh: Maktabah al-ʿUbaykān, 1993.

Ibn Kathīr *Al-bidāyah wa-l-nihāyah*. Beirut: Dār Ibn Kathīr, 2010.

Ibn Mullā Farrūkh. *Al-qawl al-sadīd fī baʿḍ māsaʾil al-ijtihād wa-l-taqlīd*. Edited by Jāsim Yāsīn and ʿAdnān Sālim. Kuwait: Dār al-Daʿwah, 1988.

Ibn Mufliḥ *Al-maqṣad al-arshad fī dhikr aṣḥāb al-Imām Aḥmad*. Riyadh: Maktabah al-Rushd, 1990.

Ibn al-Najjār. *Sharḥ al-Kawkab al-munīr*. Riyadh: Maktabah al-ʿUbaykān, 1997.

Ibn al-Naqīb. *Reliance of the Traveller: The Classic Manual of Islamic Sacred Law ʿUmdat al-Salik by Ahmad Ibn Naqib Al-Misri (d. 769/1368) in Arabic with Facing*

*English Text, Commentary, and Appendices*. Edited and translated by Nuh Ha Mim Keller. Evanston IL: Sunna Books, 1994.

Ibn al-Qayyim. *I'lām al-muwaqqi'īn 'an rabb al-'ālamīn*. Edited by Mashhūr Ḥasan Āl Salmān. Riyadh: Dār Ibn al-Jawzī, 1423/2002.

Ibn Qudāmah. *Al-mughnī*. Edited by 'Abdallāh 'Abd al-Muḥsin al-Turkī and 'Abd al-Fattāh Muḥammad al-Hulw. Cairo: Hajr, 1986–1990.

Ibn Rajab. *Dhayl 'alā Ṭabaqāt al-Ḥanābilah*. Mecca: Maktabah al-'Ubaykān, 2005.

Ibn al-Ṣalāḥ. *Fatāwā wa-masā'il Ibn al-Ṣalāḥ*. Beirut: Dār al-Ma'rifah, 1986.

Ibn al-Shāṭṭ. *Idrār al-shurūq 'alā anwār al-furuq*. Published with al-Qarāfī, *al-Furūq*. N.p.: Ālam al-Kutub, n.d.).

Ibn al-Taghrībirdī. *Al-manhal al-ṣāfī wa-l-mustawfā ba'd al-wāfī*. Cairo: Maṭba'ah Dār al-Kutub wa-l-Wathā'iq al-Qawmiyyah, 2002.

Ibn Taymiyyah. *Al-fatāwā al-kubrā*. Edited by Muḥammad 'Abd al-Qādir 'Aṭā' and Muṣṭafā 'Abd al-Qādir 'Aṭā'. Beirut: Dār al-Kutub al-'Ilmiyyah, 1987.

———. *Kitāb al-tis'īniyyah*. Edited by Muḥammad Ibrāhīm al-'Ajlān. Riyādh: Maktabah al-Ma'ārif lil-Nashr wa-l-Tawzī', 1999.

al-'Imrānī, Yaḥyā b. Abī al-Khayr. *Al-bayān fī madhhab al-Imām al-Shāfi'ī*. Edited by Qāsim Muḥammad al-Nūrī. Damascus: Dār al-Minhāj, 2000.

Jackson, Sherman A. "The Alchemy of Domination? Some Ash'arite Responses to Mu'tazilite Ethics." *International Journal of Middle East Studies* 31, no. 2 (1999): 185–201.

———. *Islamic Law and the State: The Constitutional Jurisprudence of Shihāb al-Dīn al-Qarāfī*. Leiden: Brill, 1996.

———. "Setting the Record Straight: Ibn al-Labbād's Refutation of al-Shāfi'ī." *Oxford Journal of Islamic Studies* 11, no. 2 (2000): 121–146.

al-Juwaynī, *al-Talkhīṣ fī uṣul al-fiqh*, (Beirut: Dār al-Bashā'ir al-Islāmiyyah, 1417/1996).

Kamali, Mohammad Hashim. *Principles of Islamic Jurisprudence*. Cambridge: Islamic Texts Society, 2003.

al-Karkhī. *Al-uṣūl allatī 'alayhā madār furū' al-Ḥanafiyyāh*. Cairo: al-Maṭba'ah al-Adabiyyah, n.d.

Khaṭīb al-Baghdādī. *Al-faqīh wa-l-mutafaqqih*. Riyadh: Dār Ibn al-Jawzī, 1417/1996–1997.

———. *Ta'rīkh Baghdād aw Madīnah al-Salām*. Cairo: Maktabah al-Khānjī, 1931.

———. *Ta'rīkh Baghdād*. Edited by Muṣṭafā 'Abd al-Qādir 'Aṭā. (Beirut: Dār al-Kutub al-'Ilmiyyah, 1417).

Kīrānwī, Ḥabīb Aḥmad. "Al-dīn al-qayyim." In Zafar 'Uthmānī, *I'lā' al-Sunan*. Beirut: Dār al-Fikr, 2001.

Krawietz, Birgit. "Cut and Paste in Legal Rules: Designing Islamic Norms with *Talfīq*." *Die Welt des Islams* 42 (2002): 3–40.

———. "Ibn Qayyim Al-Jawzīyah: His Life and Works," *Mamlūk Studies Review* 10, no. 2 (2006): 19–64.

———. "Transgressive Creativity in the Making: Ibn Qayyim al-Gawziyyah's Reframing within Ḥanbalī Legal Methodology." In *A Scholar in the Shadow: Essays in the*

*Legal and Theological Thought of Ibn Qayyim al-Ǧawziyyah*, edited by Caterina Bori, 47–66. Rome: Istituto per l'Oriente C. A. Nallino, 2010.

Kugle, Scott Alan. "Framed, Blamed and Renamed: The Recasting of Islamic Jurisprudence in Colonial South Asia." *Modern Asian Studies* 35, no. 2 (2001): 257–313.

al-Laknawī. *Fawātiḥ al-raḥamūt*. Beirut: Dār al-Kutub al-ʿIlmiyyah, 2002.

Landau-Tasseron, Ella. "The 'Cyclical Reform': A Study of the Mujaddid Tradition." *Studia Islamica* 70 (1989): 79–117.

Lowry, Joseph E., and Devin J. Stewart. *Essays in Arabic Literary Biography*. Wiesbaden: Harrassowitz, 2009.

Lucas, Scott. "Abū Bakr Ibn al-Mundhir, Amputation, and the Art of *Ijtihād*." *International Journal of Middle Eastern Studies* 39 (2007): 351–368.

———. "Where Are the Legal "*Ḥadīth*"?: A Study of the "*muṣannaf*" of Ibn Abī Shayba." *Islamic Law and Society* 15, no. 3 (2008): 283–314.

———. "The Legal Principles of Muhammad b. Ismāīl al-Bukhārī and Their Relationship to Classical Salafi Islam." *Islamic Law and Society* 13, no. 3 (2006): 289–324.

al-Mardāwī. *Al-inṣāf fī māʿrifah al-rājiḥ min al-khilāf ʿalā madhhab al-imām al-mubajjal Aḥmad b. Ḥanbal*. Edited by Muḥammad Ḥāmid al-Fīqī. Cairo: Maṭbūʿah al-Sunnah al-Muḥammadiyyah, 1955.

Makdisi, George. "Ashʿarī and the Ashʿarites in Islamic Religious History. I." *Studia Islamica* 17 (1962): 37–80.

———. *Ibn ʿAqil: Religion and Culture in Classical Islam*. Edinburgh: Edinburgh University Press, 1997.

———. "The Juridical Theology of Shāfiʿī: Origins and Significance of Uṣūl al-Fiqh." *Studia Islamica* 59 (1984): 5–47.

———. "The Significance of the Sunni Schools of Law in Islamic Religious History." *International Journal of Middle East Studies* 10, no. 1 (1979): 1–8.

Makdisi, John. "Legal Logic and Equity in Islamic Law." *American Journal of Comparative Law* 33, no. 1 (1985): 63–92.

Al-Matroudi, Abdul Hakim I. *The Hanbalī School of Law and Ibn Taymiyyah: Conflict or Conciliation*. Routledge: New York, 2006.

———. "The Hanbalī School of Law in the Light of Contemporary Western Studies." *Journal of Qurʾanic Studies* 8, no. 2 (2006): 260–203.

al-Māwardī. *Al-ḥāwī al-kabīr fī fiqh madhhab al-Imām al-Shāfiʿī*. Beirut: Dār al-Kutub al-ʿIlmiyyah, 1994.

Mawdudi, S. A. A. *The Islamic Law and Consitution*. Lahore: Islamic Publications, 1980.

Meri, Josef W. *The Cult of Saints Among Muslims and Jews in Medieval Syria*. Oxford: Oxford University Press, 2002.

Murad, Abdal Hakim (Timothy Winter). *Understanding the Four Madhhabs: The Facts about Ijtihād and Taqlīd*. Oneonta NY: Islamic Publications, 1998?

Metcalf, Barbara D. *Islamic Revival in British India: Deoband, 1860–1900*. Princeton: Princeton University Press, 1982.

al-Nawawī. *Al-majmū': Sharḥ al-muhadhdhab*. Beirut: Dār al-Fikr, 2000.

———. *Rawḍah al-ṭālibīn*. Beirut: Maktab al-Islāmī, 1991.

Opwis, Felicitas M. M. *Maslaha and the Purpose of the Law: Islamic Discourse on Legal Change from the 4th/10th to 8th/14th Century*. Leiden: Brill, 2010.

Peters, Rudolph. "*Ijtihād* and *Taqlīd* in 18th and 19th Century Islam." *Die Welt des Islams* 20 (1989): 132–145.

Pound, Roscoe. "The Decadence of Equity." *Columbia Law Review* 5 (1905): 20–35.

Qaraḍāwī, Yūsuf. *Kayfa nata'āmal ma' al-turāth wa-l-tamadhhub wa-l-ikhtilāf*. Beirut: Mu'assasat al-Risālah, 2005.

al-Qarāfī. *Al-furūq*. N.p.: 'Ālam al-Kutub, n.d.

———*Nafā'is al-uṣūl fī Sharḥ al-Maḥṣūl*. Edited by 'Ādil Aḥmad 'Abd al-Mawjūd, 'Alī Muḥammad Mu'awwaḍ, and 'Abd al-Fattāh Abū Sinnah. (Makkah: Maktabah Nizār Muṣtafā al-Bāz, 1416/1995).

al-Qurṭūbī, *Al-jāmi' li-aḥkām al-Qur'ān*. Edited by 'Abd al-Razzāq al-Mahdī. Beirut: Dār al-Kitāb al-'Arabī, 1423/2003.

Rapoport, Yossef, and Shahab Ahmed. *Ibn Taymiyya and His Times*. Karachi: Oxford University Press, 2010.

al-Raysūnī, Aḥmad. *Imām al-Shātibī's Theory of the Higher Objectives and Intents of Islamic Law*. London: International Institute of Islamic Thought, 2005.

al-Rāzī, Fakhr al-Dīn. *Al-maḥṣūl fī 'ilm uṣūl al-fiqh*. 2 vols. in 6. Edited by Ṭaha Jābir al-'Alwānī. Riyadh, 1979–1981.

———. *Tafsīr Mafātīḥ al-ghayb*. Beirut: Dar al-Kutub al-'Ilmiyyah, 2000.

Rheinstein, Max, ed. *Max Weber on Law in Economy and Society*. Cambridge MA: Harvard University Press, 1954.

Rashīd Riḍā, Muḥammad. *Al-manār*. Egypt: n.p, 1897.

Sabra, Adam. "Review of *Islamic Law and the State: The Constitutional Jurisprudence of Shihāb al-Dīn al-Qarāfī*." *The Journal of Law and Religion* 15, no. 2 (2001): 413–416.

al-Ṣafadī, *Kitāb al-wāfī bi-l-wafayāt*. Beirut: Dār Iḥyā' al-Turāth al-'Arabī, 2000.

al-Ṣan'ānī. *Irshād al-nuqqād ilā taysīr al-ijtihād*. Edited by Ṣalaḥ al-Dīn Maqbūl Aḥmad. Kuwait: Dār al-Salafiyyah, 1405/1985.

Schacht, Joseph. *An Introduction to Islamic Law*. Oxford: Clarendon Press, 1964.

———. *The Origins of Muhammadan Jurisprudence*. Oxford: Clarendon Press, 1950.

al-Shāfi'ī. *Al-risālah*. Translated by Majid Khadduri. Cambridge: Islamic Texts Society, 1997.

Shāh Walī Allāh. *Al-inṣāf fī bayān sabab al-ikhtilāf*. Lahore: Auqāf Department, Government of the Punjab, 1971.

———. *The Conclusive Argument from God: Shah Wali Allah of Delhi's Hujjat Allāh al-Bāligha*. Translated by Marcia K. Hermansen. Islamabad: Islamic Research Institute, 2003.

———. *'Iqd al-jīd fī aḥkām al-ijtihād wa-l-taqlīd*. Cairo: al-Maṭba'ah al-Salafīyyah, 1965.

al-Sha'rānī. *Al-mīzān al-kubrā*. Beirut: Dār al-Kutub al-'Ilmiyyah, 1997.

al-Shawkānī. *Al-qawl al-mufīd fī adillah al-ijtihād wa-l-taqlīd*. Edited by 'Abd al-Raḥmān 'Abd al-Khāliq. Kuwait: Dār al-Qalam, 1976.

al-Shirāzī, *Sharḥ al-Luma'*. Edited by 'Abd al-Majīd Turkī. (Beirut: Dār al-Gharb al-Islāmī, 1408/1988).

al-Shithrī, Sa'd. *Al-taqlīd wa-aḥkāmuh*. Riyadh: Dār al-Waṭan, 1995.

al-Shurunbulālī. *Al-'iqd al-farīd li-bayān al-rājiḥ min al-khilāf fī jawāz al-taqlīd*. Edited by Khālid Muḥammad al-'Arūsī. *Majallah Jāmi'ah Umm al-Qurā li-'Ulūm al-Sharī'ah* 17, no. 32 (1425/2004): 674–768.

al-Subkī, 'Alī b. 'Abd al-Kāfī, and Tāj al-Dīn al-Subkī. *Al-ibhāj fī sharḥ al-minhāj*. Beirut, Dār al-Kutub al-'Ilmiyyah, 1995.

al-Suyūṭī. *Bughyah al-wu'āh fī ṭabaqāt al-lughawiyyīn wa-l-nuḥāh*. Beirut: al-Maktabah al-'Aṣriyyah, 1964.

al-Ṭabarī. *Jāmi' al-bayān fī ta'wīl al-Qur'ān*. Edited by Aḥmad Muḥammad Shākir. N.p: Mu'assasah al-Risālah, n.d.

Taylor, Christopher S. *In the Vicinity of the Righteous: Ziyāra and the Veneration of Muslim Saints in Late Medieval Egypt*. Leiden: Brill, 1998.

al-Turkī, 'Abdallāh b. 'Abd al-Muḥsin. *Uṣūl madhhab al-Imām Aḥmad*. Beirut: Mu'assasah al-Risālah, 1996.

Usmani, Taqi. *The Legal Status of Following a Madhhab*. Translated by Mohammad Amin Kholwadia and edited by Muhammad Dhakir Shaikh. Karachi: Zam Zam Publishers, 1998.

'Uthmānī, Zafar. *I'lā' al-sunan*. Beirut: Dār al-Kutub al-'Ilmiyyah, 1997.

———. *I'lā' al-sunan*. Beirut: Dār al-Fikr, 2001.

Vogel, Frank E. *Islamic Law and Legal System: Studies of Saudi Arabia*. Leiden: Brill, 2000.

Voll, John O. "Renewal and Reform in Islamic History: *Tajdīd* and *Islāh*." In *Voices of Resurgent Islam*, edited by John Esposito, 32–48. New York: Oxford University Press, 1983.

Watt, W. M. *Islamic Political Thought*. Edinburgh: Edinburgh University Press, 1998.

Weiss, Bernard G., ed. *Studies in Islamic Legal Theory*. Leiden: Brill, 2002.

———. "Ibn Taymīyya on Leadership in the Ritual Prayer." In *Islamic Legal Interpretation: Muftīs and their fatwās*, edited by Khalid Masud, Brinkely Messick, and David Powers, 63–71. Karachi: Oxford University Press, 2005.

Tim Winter, ed. *The Cambridge Companion to Classical Islamic Theology*. Cambridge: Cambridge University Press, 2008.

al-Yāfi'ī, 'Abd al-Fattāḥ. *Al-tamadhhub: Dirāsah ta'ṣīliyyah muqāranah li-masā'il wa-aḥkām al-tamadhhub*. Beirut: Mu'assasat al-Risālah Nāshirūn, 2006.

al-Ziriklī. *Al-a'lām*. Beirut: Dār al-'Ilm lil-Malāyīn, 2002.

Zaman, Muhammad Qasim. *Ashraf 'Ali Thanawi: Islam in Modern South Asia*. Oxford: Oneworld, 2008.

# Index

www.ingramcontent.com/pod-product-compliance
Lightning Source LLC
Chambersburg PA
CBHW020624250426
43813CB00002B/77
*9780199937516*